SCHOOLING THE DAUGHTERS OF MARIANNE

LINDA L. CLARK

Schooling the Daughters of Marianne

TEXTBOOKS AND THE SOCIALIZATION OF GIRLS
IN MODERN FRENCH PRIMARY SCHOOLS

State University of New York Press
ALBANY

Published by
State University of New York Press, Albany

© 1984 State University of New York

For information, address State University of New York
Press, State University Plaza, Albany, N.Y., 12246

Library of Congress Cataloging in Publication Data

Clark, Linda L., 1942–
    Schooling the Daughters of Marianne.

    (SUNY series on European social history)
    Bibliography: p. 205
    1. Women—Education—France—History. 2. Education, Primary—France—
History. 3. Textbooks—France—History. 4. Sexism in textbooks—France—
History. 5. France—History—1870–1940. I. Title. II. Series.
LC2094.C58   1984   396'.944   83-5035
ISBN O-87395-787-3
ISBN O-87395-786-5 (pbk.)

10 9 8 7 6 5 4 3 2 1

Contents

List of Tables   vi

Illustrations   vii

Acknowledgments   viii

Introduction   1

CHAPTER ONE   *Girls' Primary Education in the Nineteenth Century:
Traditions and Innovations*   5

TWO   *Prescribing Values and Behavior: Feminine Images
in Textbooks, 1880–1914*   26

THREE   *The School's Dissemination of Feminine Images and
Reactions to Them, 1880–1914*   60

FOUR   *From World War I to World War II: Continuity and
Change in Curriculum and Textbooks*   81

FIVE   *The Feminine Image and Social and Economic Realities, 1880–1940*   102

SIX   *From Vichy through the Fourth Republic*   133

SEVEN   *The Fifth Republic: Educational Reforms and
Reevaluations of Girls' Schooling*   151

NOTES   169

BIBLIOGRAPHY   205

INDEX   219

List of Tables

1. Number of Pupils Taught by Secular and Religious Teachers, 1863–1914   12
2. Percentage of Primary Pupils in Private Primary Schools, 1850–1963   15
3. Enrollments in Special Primary Classes of Public Secondary Schools, 1896–1936   38
4. Girls Earning the *Certificat d'Etudes Primaires*   109
5. Pupils Earning the *C.e.p.* from Paris Schools   111
6. Primary School Statistics for Departments Where Girls Earned High and Low Percentages of the *C.e.p.* in 1907   112
7. Women's Occupational Patterns and Illiteracy Rates in 1901 in Departments Where Girls Earned a Low Percentage of the *C.e.p.*   114
8. Educational Trends in Departments Where Girls Earned High and Low Percentages of the *C.e.p.*   115
9. Women's Occupational Patterns and Illiteracy Rates in 1901 in Departments Where Girls Earned a High Percentage of the *C.e.p.*   117
10. Women's Representation in Different Economic Sectors in Southeastern France, 1901   118
11. Enrollments in Public Post-Primary Education, 1881–1938   120
12. Future Activities of Pupils Leaving *Ecoles Primaires Supérieures* and Public *Cours Complémentaires*, 1898–1907   126
13. Future Activities of Girls Leaving *Cours Complémentaires* in Six Southern Departments, 1896–1898, and Occupations of Parents   128
14. Future Activities of Girls Leaving *Cours Complémentaires* in Vienne (Isère), 1896–1898, and Occupations of Fathers and Mothers   129
15. Evolution of Women's Work, 1896–1936   130
16. Adolescents' Criteria for Success in Life   146
17. Enrollments in Post-Primary Education, 1938–1958   149
18. Coeducation in Primary Schools   155

Illustrations

1. The woman tries to persuade her husband not to strike 34
2. A textbook preparing girls for work and housework 44
3. Suzette's class comments on the utility of school 45
4. Bringing the daughters of the bourgeoisie and working class together: Madeleine lends Jeanne books 50
5. Madeleine shows Jeanne that flowers and pictures beautify a simple room 51
6. The presentation of distinguished role models 53
7. The presentation of distinguished role models 53
8. Domestic economy for the farm girl 55
9. Education to combat depopulation 84
10. The care and feeding of children 95

Acknowledgments

I wish to thank the Bunting Institute of Radcliffe College and the National Institute of Education for an Educational Research Grant in 1979–1980 which made possible much of the research for this study. I also wish to offer special thanks to Mme Héraud of the Institut national de recherche pédagogique, who provided me with access to the textbook collection housed at 29 rue d'Ulm in Paris; to Serge Chassagne and his staff for facilitating my use of a collection of student notebooks at the Musée national de l'éducation at Mont-Saint-Aignan; to Mme Paule René-Bazin of the Archives Nationales, who allowed me to consult documents not yet formally classified; to Philippe Grand of the Archives de Paris for much assistance; to Alain Choppin of the Service d'histoire de l'éducation for much helpful advice; to Mlle Jeanne Séguin, former *inspectrice* of schools in the department of the Seine, for insights into textbook writing during the 1950s; and to the archivists at several publishing houses who graciously provided information about textbook sales: Mlle Boulet at Armand Colin, M. Lanthoinette at Hachette, M. Blaise at Delagrave, and Mmes Buc and Laine at Larousse. The Press and Information Division of the French Embassy in New York and the Association pour une école non sexiste supplied useful contemporary materials. Librarians at the National Institute of Education in Washington, D.C., were extremely helpful in locating French pedagogical materials housed in basement storage areas. Evelyn Lyons and Leo Shelley provided invaluable assistance in securing scores of publications through interlibrary loan.

Along the way I have also accumulated numerous debts to fellow historians and academicians who have offered advice and encouragement. I am grateful to Lenard Berlanstein, Jack Censer, George Chase, Arlene Clift, Cissie Fairchilds, Marjorie Farrar, Kurt Fischer, Paul Gagnon, Shirley Garrett, Ingrun Lafleur, Frances Malino, Theresa McBride, Father Joseph Moody, Karen Offen, John B. Osborne, Harry Paul, Laura Strumingher, Gillian Thompson, Louise Tilly, Simone

Vincens, and Eugen Weber. Margaret Weitz generously supplied a wealth of information about women in contemporary France.

Some of the phrasing in this book is taken from my previously published articles: "The Molding of the *Citoyenne:* The Image of the Female in French Educational Literature, 1880–1914," *Third Republic/ Troisième République,* nos. 3–4 (1977), pp. 74–103: "The Primary Education of French Girls: Pedagogical Prescriptions and Social Realities, 1880–1940," *History of Education Quarterly* 21 (Winter 1981): 411–428: "The Socialization of Girls in the Primary Schools of the Third Republic," *Journal of Social History* 15 (Summer 1982): 685–697.

Illustrations were supplied by Larousse, by the photographic services department of Widener Library, and by Ed Hall and the printing and duplicating office of Millersville University of Pennsylvania.

Joyce Allen helped with the proofreading and indexing.

Introduction

Soon after Françoise Giroud assumed the newly created post of Secretary of State for the Feminine Condition in 1974, she requested a study of the depiction of women in contemporary French textbooks. Accordingly, researchers at the Institut national pour la recherche et documentation pédagogiques (INRDP) surveyed more than seventy books used in urban and rural elementary schools. A sign of the renascence of French feminism during the 1970s, the governmental project demonstrated a heightened awareness that a girl's sense of self-importance and ideas about adult roles are influenced from an early age by institutions transmitting cultural values, the school being one of the most important of these, along with the family, peer groups, government, church, and mass media.[1] The INRDP report concluded that the Fifth Republic's school literature presented women engaged primarily in domestic activities and subordinate roles and thus failed to project an accurate and positive image of the multifaceted feminine role in modern society.[2] A few years later a feminist's assessment of the portrayal of women in forty-two contemporary school texts appeared with the revealing title, *Papa lit, Maman coud* [Father Reads, Mother Sews].[3]

Encountering such verdicts about French schoolbooks of recent vintage, one might readily assume that an investigation of the depiction of women in the school literature of earlier eras would simply produce the not surprising conclusion, "plus ça change, plus c'est la même chose." Why study older pedagogical materials for girls when critiques of recent textbooks seem to pinpoint some of the major themes in past literature? Undeniably, the image of women in French textbooks during the last century was often far removed from the feminist ideal of equality between the sexes. Educators, like most other molders of public opinion, long accepted for women a series of psychological, social, economic, and legal constraints not applied to men. Yet an investigation of the representation of women in earlier school materials has much to offer historians if feminine images are placed within the social, economic, political, and cultural context.

1

Focusing on pedagogical literature used in primary schools since 1880, this study explains how girls' primary education has differed in certain respects from that for boys and suggests how educators' images of women have been related to social and political issues.

Why a concentration on the primary school when materials for secondary schools, intended for older girls, might offer a more sophisticated view of women? And why so much attention to the Third Republic and then the short-lived Fourth Republic in the chronological setting?

Primary school materials are the logical choice for a study of the school literature that reached the largest number of French girls before the Fifth Republic. Prior to the 1960s the majority of French adolescents, male and female, did not attend school after the primary grades. During the Third Republic secondary education was often the preserve of the middle classes. Educators themselves testified to the social separation of primary from secondary when they referred to the primary schools as schools for the masses or "le peuple."[4] Middle class children frequently attended special elementary classes attached to secondary schools and so avoided mixing with the "children of the people" in the classroom.

The Third and Fourth Republics are important periods in the history of French primary education because grade schools then held a significance that they can no longer claim. Because school was compulsory only until age thirteen (or fourteen, as of 1936), it was in the primary school that the majority of French men and women experienced the process of acculturation designed for them either by the state authorities in control of the Ministry of Public Instruction—renamed the Ministry of National Education in 1932—or by officials presiding over the competing and largely Catholic private schools.

The early Third Republic ushered in important reforms that delineated the essential features of a public primary school that underwent few significant changes before World War II. Building upon the educational legacy of the July Monarchy and Second Empire, Minister of Public Instruction Jules Ferry sponsored legislation in 1881–1882 to make primary schooling compulsory for children aged six to thirteen and to make public primary schools free and secular. For the first time public primary schools also became as readily available for girls as for boys, but generally males and females did not share the same classroom. The Third Republic continued the segregation of the sexes characteristic of many earlier schools, whether Catholic or public. Communes with a population of more than five hundred were to maintain separate primary schools for boys and girls, while those with smaller populations were permitted to have a coeducational school (école mixte).

During the Fourth Republic, as opportunities for various types of secondary schooling expanded, the role of the primary school began to change, as many of its personnel noted sadly.[5] Retaining its mission of introducing children to reading, writing, and arithmetic, the primary school became less important in the preparation of pupils for work and family life after school; it now shared the dissemination of moral and civic values with other parts of the educational establishment, to which larger numbers of primary pupils obtained access.[6] A 1959 law which raised the school-leaving age to sixteen for children enrolling in first grade that year ensured that during the Fifth Republic the primary school's loss of importance in the process of acculturation would continue. At the same time, the adoption of coeducation (*mixité*) in public and many private primary schools during the 1960s and 1970s ended segregation of the sexes at an early age in urban areas. Coeducation made girls' elementary schooling less distinct from boys' than it once had been.

Clearly the history of girls' primary education cannot be separated from the general history of French education or from changes in the larger society which affected the classroom. Four questions addressed in this study will help illuminate the relationship of girls' schooling to modern French society and explain how pedagogues have prepared girls for roles that differed from those assigned to boys. (1) What did educators find distinctive in the personalities of girls and women? (2) How did textbooks depict woman's responsibilities within the family and her relationship to husband, parents, and children? (3) What relation was envisioned between women and the larger world beyond the domestic foyer—the forum of work, politics, and community life? (4) Finally, have the answers to the preceding questions changed significantly since the 1880s? The public school's program for the daughters of Marianne, the feminine figure whose symbolic connection with a republic dates from the first French Revolution,[7] is the primary focus, but comparisons are also made between public school offerings and the Catholic school's textbooks for the daughters of Mary (Marie in French). We shall see that pedagogues' depictions of the feminine mission reveal much about the political and social preoccupations of France's leaders.

Questions about educators' programs for girls do not, of course, address the whole story of French girls' experience in primary schools. Textbooks and pedagogical manuals cannot tell us all that we might like to know about a teacher's interactions with students, a school's relationship to a community, or a student's absorption of and reactions to the school's offerings. But curricular materials do tell us what educators believed *ought* to exist, even if textbook images have not always mirrored the reality conveyed by census statistics on the participation of women in the work force. That this study can also demonstrate that formal education has helped many young women assume work roles at odds with those dominating the schools' prescriptive literature is not surprising. We shall see, however, that for a long time women's assumption of nondomestic roles did not, in many instances, indicate fundamental rejection of what they had learned at home and school about woman's place.

Girls' Primary Education in the Nineteenth Century: Traditions and Innovations

Girls' schools were already numerous in France when the Third Republic made primary schooling compulsory for both sexes. Although republicans sometimes presented themselves as the first significant providers of enlightenment for the masses previously left in darkness, historians studying education under earlier regimes have presented a more nuanced picture of the Republic's educational innovations.[1] Prior to the 1870s a large majority of children obtained some schooling, but there were significant regional variations in literacy rates. Moreover, girls' education had often been more neglected than boys', especially in rural areas. In 1865 the Abbé Hébert-Duperron, an inspector of schools in the Dordogne, spoke frankly to women teachers about this past neglect and judged it highly unfortunate. The *Dictionnaire pédagogique*, the Republic's standard reference work on education, thus claimed correctly that before the 1880s "the education of girls had not occupied in the concerns of government leaders the same place as that of boys."[2] We must review the important traditions, values, and laws that shaped girls' primary education before 1880 and then note the formal changes ushered in by the Ferry Laws.

During the Old Regime, the Reformation and Counter-Reformation had spurred the interest of religious leaders in teaching reading to the popular classes. A literate population could read devotional materials. Religious and governmental leaders also recognized that educated girls grew up to become mothers whose influence on families might contribute to the maintenance of religious observance and public order.[3] The royal declaration of 13 December 1698 that proclaimed the desirability of a schoolmaster and schoolmistress for each parish stipulated the importance of teaching "the catechism and prayers" and then added that instruction could also be given in reading and "even" writing to those needing such skills.[4]

The wording of that royal declaration is also a clue to an old educational practice that now seems especially curious: namely, instruction in reading was often unaccompanied by instruction in writing—more often, it seems, in the case of girls than of boys. The Catholic Church's wish to prevent girls from being able to write love letters has been cited as an explanation for the separation of reading and writing. More important determinants, however, were the absence of any compelling economic need for writing, a shortage of teachers, and the slow pace of learning caused by the common practice of instructing one pupil at a time rather than an entire class.[5] Large numbers of adults able to read but not to write were to be found in some areas well into the nineteenth century. According to the 1866 census, 50 percent of the population could read and write; 10 percent could read but not write.[6]

Social, economic, and geographical settings also greatly influenced literacy levels in early modern France. Urban literacy rates were higher than rural ones for both men and women. By 1700, for example, more than 70 percent of merchants' wives in Montpellier wre literate; by 1800, nearly 100 percent. Similarly, nearly all aristocratic and bourgeois men and women in the region that became the department of Seine-et-Marne were literate by the end of the eighteenth century. Regional literacy rates varied from a high of 89 percent for men and 65 percent for women in Lorraine to 14 percent for men and 6 percent for women in the Nivernais, often being particularly low in rural regions where the Catholic Church had experienced little or no competition from Protestants. For the total population on the eve of the French Revolution the literacy rates, as measured by ability to sign the marriage register, were 47 percent for men (as compared to 29 percent in 1700) and 27 percent for women (14 percent in 1700). In general, literacy rates were significantly higher north of a line that could be drawn between Saint Malo and Geneva than south of it.[7]

The gap between male and female literacy rates demonstrates that Old Regime society attached less importance to the formal education of women than of men. Officially church and governmental regulations required separating the sexes in schools in order to preserve feminine purity. However, the near doubling of women's literacy rates during the eighteenth century, unaccompanied by a comparable increase in the number of girls' schools, suggests that in practice coeducation sometimes existed or that girls were taught during hours when boys were not in class. According to Marie-Laurence Netter, the use of coeducation in the "petites écoles" maintained by localities explains why, in both 1690 and 1820, the area that became the department of the Yonne (north of the Saint Malo-Geneva line) exhibited a significantly higher female literacy rate than did the Haute-Garonne (in the south) where elementary education was more elitist and there was virtually no coeducation.[8] Religious orders also sponsored many girls' schools, some orders specializing in education for the upper classes and others for the masses. However, for many daughters of the aristocracy and bourgeoisie home instruction by mothers or governesses was the norm. Literate women of humbler station presumably passed on their knowledge to offspring, too.[9]

There were qualitative as well as quantitative differences between girls' and boys' schooling. Sewing and religion were the major subjects in many girls' schools, although religion was certainly not absent from boys' schools.[10] The emphasis on teaching girls needlework and memorization of the catechism explains why Jean Perrel can demonstrate, on the one hand, that contrary to old assumptions about the lack of girls' schools before 1880, some rural areas like Auvergne and the Bourbonnais actually had more classes for girls than for boys but that, on the other hand, literacy was not a necessary consequence of attending school.[11]

On the eve of the French Revolution some framers of *cahiers de doléances* asked for expansion of schooling, and after 1789 most leaders of the Revolution agreed that all citizens had a right to become literate. Discarding the religious purposes of previous popular instruction, revolutionaries also hoped to use schools to teach patriotism to free and equal citizens. In practice the Revolution's educational accomplishments were disappointing and, by persecuting the clergy, it actually hindered instruction in some regions. The Constitution of 1791 envisioned free public primary schools for all children, but detailed plans for such a system often contained disparities between boys' and girls' education. Thus in 1791 Talleyrand proposed that girls' schools teach the "virtues of domestic life" and "talents useful in the government of a family." He also recommended that girls, unlike boys, leave school at age eight because thereafter parents were their most suitable educators. By contrast, the progressive Marquis de Condorcet advocated the same primary education for girls and boys; he believed in the intellectual equality of the sexes and even in coeducation but agreed that women should not be admitted to advanced courses providing training for jobs that only men could hold. The Convention in 1793 considered Lakanal's plan for separate sections for boys and girls within one school and passed a version of it in November 1794. Then under the Directory the government's interest in providing free public schools for all children waned in the midst of crisis, and at the end of the 1790s private schools remained more numerous than public ones.[12]

The lack of formal schooling opportunities for many children notwithstanding, the First Republic's and the Directory's emphasis on inculcating republican civic and secular values helped lay the basis for the national school system of the nineteenth century.[13] As for revolutionary pedagogy specifically for girls, Poisson de la Chabeaussière's famous textbook, *Catéchisme français ou principes de morale républicaine à l'usage des écoles primaires*, which spoke of the "equality" of the sexes, seems to have been unusual. Typical school manuals of the 1790s were often "antifeminist," scorning women who strove for independence or citing women as the most common cause of the ruination of families.[14]

The record of the First Empire on primary education was also disappointing. Napoleon was more preoccupied with secondary and professional education for military and technical elites than with expanding primary schooling. His regime ushered in the *Université*, establishing state administrative control over all levels of education from university on down. But Napoleon was content to leave many primary schools to the church, with which he had reestablished relations in the Concordat of 1801. Unlike Condorcet, who had viewed educating women as a key to uplifting all humanity, Napoleon scorned the "faiblesse" of feminine brains and wanted simply to train women to be docile and devout wives and mothers. Girls did not need "public education" because they were "not called to live in public." The only landmark in girls' education from the First Empire was the opening of a school for daughters of members of the Legion of Honor, and for them Napoleon recommended that three-fourths of the day be devoted to sewing and instruction in housekeeping.[15]

Under the Bourbon Restoration additional primary schools, public and private, were opened. Expenditures for primary education were placed in the national budget for the first time in 1816, although parents and local governments continued to be the main source of funding. Statistics are inadequate for measuring the Restoration's record on girls' schooling. For boys additional schools meant that whereas in 1815 less than one-third (865,000) went to school, by 1829 1,372,206 did so.[16] The *brevet de capacité*, a certificate attesting to a male teacher's possessing sufficient knowledge to instruct children, was also introduced in 1816. It became a requirement for women teachers in 1819. However, members of religious orders teaching in communal schools could substitute "letters of obedience" from religious superiors for the professional credential.

The July Monarchy laid more substantial foundations for public primary schools in 1833 with a law which François Guizot, Louis Philippe's education minister, dubbed the "charter of primary education." The Guizot Law required communes to provide a school building and a minimum income for a teacher. A department not already having a normal school should establish one. Teaching brothers now had to present the *brevet* to teach in public schools, but nuns still needed only a "letter of obedience." Although the law did not make primary education free or compulsory, it contributed to a significant increase in school enrollments just at a time when the economic value of literacy was becoming more apparent to rural as well as urban parents.[17] Between 1833 and 1847 the number of primary schools doubled, leaving only one-tenth of communes without at least one school, either public or private. Boys benefited more than girls, for by 1847 the number of girls in school (1,354,056) was just under two-thirds the number of boys (2,176,079).[18] Because of financial considerations the government had omitted requirements for girls' schools from the Guizot Law. An ordinance of 1836 which included regulations for girls' schools also did not obligate communes to set up separate girls' facilities, even though public opinion and officialdom still frowned upon coeducation as a moral danger causing girls to lose "that reserve, that decency which is natural to them."[19] In practice, many small village schools were "mixed" but had partitions one and one-half meters high in the middle of the classroom to separate the sexes. By the last year of the July Monarchy some 40 percent of girls still received no formal schooling, and in the department of Finistère in Brittany the figure was 81 percent.[20]

The July Monarchy's prescriptions for girls' education appeared in the official curriculum and were elaborated upon in teachers' manuals. In theory, if not always in practice, boys and girls studied the same general subjects: religion and moral instruction, reading, writing, arithmetic, singing, and drawing. Girls also received lessons in sewing, that specialty of parish schools of the Old Regime and contemporary Catholic boarding schools. In reality, many girls' schools devoted more time to religion and sewing than to the academic subjects prescribed by law.[21]

How to adapt the curriculum and school setting to feminine needs was the subject of Lucille Sauvan's *Directions*, an outgrowth of lessons for aspiring teachers attending the *cours normaux* that she offered in Paris for thirty-five years. Girls' education had the same basic goals for all social classes: to produce "a good Christian, respectful child, virtuous woman, faithful spouse, tender but not weak mother, . . . [and] thrifty and prudent housewife."[22] Certainly there was a timeless quality to Sauvan's aims. Her list mirrored the educational design for aristocratic girls that the Abbé Fénelon and Madame de Maintenon shared during the late seventeenth century, although their model woman differed significantly from the salon women of the age of Louis XIV.[23]

Sauvan knew in the 1840s that she was addressing the education of humble Parisian girls, not aristocrats, and so also recommended that instruction be tailored to the situation of each social class. Most urban public school girls would become not only wives and mothers but also, for at least part of their adult lives, workers (ouvrières). Stating that workers' daughters generally received less care and attention than middle class girls educated at home or in pensionnats, Sauvan advised women teachers (institutrices) to teach their charges "sobriety, patience, love of work, resignation, moderation in desires, simplicity in tastes." Teachers themselves should set excellent examples of proper behavior and attitudes. Sauvan was also explicit about the utility of Christianity for maintaining social order: those who endured earthly deprivations would be rewarded in heaven. That Jesus was born in a stable and grew up in a carpenter's household should help poor children accept their dismal lot in life. If proper instruction failed to inspire love of God in a child, then a teacher should invoke fear of God to produce good conduct. The masses must believe that God surveyed every second of their existence.[24]

Sauvan's manual is but one illustration of how nineteenth-century governments increasingly utilized advice-givers whose pronouncements about the nature of the family and the responsibilities of its members could be convenient rationalizations for existing social and economic realities. As Jacques Donzelot has argued, an increase in governmental intrusions into private life went hand in hand with the growing needs of employers in an industrializing age for a literate labor force imbued with the values of hard work, punctuality, and self-discipline. If schools taught these values to girls as well as to boys, then mothers could transmit them to children. Appropriately, sociologists Pierre Bourdieu and Jean-Claude Passeron have termed the school's transmission of values a process of "cultural reproduction."[25]

It was the religious foundation in manuals like Sauvan's that differentiated the inculcation of values in mid-nineteenth-century public schools from that of the Third Republic. Subsequent regimes did not change the behavioral patterns of hard work, thriftiness, and resignation which middle class educators of the July Monarchy found suitable for both men and women of the people, but with the Ferry Laws the religiosity which often permeated earlier public education would disappear. Before the 1880s, however, religious foundations were implanted still more deeply in public schools, and especially in girls' schools, by the educational policies of the Second Republic and Second Empire. The plan of revolutionary leaders of 1848 to eliminate religion from public schools was abandoned after the "June Days" uprising heightened the middle classes' preoccupation with maintaining law and order.

The expansion of schooling after 1850 was a veritable "silent revolution" presided over by Louis Napoleon Bonaparte, president of the Second Republic and emperor after December 1852. By the end of the Second Empire the overwhelming majority of girls as well as boys obtained some formal schooling. The number of girls in school in 1866 was 93 percent of that of boys, but perhaps one-fifth of all boys and one-third of all girls "were escaping effective education."[26] Article 51 of the Falloux Law of 1850 had called for separate girls' schools in communes with a population of 800 or more, but it hedged on a commune's obligation to create a girls' school by also stating, "if its own resources provide the means." Supporters of Catholic schools were appeased with the provision that if a free private school existed in a commune, a departmental council could excuse the commune from founding a public one. Although the right to free primary schooling was not yet established, by 1866 41 percent of children in public schools received a free education and by 1872, 54 percent.[27]

Like the July Monarchy, the Second Empire permitted religious personnel to teach in public schools but continued to exempt nuns and some male clerics from the requirement of the *brevet*.[28] Not surprisingly, secular critics like Jules Simon questioned the intellectual preparation of teaching *soeurs* whose only credential was a "letter of obedience."[29] Between 1850 and 1853 religious teachers were entrusted with 47 percent of newly created public schools for boys and 60 percent of those for girls. If public and private school pupils are counted together, 21 percent of boys and 55 percent of girls were taught by religious orders in 1866. In the public schools alone, 19 percent of boys and 53 percent of girls had religious teachers in 1866 (Table 1).[30]

The Catholic Church's strength in primary education and its parallel gains in secondary schools led two imperial education ministers, Gustave Rouland and Victor Duruy, to attempt to check its influence in public schools. Although the Second Empire had at first eagerly sought clerical backing, by the 1860s church-state relations had been strained by French support for the unification of Italy, a threat to the continuing existence of the Papal States. Moreover, the government had come to see the church as a _ival for the first allegiances of French men and women. In many communes religious teachers had driven out la teac rs, partly because subsidies from their

Table 1. Number of Pupils Taught by Secular and Religious Teachers, 1863–1914 (in 1000s of pupils)

Type of Teachers:	Public Schools				Private Schools			
	Boys		Girls		Boys		Girls	
	Lay	Relig.	Lay	Relig.	Lay	Relig.	Lay	Relig.
1863	1,667	412	636	697	126	82	296	418
1866	1,717	398	669	753	135	94	299	450
1876	1,626	587	712	1,041	94	94	218	345
1881	2,188	254	1,161	755	66	200	152	564
1886	2,293	169	1,351	630	60	267	114	640
1891	2,518	37	1,435	491	54	397	94	731
1896	2,293	26	1,488	384	48	416	83	794
1901	2,313	16	1,609	237	46	401	73	856
1906	2,468	3	2,074	38	287	50	527	138
1912	2,474	.2	2,125	2	360	8	672	28

SOURCE: Antoine Prost, *Histoire de l'enseignement en France, 1800–1967* (Paris: Armand Colin, 1968), p. 218.

orders or private benefactors made them less costly to a locality. To counter this trend, Rouland made authorizations for new congregations more difficult to obtain. In 1860 he also instructed prefects, who had received the power to appoint teachers in 1854, to reject municipal councils' requests for engaging *congréganistes* if suitable lay teachers could be found. Duruy continued these policies.[31]

Wishing to lessen the church's predominance in girls' education, the liberal Duruy inserted in the education law of 1867 a provision which reduced to five hundred the population of communes required to maintain a separate girls' school. Yet there was little likelihood that many public schools for girls would lose their religious character as long as the government neglected to train women teachers. While most departments had provided normal schools for men since the July Monarchy, most *cours normaux* for women were not secular. In 1863 congregations ran seven of the eleven normal schools for women and thirty-five of the fifty-seven "normal courses"; by early 1870, when the number of female teacher training schools and courses had risen to seventy-four, congregations still directed two-thirds of them.[32] Furthermore, Duruy did not eliminate religion from the official primary curriculum because, like predecessors, he judged it an important foundation of social order. Thus public school pupils might still fill entire notebooks with dictations from the gospels, catechism, or rules for a holy life.[33] To bring a secular education to a select group of middle class adolescent girls, Duruy did introduce the first public secondary level courses for females. But protracted church opposition, orchestrated by Bishop Dupanloup, prevented these courses from gaining a substantial clientele by the time the Second Empire went down to defeat in 1870.[34]

The identification of the church with conservative and monarchical politics at the start of the Third Republic was a major cause of republican anticlericalism. However, the republicanizing and secularizing of public schools which would indoctrinate future generations could not begin until republicans had gained control of the Chamber of Deputies in the elections of 1876 and protected that position by winning the elections of October 1877, the aftermath of the *seize mai* crisis initiated by President MacMahon and his monarchist backers. MacMahon's early resignation in 1879 left republicans firmly in charge of the government.

Recognizing the desirability of literacy for voters in a democratic state and realizing also, like Duruy, that an industrializing society required a literate work force, republican politicans committed themselves to universal primary schooling. The Ferry Laws of 1881–1882 made public schools free and secular and made school attendance compulsory for all children aged six to thirteen. In the realm of girls' education the Third Republic attempted in three ways to make up for past neglect: the creation of additional public primary schools, the opening of normal schools, and the foundation of state secondary schools. Since the Second Empire republicans had been explicit about their motivations for supporting reforms in girls' education. Decrying the intellectual gulf between husband and wife as a cause of marital discord, Jules Ferry had contended in April 1870, using the positivist rhetoric of the day, that domestic harmony could be restored if the influence of science replaced the church's hold on women. Like Catholics, republicans recognized the importance of woman's influence on members of the family circle. A decade later Ferry was both Minister of Public Instruction and premier and ready to change educational policy so that the next generations would have wives and mothers imbued with secular and republican values. He and his supporters would also make war on illiteracy, more common for women than for men. In 1880 25 percent of women were still unable to sign the marriage register, as compared to 16 percent of men.[35]

Legislation concerning the training of lay teachers preceded the formal secularization of public schools. A law of August 1879 required all departments to maintain normal schools for women as well as men. Subsequently sixty-four new normal schools for women and six for men opened, the numerical disparity testifying to the state's prior neglect of girls' education.[36] An increase of 56 percent in the corps of lay *institutrices* between 1876 and 1881 meant that there were more lay women teachers than teaching nuns for the first time since the July Monarchy. By 1886 there were 114 percent more lay *institutrices* than in 1876.[37] With the normal schools in place, republicans passed a law in October 1886 to eliminate all clerical personnel from public school teaching ranks. By then certain municipalities like Paris, where anticlericals dominated the city council, had already decreed that all public school personnel should be laymen and laywomen. In many places, however, another two or three decades elapsed before the *congréganiste* became as much a rarity in girls' schools as in boys' schools. In 1901 237,000 girls in public schools still had religious teachers, as compared to only 16,000 boys (Table 1).[38]

Furthermore, many lay female teachers had themselves received and been deeply influenced by religious schooling. Despite Ferry's elimination of religion from public schools, many *institutrices* of the 1880s and 1890s and even later neither understood nor embraced the secularized moral instruction that replaced religion in the curriculum.[39] In the normal school of the Lozère in the 1880s Catholic pupils deliberately separated themselves from Protestants, Catholics being determined to belie predictions that they would lose their souls in this republican institution. At the normal school of Grenoble in the early 1880s attendance at mass or a Protestant service was required, but by the 1890s unbelievers or nonpractitioners were free to stay away from church, a *décret* of 9 January 1883 having made religious observance optional for *normalien(ne)s*.[40] Because of personal conviction or the need to accommodate local preferences, some rural *institutrices* of the Belle Epoque still gave religious instruction, at least when a school inspector was not around, and accompanied their charges to mass on Sunday.[41]

Parental tastes undoubtedly contributed to the longer duration of religious overtones in girls' public schools than in boys', although some aging *instituteurs* also defied republican authorities and displayed the crucifix in public school classrooms at the end of the century.[42] Enrollment statistics for private schools (*écoles libres*), eventually largely Catholic, further illustrate parental belief that religious schooling was far more important for girls than for boys. After the secularization of public schools in March 1882, there was a rush to enroll more children in Catholic schools, but noticeably more girls than boys were entered. Whereas 29 percent of girls had attended private schools in 1880, 38 percent did so in 1886. In comparison, 10 percent of primary school boys attended private schools in 1880 and 12 percent in 1886. The less exclusive Catholic schools often competed openly with public schools by offering free tuition, but after 1882 Protestants and Jews largely abandoned denominational schools in favor of the now free public institutions. Secular private schools also became a rarity. A major reason why girls outnumbered boys in Catholic schools was that parents wanted boys to receive the public school instruction qualifying them to pass the state examination for the certificate of primary studies. Parents viewed that credential as less important for girls. The number of girls in private schools subsequently declined during the next wave of republican anticlericalism following the Dreyfus Affair, but by 1911 25 percent of girls still attended private schools, as compared to 13 percent of boys. The preponderance of girls in private schools would continue throughout the twentieth century, although after World War II the gap between the sexes in enrollments narrowed (Table 2).[43]

Girls in public primary schools attended either separate girls' schools or *écoles mixtes*. Although the *écoles maternelles* for ages two to six were coeducational, republicans continued the regulation of 1867 calling for separate girls' primary schools in town of five hundred or more.[44] They also stipulated that *écoles maternelles* and mixed primary schools be staffed by women. As of 1910 only 12.5 percent of children in public schools were in mixed classes where, as previously, "principles of decency" were often preserved by seating boys and girls on different sides of the room. Catholic educators boasted that their schools offered more certainty of avoiding the dangers of

Table 2. Percentage of Primary School Pupils Enrolled in Private Primary Schools, 1850–1963

	Girls	Boys	All Pupils
1850	33	13	22
1865	32	10	20
1875	24	8	17
1880	29	10	19
1886	38	12	20
1891	30	16	23
1896	32	17	24
1901	34	16	25
1906	24	12	18
1911	25	13	19
1925	26	14	23
1935	23	12	18
1945	26	16	21
1955	19	13	16
1963	17	13	15

Calculated from statistics in Pierre Chevallier, ed., *La Scolarisation en France depuis un siècle* (Paris and The Hague: Mouton, 1974), p. 42.

coeducation: only 1.7 percent of Catholic students were in mixed classes in 1910.[45] Many republican educators, like Catholic colleagues, rejected the American penchant for coeducation on the grounds that the nature and destiny of women differed from that of men.[46]

The education ministry also assigned different missions to boys' and girls' schools: primary schools should prepare boys to become workers and soldiers and initiate girls in the "care of the household and *ouvrages de femmes.*"[47] This directive and the content of many instructional materials for girls' schools make it necessary to revise a generalization about the identity of boys' and girls' primary schooling in a standard history of French education. According to Antoine Prost, primary schools did not exhibit the striking differences between girls' and boys' education evident in secondary schools during much of the Third Republic. The founders of public secondary schools for girls in 1880 never intended them to prepare pupils for professional careers, as was the case with boys' *lycées* and *collèges.* The girls' secondary program, lasting five years, was two years shorter than the boys' program, and the exclusion of Latin from girls' secondary schools meant that their pupils lacked an essential subject for the examination for the *baccalauréat,* the credential needed for admission to university study. Girls' secondary schools were instead expected to familiarize future ladies of the republican bourgeoisie with domestic virtues and social graces as well as with an academic "general culture." In contrast, wrote Prost, the primary schools served the children of the people and aimed to prepare both sexes for a lifetime of hard work.[48] Certainly, as Prost emphasized, the primary and secondary schools were designed to serve different social classes. But the republican primary school's transmission of middle class values and role models to "le peuple" indeed included attention to gender roles. Although boys and girls studied the same academic subjects, textbooks for reading, moral lessons, and science and ministerial instructions for practical subjects highlighted differences between girls' and boys' expected destinies.

The primary school curriculum of 1882 included the July Monarchy's staples of moral instruction, reading, writing, grammar, arithmetic, singing, and drawing and the Second Empire's additions of history, geography, science, and hygiene. The nonacademic subjects of "manual works" *(travaux manuels)* and physical education rounded out the program, which was graded according to the levels of the *cours préparatoire* (ages 6–7), *cours élémentaire* (7–9), *cours moyen* (9–11), and *cours supérieur* (11–13). Frequently, however, separate classrooms were not available for each grade because many rural schools were one-room affairs. In 1906 one-room schools were more than twice as numerous as those with at least two classrooms; and in only nine departments were schools with more than one classroom the norm, the Seine leading the way with an average of 7.5 classes, followed by Calvados with 3.3 and the Nord with 2.7.[49]

The detailed primary program of 1887 and later additions referred explicitly to differences in physical education and "manual works" for boys and girls. For "gymnastique" teachers should use separate girls' and boys' manuals published by the education ministry, girls' exercises being designed to develop a "comfortable gait" and "graceful bearing." Initially boys also learned military exercises, for these seemed essential to an angry nation wounded by losing a war to the Germans. "Manual works" meant instruction in the use of common tools for boys and sewing for girls. Although the education ministry specified that the primary school must not lose "its essential character as an educational establishment" and become "an atelier," it nonetheless told teachers to give "manual exercises" sufficient attention so that boys and girls were prepared for future roles as men and women. "Domestic economy" *(économie domestique)* for girls was also endowed with moral value: it could teach them "love of order, make them acquire the serious qualities of a housewife, and put them on guard against frivolous and dangerous tastes."[50]

Normal schools instructed future teachers in all parts of the required primary program. Over the course of three years, aspiring teachers studied academic subjects and pedagogical techniques. Instruction in "practical" topics varied according to gender. For women, drawing lessons stressed "ornamental" more than "geometrical" design, and "manual works" meant sewing and home economics. In 1905, after numerous complaints that many *institutrices'* preparation in home economics was more theoretical than practical, the third year of the normal school program for women was revised to devote fully eleven hours a week to sewing and domestic economy. Classes in child care *(puériculture)* of one hour per week were also added.[51] Examinations for the *brevet supérieur* and later for the certificate of professional aptitude measured the *normalien(ne)s'* command of the subject matter.

Many women attending the normal schools probably found their atmosphere as important in the educational process as the formal curriculum. Descriptions of normal schools as "lay convents" abound in teachers' memoirs and contemporary reports.[52] The label was appropriate not only because *normaliennes* had their mail censored, could not bring unapproved books into the school, and were kept apart from *normaliens* but also because normal school professors taught students that they were preparing for a special vocation, not just a job. Félix Pécaut, the influential head of the Ecole normale supérieure pour l'enseignement primaire at Fontenay-aux-Roses, founded in 1880 to train women to teach in the departmental normal schools, wanted teachers to have a strong moral presence. In his morning talks at Fontenay this former Protestant set such an example for students. He advised these teachers of future teachers to give sound instruction in a simple, natural fashion. They should avoid intellectual pretensions because girls of the people did not need a bluestocking as a role model.[53] Complementing Jules Ferry's famous assertion that the *père de famille* was the desired model for *l'instituteur*,[54] normal schools encouraged women teachers to think of themselves as exercising a maternal function in the classroom. Indeed, it was because motherly qualities were assumed to be natural attributes of women that the coeducational nursery schools were named *écoles maternelles* and taught exclusively by women. Once on the job, *institutrices* should be exemplary in conduct, avoiding local disputes and gossip and keeping a distance from men.[55] Much in their training thus resembled the moral advice given to Catholic teachers, religious and lay.[56]

Normal schools greatly enhanced the professionalism of women teachers. Presumably classes in which a teacher dozed off and was awakened by her charges only when a word in a reader stumped them, as was the case in two Deux-Sèvres schools in the mid-nineteenth century, became a rarity.[57] Certainly inspectors' reports on Parisian teachers during the 1880s and 1890s indicate that most efficiently performed their obligations in the classroom. To the extent that teachers' incompetency presented problems during the first decades after the Ferry Laws, it was often because holdovers from an earlier period could not adjust to new standards—as when a sixty-year-old woman in the nineteenth arrondissement of Paris baffled six- and seven-year-olds with incomprehensible ramblings, sometimes in Latin and Greek, about philosophy and ancient history. As late as 1907 about one-sixth of public school *institutrices* lacked the *brevet supérieur*, not required of all women teachers before the Ferry reforms. Younger teachers knowledgeable enough to obtain certification but unable to impose discipline on unruly charges received low ratings from inspectors and did not obtain tenure.[58]

On the eve of the passage of the Ferry Laws *institutrices* already had available both special girls' textbooks and assorted treatises on girls' education. Of the old discourses by clerics and lay authors on the goals of girls' education, probably none was better known than *De l'éducation des filles*, first published in 1687 by François de Salignac de la Mothe-Fénelon, future archbishop of Cambrai. Like Sauvan's later manual, Fénelon's book advised instilling religious principles, certainly a topic far removed from republicans' secular concerns. But

Fénelon's notions about the special nature of woman were long acceptable to lay as well as congregational educators. Fénelon judged feminine minds and bodies to be different from and weaker than those of men. Nature compensated for these weaknesses by endowing women with the qualities of industry, neatness, and thrift so that they might be quietly occupied with their homes. Significantly, women's differences did not make them inferior human beings. Their domestic functions were "no less important to the public than those of men" because men's success and the education of children were dependent upon women's performance of their duties. "A discreet, diligent, pious woman is the soul of an entire household; she provides in it alike for temporal and spiritual welfare."[59]

To make Fénelon available to contemporary educators, Hachette, publisher of many textbooks and pedagogical materials, brought out a new edition of *De l'éducation des filles* in 1881. Annotations were added by Charles Defodon, editor of the *Manuel général de l'instruction primaire*, an important teachers' journal dating from the July Monarchy. Between 1880 and 1914 at least twenty-five editions of Fénelon's classic were published, including ten of the Defodon version; between 1811 and 1880 at least twenty-six editions had also appeared.[60] Republican pedagogues discarded Fénelon's emphasis on feminine piety but accepted much of his teaching on woman's personality and domestic role. Defodon's primary complaint was that Fénelon excessively restricted feminine studies in important subjects such as history, now very important for the molding of a patriotic woman. Although Pécaut in 1885 criticized Fénelon for being more interested in educating women to please husbands than to develop themselves as human beings, in 1894 education minister Eugène Spuller readily cited both Fénelon and Madame de Maintenon to reinforce his argument that French women, unlike some presumably more adventurous American sisters, belonged at home.[61]

Pécaut's criticism of the *abbé* notwithstanding, a less traditional interpretation of his message was also possible. An inspector general who observed one normal school directress's lesson on Fénelon's treatise in 1886 complained that she was unwisely implanting in country girls, destined for the most part to return to rural schools, notions about "their superiority or their equality to men." Furthermore, the feminist *directrice* of the Nord's normal school for women in 1907 saw in Fénelon an early example of "the idea of the fundamental equality of the sexes" because he had asserted that women were as virtuous as men.[62] As we shall see, these were not the only women educators or feminists who utilized ideas about gender differences to promote the cause of equal rights for women.

Fénelon's conviction that women could make or unmake a household was implicit, if not explicit, in much republican pedagogical literature about the teacher's role in preparing young women to be wives and mothers. Jules Payot's book for fledgling teachers revealed how the Parisian educational leadership expected the school to "civilize" backward rural areas in the year 1897. *Institutrices*, many of whom also came from humble backgrounds, should prepare for considerable activity outside as well as inside classrooms because poor peasant women were deficient in many respects:

> They are ignorant of housekeeping, they cannot cook or sew. . . . The young men of the village who marry them, raised in hardship, badly nourished by their mothers, used to the lack of comfort and elegance, find nothing to criticize about the wife: if she is negligent, slovenly, they do not perceive it, they do not suffer from it. They suffer nonetheless . . . from the indifference provoked by this lack of attention, and soon, their household resembles so many country households, gloomy, without affection, made of habits rather than of love. The *institutrice* can do much to change this state of things.

One way teachers could bring improvement was to conduct evening gatherings once or twice a week to teach local women more about cooking and housekeeping. With such training young women who kept homes spotless would "slowly give their parents, brothers, and husbands, the taste for tidiness, and consequently disgust for the cabaret. Walls and ceilings washed, the irreproachable floor, clean windows letting all light enter, furniture washed . . . or waxed and shining suffice already to give the house a festive air." Hang white curtains at the window, put a bowl of flowers on the table, hang some photographs or prints on the wall, and "*voilà*—a house . . . that men will love to stay in," especially if the children are well behaved and clean and the wife well dressed, she having learned dressmaking from the teacher, too. By being dedicated, setting a good example, and organizing her time well, a "clever *institutrice* can accomplish a revolution in each village."[63]

While the treatises of Fénelon and Payot exemplified the kind of advice teachers received, textbooks presented a simpler version of the school's messages about gender roles to children. Book selection was a largely decentralized process for both public and private schools. In 1865 Duruy had abandoned the previous policy of having each schoolbook approved by a governmental textbook commission before it was given to children. In practice many teachers before

1865 had paid little attention to official recommendations of books, sometimes because there was no hope of getting poor parents or town councils to buy new ones. During the July Monarchy the education ministry had purchased several hundred thousand copies of a few readers and catechisms and distributed them to communal schools, but the practice had not been continued. In impoverished areas teachers frequently resorted to asking children to bring books from home—a tactic which created difficulties for group instruction in reading unless all children brought a Bible, as many did.[64]

The central textbook commission was reinstated briefly in 1873 by the conservative forces of the *ordre moral,* but Ferry eliminated it. Instead schoolteachers met once a year at the cantonal level to draw up or modify a list of suitable textbooks from which teachers either made their own selections or picked those recommended by their school's inspector. A departmental commission reviewed cantonal lists but only for the purpose of deleting books judged unsuitable by the education ministry on the grounds of containing material offensive to public morality or hostile to the constitution—a veto power carried over from previous regimes. The Third Republic did not require communes to furnish books free to pupils, but in practice many did. If parents paid for textbooks, they belonged to students; when communes supplied them, students returned them at the end of the school year. In private schools each principal selected books, sometimes with the advice of diocesan educational officials. The only state control over textbooks for *écoles libres* was the prohibition on books banned by the education ministry. In practice, relatively few were banned.[65]

Girls' schools, public and private, could choose texts written for boys or for coeducational audiences, but many *institutrices* preferred special girls' books. Separate readers for boys and girls predated the Third Republic, for such publishers as Belin and Hachette had issued girls' readers during the July Monarchy and Second Empire, and some of these remained in use during the 1870s and 1880s. Comparing the content of older books with the batches of new texts introduced after the Ferry Laws (and discussed in the next chapter) will demonstrate the extent to which older and Catholic models of French womanhood still figured in the educational literature of a regime whose first decades were marked by bitter feuding between anticlerical republicans and Catholics, both eager to enlist women's support.

One girls' textbook first published during the July Monarchy and still available after 1870 was Josephine Sirey's *Petit manuel d'éducation, ou lectures à l'usage des jeunes filles de 8 à 12 ans.* Madame Sirey, editor of two women's magazines, set forth the familiar dichotomy between man's exterior role and woman's interior one. Although this differentiation of spheres was of classical vintage—having been enunciated by Xenophon in *The Economist* in the fourth century B.C.—it long mirrored a reality far more familiar to the upper classes than to peasants whose everyday lives were marked by a less rigid division of farm labor between the sexes.[66] The ubiquitousness of this explicit dichotomy in textbooks by the mid-nineteenth century testified to the separation of home and work place made increasingly common by industrialization and urbanization. Whereas her contemporary, Sauvan, expected urban working class girls to spend part of their lives toiling outside the home, Sirey reserved that destiny for boys. Girls would either become *mères de famille* or devote their lives to God. The purpose of girls' education was to enable women to instruct their children, not to prepare them for work or additional study. Barbara Pope has written about the vogue for the image of the woman as "mère-éducatrice" among the aristocracy and bourgeoisie after 1815 and has argued that these social groups utilized the image in their efforts to restore social stability after a generation of upheaval. A "mother-educator" could not be accused of the frivolity presumably indulged in by salon women before the Revolution of 1789. Sirey's manual shows the dissemination of the image of "mother-educator" to other social classes. Although she described her book as suitable for girls from all social groups, Sirey included a point commonly used by educators to divert the laboring classes from envy of the more prosperous: rich children were often less happy than artisans' offspring. Religiosity also permeated the book, for heroine Marie said daily prayers and went to confession and Sunday services. On the day for distributing school prizes and celebrating the *fête* of Saint Anne at the end of the book, villagers went first to church to hear the priest discuss woman's role as mother and manager of family life. Then the festivities moved to the school where the mayor gave out prizes which he, the priest, and the two village teachers (husband and wife) had awarded to the best pupils.[67] Under the Third Republic the prize ceremonies remained the climax of the school year but were strictly secular affairs in public schools.

Religion also had a significant place in the rural commune depicted in *La petite Jeanne ou le devoir*, a popular text published in 1852 by Zulma Carraud and approved by the imperial textbook commission in 1859. Hachette sold more than 500,000 copies of *Petite Jeanne* between the 1850s and World War I.[68] Whereas Sirey's manual was for girls of all social classes, Carraud's was intended for poor rural girls. Readers followed Jeanne's path from an impoverished childhood to domestic service, maturity as a hardworking farm wife, and, finally, widowhood. They learned that misfortunes were the common lot of the masses and should be borne without complaint. Far from questioning the social hierarchy, Jeanne entrusted her earnings to the master in whose household she was a servant and often sought his advice. In marriage Jeanne and her less educated mate were partners who fulfilled complementary roles, Jeanne well illustrating Fénelon's dictum that women could make or unmake households. *Jeanne* remained on the approved textbook lists of twenty-one departments, mostly rural, as late as 1889, but its religious content made it unsuitable for the secularized public schools of the Third Republic and sales of it dropped dramatically after the mid-1880s.[69] In Jeanne's village the priest had been the main moral and intellectual leader and took it upon himself to burn trashy books brought to town by a *colporteur*. Secularized texts of the Third Republic would assign the priest's role to a lay *instituteur* or *institutrice*, nowhere in evidence in *Jeanne*, although a male teacher was prominent in *Maurice ou le travail*, Carraud's companion volume for boys. Certain social mores accepted as normal in *Jeanne* also disappeared in later textbooks designed to bring urban middle class norms to the countryside. Henceforth, men would not find it unacceptable for women to sit at the table at mealtime, as was the case in Jeanne's master's house in the Cher at mid-century; and heroines would not continue to hire themselves out as wet-nurses when the Republic wished to control the wet-nursing profession and reduce its importance.[70]

Republican educators' elimination of religiosity and rude customs from school literature also explains the declining fortunes of *Madame Adeline* (1867), written by the *institutrice* Lilla Pichard. Five editions had appeared by 1879 and two more were produced in 1882 and 1889, but only two cantons of one department, the Haute Saône, retained it as a public school reader as of 1883. *Madame Adeline* told the story of a long suffering farm wife beaten by her husband but finally able, through her example of piety and hard work, to transform the brute into a civilized mate. The female narrator moralized: "It is in the heart of woman that God has engraved his conservative laws, and this essentially conservative sentiment which is in us is the dike which he opposes to the bad passions of men. . . . Courage, woman has a regenerating mission: there where God had placed her, evil can be transformed into good."[71]

Also inappropriate for secularized public schools was Madame Paul Caillard's *Entretiens familiers d'une institutrice avec ses élèves*, published in three editions between 1863 and 1874 and approved by the imperial textbook commission in 1863. The Bishop of Meaux praised its "truly Christian sentiments," and the secular educational official responsible for schools in the departments under the Academy of Toulouse commended the linkage of women's education to the "lessons of the catechism, that only infallible science," and the delineation of duties and qualities appropriate for girls' "destination in the family and in social relations." As we shall see, most items on Caillard's list of feminine qualities well matched the ideal woman's personality outlined by republican textbooks. Caillard wrote about order, good manners, cleanliness, love of one's fellow man, obedience to parents, affability, charity, goodness, modesty, sweetness, patience, sincerity, discretion, honesty, and, finally, "firm and enlightened piety." What successful authors of later republican textbooks would not do, however, was to link good behavior with injunctions such as "God is order, and order leads us to God."[72] Caillard's advice that arousing the fear of God in pupils could help prevent faults and ensure performance of duties echoed Sauvan's pedagogy of earlier decades but would disappear in secularized manuals of moral instruction.[73]

That Delagrave still published one edition of Caillard's *Entretiens* and four editions of its short version during the 1870s is a sign that the political changes of 1870–1871, ushering in the conservative *ordre moral*, had less impact on the content of textbooks than the Ferry Laws of the 1880s.[74] The most important girls' textbooks introduced during the first decade of the Third Republic were Ernestine Wirth's two-volume *Livre de lecture courante des jeunes filles chrétiennes*, published by Hachette in 1870 and 1872. Whereas Hachette's now classic *Petite Jeanne* combined moral messages with one long story, Wirth's readers were collections of stories and didactic passages. Bishop Dupanloup and Cardinal Donnet enthusiastically endorsed them, Donnet noting that "men and women have different duties to fill, they thus need special instruction." Although the religious element in Wirth's title is obvious, she was actually trying to meet teachers' complaints that too many textbooks for girls were simply for religious instruction and unsuitable as readers.[75]

Wirth's selections—ninety-five in the first book and one hundred forty-nine in the more advanced one—focused on family scenes and lives of famous women and illustrated "domestic virtues" and the traits of "self-sacrifice" and "resignation." Convinced that it was more useful for girls to know about illustrious women like Saint Genevieve than about Alexander the Great, Wirth deliberately provided notable female role models but, at the same time, chose examples to underscore the message that domestic economy was more important for a girl's future than algebra and geometry. In the first volume, eight historical heroines were queens or female relatives of heroes, two functioned in motherly roles, two were saints, one a nun, one a laywoman engaged in charity, and two rendered military services to France. Although the military feats of Joan of Arc and

Jeanne Hachette were hardly traditional feminine activities, these two shared with such women as Louis IX's mother or Madame de Maintenon the virtue of serving others. Some girls' aspirations must have been dampened by Wirth's story about James I of England who, on hearing about a young girl who knew many languages, living and dead, supposedly admitted that these were "rare qualities" for a female but then asked, "Does she know how to sew?" Readers learned that a married woman should do "everything which pleases" her husband and suffer "patiently" when he displeased her.[76]

As of 1883, Hachette had published 122,065 copies of the first volume of Wirth's *Livre de lecture* and 78,031 copies of the second. Like Carraud's *Petite Jeanne*, Wirth's readers also remained on twenty-one departmental reading lists for public schools in 1889.[77] Yet it is obvious why they, like *Jeanne*, were inappropriate for most girls' public schools after the Ferry Laws, even if pleasing to the nuns who still taught one-quarter of all girls in public schools in 1891. Flattering vignettes about Marie Antoinette were hardly desirable for a regime eager to rehabilitate the French Revolution by creating the first Sorbonne chair for a specialist in its history. Anticlericals would also want to replace religious role models like the Virgin Mary, Saint Theresa, or Saint Genevieve with suitable secular figures. It remains to be seen whether the many new textbooks quickly issued after the Ferry Laws of 1881–1882 altered Wirth's emphasis on "self-sacrifice" and "resignation" as cardinal virtues for women. To free women from the "spiritual rods" that priests allegedly used to beat them into submission to the church,[78] would anticlerical republicans significantly alter older Catholic images of womanhood?

CHAPTER TWO

Prescribing Values and Behavior: Feminine Images in Textbooks, 1880–1914

"Le grand bienfait dont jeunes filles sont redevable à la République, c'est l'émancipation de l'âme féminine par l'instruction."[1] The opinion of Madame Albertine Eidenschenk-Patin, *directrice* of the normal school for women in the department of the Nord, this boast about the liberating effects of republican education for women came from one whose professional success would not have been possible before the state assumed responsibility for training women teachers. Because girls' primary schools had by 1914 virtually eliminated illiteracy among women under age forty, they certainly deserved praise for emancipating some women from ignorance and better preparing them to cope with modern society. But should Eidenschenk-Patin's claim about the public school's emancipation of woman's mind and spirit also be equated with freeing women from any confining notions about female roles which feminists, then and now, find barriers to achieving equality between the sexes? An examination of feminine images in textbooks used between 1880 and 1914 will supply a partial answer.

Between the 1880s and 1914 the selection of textbooks offered by publishers expanded enormously. Educators, professional authors, and politicians wrote many new texts for the republicanized and secularized schools of Jules Ferry. In 1890 one educator estimated that some 2000 books were available from 130 different publishers, and his calculation may have been too low, for recent estimates suggest that between 60,000 and 120,000 textbooks were published in France between 1789 and 1959.[2] Textbooks sales were undoubtedly spurred by a ministerial decree of 29 January 1890 specifying the types of books a primary school student must have: for the *cours élémentaire*, a reader; for the *cours moyen*, a reader plus an atlas and books for grammar, arithmetic, and French history; for the *cours supérieur,* all the preceding plus a textbook for moral and civic instruction.[3] Covering themes required by the official program of instruction, textbooks were an invaluable teaching aid in classes whose average size of thirty-five to thirty-seven pupils hampered teachers' ability to give special attention to individual students.[4] In one-room schools textbook lessons kept pupils of one grade level busy while the teacher guided another group.

Special textbooks for girls also became more numerous by the 1890s.[5] As of 1889 at least 35 titles for girls were on the Ministry of Public Instruction's list of schoolbooks approved by departmental authorities for public school use; 4 were for moral and civic instruction, 16 were readers, and 15 were sewing and home economics manuals. Admittedly, girls' texts were only a small part of the complete list; the 35 girls' titles appeared in three sections containing a total of 624 texts.[6] By 1909, when the ministry accumulated another set of departmental book adoptions, at least 90 girls' books figured on public school lists.[7] For this chapter 136 textbooks first published before 1914 have been utilized. Of these 76 were girls' books and 25 were published by Catholic presses.[8] The majority (112) were for pupils aged 9 to 13 in the cours *moyen* or *supérieur* and so devoted more attention to preparation for adult life than books for earlier grades.

Some titles on public school lists also found favor in Catholic schools. Such was the case with the most popular reader of the Third Republic, Bruno's *Tour de la France par deux enfants* (1877), a tale about two ingenious male orphans.[9] Furthermore, the ministry's list of 1889 included books first published before 1880 and thus dispensing religious messages later eradicated by republican authors who either ignored religion altogether or, more commonly during the 1880s and 1890s, dealt in a vague deistic fashion with the topic of "duties to God" officially prescribed for moral instruction. Carraud's *Petite Jeanne* and Wirth's *Lecture courante* typified older books for girls, and twenty-one rural departments—most of which did not have an above average percentage of nuns teaching in public schools—kept them on public school lists.[10] However, after 1889 Hachette published less than 16,000 copies of its once popular *Petite Jeanne;* Wirth's two volumes of *Lecture courante* did sell more than 100,000 copies after 1889, but presumably Catholic schools eventually used them more than public schools, not finding them as archaic as *Petite Jeanne.*[11] For boys twenty-three departments in 1889 still approved of Carraud's *Maurice,* twenty-one of the *morale* text of the Frères de l'instruction chrétienne, and twenty of Charles Jeannel's *Petit Jean* (1843), a Catholic equivalent of *Tour de la France.*[12]

That public and Catholic schools shared certain textbooks during the 1880s did not mean that republican and Catholic educators generally considered most textbooks interchangeable or that dual usage would continue indefinitely once republican educators intensified efforts to secularize public schools. Anticlericals on the Paris municipal council objected to the religious content in certain books accepted for public schools in more traditional departments, and by 1889 the city's list of books furnished free to public schools no longer contained the popular *Tour de la France*, which offended by making God the creator of the universe.[13] Carraud's *Jeanne* and Wirth's *Lectures* were also absent. By 1901 the education ministry had banned eleven books from both public and private schools and another five from public schools. Although most were Catholic history texts, two were girls' home economics books. Since Catholic history texts treated such topics as the Reformation, wars of religion, and the French Revolution in a fashion that was noticeably different from that in secular tomes, their predominance on the banned list was not surprising. No school could use Théophile Valentin's *Fleurs de l'histoire* (1890) which ridiculed enemies of religion and proclaimed that it was "better to have a false or erroneous religion than to have none at all." Public schools could not adopt a home economics book which insisted that Christian mothers must send their children to Catholic schools.[14]

The exacerbation of republican anticlericalism in the wake of the Dreyfus Affair and the separation of church and state in 1905 also prompted publishers to expurgate the small amount of religious content in some old favorites. After 1905 Belin published two editions of *Tour de la France:* the original version of 1877 and another without sections on Notre Dame, notable Old Regime clerics, and prayers. Similarly, in 1909 Larousse issued secularized versions of two popular girls' readers by Clarisse Juranville. By that year five pre-1880 girls' titles with religious content which were still utilized in 1889 had also disappeared from public school book lists.[15] Catholic educators were, of course, not limited to textbooks used by state schools. They could turn to distinctly Catholic publishers like Alfred Mame of Tours, Emmanuel Vitte of Lyon, and A. Hatier and Charles Poussielgue of Paris. As of 1913 the *Annuaire officiel de l'enseignement libre catholique* also published a list of recommended Catholic texts.

Didactic behavioral prescriptions were most prominent in textbooks for moral instruction or a combination of moral and civic instruction, topics studied at all three primary levels. Civics dealt with the functioning of national and local government. *Morale* supposedly belonged to a "sphere completely different from the rest of the program of instruction," being intended to develop the conscience as well as the intellect. The teacher should "fortify and implant in the conscience of pupils . . . [and] bring into daily practice those essential notions of human morality, common to all doctrines and necessary for all civilized men." The official program listed the child's "duties" (*devoirs*) to self, family, other people, animals, and God and called for making him or her conscious of belonging to three social units: the family, school, and nation. In elementary and middle courses teachers gave *morale* lessons in conversational form at the start of each day—a replacement for Catholic prayer and catechism—and, ideally, exhibited "warmth" and "intensity" when presenting important principles or actions. Children also found numerous *morale* lessons in elementary and middle level readers and at age eleven or twelve, at the superior level, received a special textbook for moral and civic instruction.[16].

The education ministry specified behavioral ideals for all children: obedience to parents and respect and love for parents and siblings; hard work and thrift, but not excessive love of money or profit; cleanliness and sobriety; truthfulness, modesty, patience; and courage in the face of adversity. The social value of these virtues is obvious. They were ideal traits for industrious and uncomplaining peasants or factory workers and for law-abiding citizens. They well illustrate the school's role in the process of "cultural reproduction." Repeating behavioral standards of earlier regimes' textbooks, republican *morale* differed from predecessors only in omitting religious components other than the officially prescribed belief in God the creator—and even that was absent from many republican texts.[17]

The official program for primary schools did not distinguish between *morale* for girls and for boys, but girls' textbooks included messages not bestowed on boys. In 1893 the education ministry also explicitly defined the "special duties for the girl" in an outline for moral instruction in girls' *écoles primaires supérieures*, the post-primary schools often called "the secondary schools of the people."[18] Most primary school girls' textbooks, republican and Catholic, incorporated all or nearly all of this behavioral model, which enumerated four types of duties: personal, familial, social, and civic. A girl was enjoined "to fortify her judgment and will in view of her special obligations and the duties which await her in the family and society." "Modesty in dress, attitudes, and language" was especially important. She should perceive her role in the family as "discreet, modest and effective" and execute "domestic tasks, not only without repugnance, but with eagerness." An older sister must assume "maternal duties" to aid her mother. As the "daughter, sister, spouse, and mother of citizens," woman also influenced men's actions. A good, patient, and even-tempered woman served society by promoting harmony—"la concorde pour la vie"—in human relationships. Her behavior showed what "persuasion, the spirit of conciliation, love of peace, and mutual respect" could accomplish. "Today she can, because of the more varied and thorough instruction which she receives, ennoble our activity. Compassion and charity are her natural gifts, and it is again natural that she will remind us, in peace and in war, of respect for laws and love of country."[19]

Madame Henry Gréville's *Instruction morale et civique des jeunes filles*, first published in 1882, well illustrates the textbook presentation of woman's personality and duties. Within ten years, twenty-nine editions appeared and, as of 1889, seventy-nine departments placed it on textbook lists, more than the number of departmental adoptions for any other girls' text and a figure equaled by few boys' books or books for both sexes.[20] In the opinion of many Catholics, the book also exemplified deficiencies in republican moral instruction and so was part of an extended textbook controversy touched off in December 1882 when the Vatican placed four republican *morale* texts on the Index. The authors condemned for neglecting religion were Gréville, the philosopher and educator Gabriel Compayré, and the Opportunist politicians Jules Steeg and Paul Bert, the latter an outspoken anti-clerical who was Léon Gambetta's education minister from November 1881 to January 1882.[21] Gréville's book was the only one of the controversial four that was addressed to girls. We shall see what was normative in girls' textbooks just after the Ferry Laws by following Gréville's delineation of female roles and then comparing her prescriptions with other republican *morale* texts, readers, and domestic economy manuals for girls and also with Catholic texts and boys' texts.

"Madame Henry Gréville" was the pen name of Alice Marie Céleste Henry, Madame Emile Durand-Gréville (1842–1902), a successful *femme de lettres* married to a writer. According to Theodore Stanton, son of the American feminist, Gréville was a "broad-minded, liberal thinker on all the great reform and progressive questions of the hour," and she made her "artistic little house on the heights of Montmartre . . . an influential center for the propagation of modern ideas." Gréville was also a Protestant, as were some other leading educators involved in implementing the Ferry Laws—most notably, Buisson, Pécaut, and Steeg.[22] Although a few girls' textbooks were written by male pedagogues, most were by women who were either teachers or, like Gréville, recognized authors. By 1900 normal school professors, *lycée* professors, or *institutrices* were more likely than writers outside the educational establishment, like Gréville, to obtain publishers' contracts for girls' public school textbooks, just as their male counterparts were the most typical authors of textbooks for boys or coeducational classes.[23]

Gréville's manual had three parts, the first two offering maxims and examples totally suitable for a boys' book because all the characters illustrating good and bad behavior were male. Although it may seem strange that no girls appeared in this section of a girls' book, Gréville was not unlike other pedagogues who, while addressing strictly feminine audiences, seemed to talk about educating males. Pécaut could exhort women students at Fontenay-aux-Roses to be conscious of their responsibility to form in each student "une âme d'homme" or "to cultivate the man."[24] Few women teachers complained openly, as did a Paris *inspectrice* of schools in 1911, about the predominance of the male gender in much school literature for girls.[25]

Unlike the first two parts of Gréville's manual, the third, "The Young Girl and Woman in Society," was in the tradition of Fénelon's treatise: women were destined for a different role than men and possessed uniquely feminine traits suitable for that role. "Woman is the *guardian of the foyer*," Gréville intoned. "Her place is at home, in the house of her parents or husband . . . ; it is for the foyer that she must reserve all her grace and good humor. . . . A woman who does not love her home, who has no taste for household duties . . . cannot remain a virtuous woman for long."[26]

Gréville's delineation of feminine traits was perfectly consistent with her instructions—and warnings—about woman's domestic mission. The ideal woman prized order and cleanliness as she set about making the home comfortable for her family. She was also *douce*, patient, modest, charitable, and reserved. She performed duties conscientiously and bore life's disappointments with "joyous resignation." Woman's natural *douceur*—that is, sweetness, gentleness, and good nature—made her a charming "mistress of the house" and kept her from becoming shrewish in giving orders. Patience, labeled a quintessentially feminine virtue, was rooted in both nature and laws, which have conditioned a woman to wait. If a woman was deficient in any of these traits or guilty of behavioral vices, such as exposing too much skin or pushiness in conversations, then her faults were more serious than those of men because her honor and virtue were, like "delicate flowers," easily damaged. A woman must never forget that "*what men require* above all in a woman, is that she be *feminine in virtues and appearance*." Her thoughts and actions should be an open book where her family could find "elevated sentiments, respect for duty, patience, and devotion."[27] In sum, this personality package assumed that women found self-fulfillment only by serving others. The virtues of patience, resignation, and setting behavioral standards for others were not likely to form individualistic rebels. Although males from the popular classes were certainly also enjoined to obey laws, work hard, and be responsible for families, they avoided the additional injunction of subservience to the opposite sex which textbooks carried over from the Civil Code.

Apart from listing feminine virtues and vices, as had many religious and secular educators over the centuries,[28] Gréville also utilized two role models, Jeanne and Cécile, to instruct girls about their destiny. Finishing school at thirteen, Jeanne ceased to be a child and became a young woman who helped her mother with housework and younger siblings. Such would be her life until death, for Jeanne had taken on the "duties of woman." Jeanne was pleasant and agreeable, as a wife should be, but did not marry because no one asked her and her parents needed her. Fortunately, she had realized that "a woman should be able to support herself" and so learned a trade. Although Gréville never bothered to specify Jeanne's métier, it enabled her to earn a living and help her aging parents. Jeanne was an "old maid" (*vieille fille*) but, Gréville concluded in italics, she was "*happy*." Her life had been full of self-sacrifice, but "sacrifice is the source of the best joys."[29]

Gréville's chapters about a married woman, Cécile, reinforced the message that the foyer rather than the forum was the proper setting for fulfillment of woman's special role. Emphasis on woman's function *inside* the *orderly* household had a lineage dating from ancient Greece and Rome to early modern Europe; Fénelon and Madame de Maintenon enshrined it in treatises on girls' education, as did Rousseau in *Emile* (1762).[30] However, idealizations of woman's role inside the household mushroomed in nineteenth-century prescriptive literature and have been variously interpreted as a reaction to the disorder of the French Revolution, a deliberate retreat from the danger and confusion in rapidly expanding cities, and a by-product of the growing separation of home from work place ushered in by the Industrial Revolution.[31] With home and work place separated in cities, the combination of domesticity and income-producing activities became increasingly difficult for married women. Gréville emphasized that a wife must keep a residence orderly and comfortable so that a husband could retreat and relax there after toiling in the outside world. And, she warned, if a woman found herself alone at night, then something was probably wrong with the household and the man's absence her fault.[32]

Gréville's model couple, Cécile and Pierre, went before the mayor of their commune for the civil marriage made obligatory in 1882 and simply ignored the option of a second religious ceremony. The marriage day was the most important one in a woman's life, Gréville intoned, because it profoundly changed her legal status and altered her existence much more than her husband's. Article 213 of the Civil Code obliged a man to give "aid and protection" to his spouse; a wife in turn owed "obedience and submission." Although possessing most of the same civil rights as a man when single, a woman, once married, had to submit to her husband's "domination" and could no longer bring a lawsuit without his consent or, prior to a reform of 1907, control her own earnings.[33]

A careful reader could detect that Gréville was not totally happy with the restrictions imposed on women by French law. She asserted that during the Middle Ages married women had enjoyed greater civil equality with men and had since suffered a diminution of rights. Thus much needed to be done to "ameliorate the moral situation of woman." This complaint was consistent with Gréville's association with such prominent and moderate French feminists as Maria Deraismes, a cultured woman from an upper class republican family. However, a textbook was not the place for political protest if one wished it to be widely adopted, and middle class feminists did not necessarily envision radical changes in the lives of humble women. Thus Gréville muted what otherwise might have been too strong a protest for a textbook by insisting that modern women were "everywhere treated with honor" and counseling that, for the moment, women should make the best of their existing rights and duties.[34]

Gréville's portrayal of the married life of Cécile and Pierre explained how Cécile combined the submission required by the Civil Code with the exercise of real psychological and economic power within the family unit. Patient and kind as an ideal woman should be, Cécile tolerated without complaint the sometimes difficult personality of her mother-in-law. Nor did she question her husband's status as "chef de la famille." Nonetheless, like most working class women, she controlled family finances. Gréville insisted that women be realistic about money. They should see that families were adequately insured and also open savings accounts in their own name, something only recently permitted by a law of 1881. In Cécile's case, her thrift carried the family through Pierre's temporary unemployment. Later, when Pierre was gravely ill, Cécile managed, by working day and night as a *repasseuse* (ironer), to earn enough to keep the family from financial ruin.

Despite complete devotion to her foyer, Cécile was not oblivious to the outside world. Like many republican politicians and educators, Gréville drew girls' attention to the potential behind-the-scenes influence exerted by women on husbands. Although women could not vote, they should take an active interest in politics in order to discuss current issues with spouses. But if husband and wife disagreed about

1. The woman tries to persuade her husband not to strike. From Mme Henry
Gréville, *L'Instruction morale et civique des jeunes filles* (Paris: E. Weill and
G. Maurice, 1882), p. 159.

politics, then she must stop the argument, the preservation of harmony within the family being her responsibility. Writing just before
the full legalization of trade unions in 1884, Gréville also counseled
women to do their bit to maintain social order by preventing husbands
from going on strike. Women should explain patiently to men that
"one obtains everything by firmness and perseverance; in our century
of progress, violence no longer has a *raison d'être*." Thus "patient
resignation—which does not exclude . . . the desire for ameliora-
tions" should "reign in the atelier as in the foyer." Patriotism was
the last social responsibility conveyed to eleven-to-thirteen-year-olds.
Women did not fight wars, but they were the wives and mothers
of soldiers whom they must encourage to fight for France if the
occasion arose. Gréville's conclusion, in keeping with previous advice,
told girls to take as their motto, "All sacrifice for duty, honor, and
country," because this slogan, although one of renunciation, offered
its practitioners "grand" and "pure" joys.[35]

Gréville's anti-strike injunctions soon became inappropriate for a
republican text, but her basic image of a cooperative, submissive,
duty-oriented woman—a duplication of models in older textbooks—
would not be substantially modified for decades. Other republican
morale books for girls are thus of interest not for a noticeably different
vision of womanhood but simply for details ignored or slighted by
Gréville. Three other popular texts for girls' moral and civic instruction

were also on the education ministry's 1889 list: Henriette Massy's *Notions d'éducation civique à l'usage des jeunes filles* (1884), Clarisse Juranville's *Manuel d'éducation morale et d'instruction civique à l'usage des jeunes filles* (1883), and Rose-Elise Chalamet's *Première année d'économie domestique* (1887).

Echoing Gréville's counsel that women accept prevailing social conventions, Massy's book, adopted by sixty-three departments as of 1889, added more behavioral prohibitions. Women needed civic instruction because of their influence on sons and husbands but should avoid public political meetings. The reminder that professional women with advanced degrees would always be exceptional among members of their sex discouraged elevated career aspirations. Yet Massy did permit the schoolgirls she depicted to raise embarrassing questions. Unlike Gréville who neglected the topic, Massy explained the types of property arrangements possible with marriage contracts. The *régime dotal* protected the wife's assets (dowry) at the time of marriage, but only the husband could administer the assets; the more common *régime de communauté*, which prevailed if no contract regarding property was made, provided for joint ownership of goods but gave the husband sole control of them. When one girl in Massy's narrative complained that a man's control of his wife's property was unfair, the teacher's defense was that someone must take charge of a family. Another girl asked why the class had lessons on "superiors" and "inferiors" if all were equal in the Third Republic. She was told that republican equality did not exclude a hierarchy of functions: superiors gave orders and inferiors took them. Like many other republican writers on moral values, Massy cited Kant for maxims. Whether dealing with equals, inferiors, or superiors, one should behave in a way that set an example for everyone.[36]

In comparison to Gréville and Massy, both of whom hinted subtly that woman's legal situation could stand improvement, Juranville eschewed complaints and wrote more sentimentally about woman's lot in life. Author of eighteen textbooks—eight of which were especially for girls—Juranville (1826–1906) was a lay *institutrice* in Orléans and had been writing schoolbooks since 1857.[37] From 1887 to 1905 she and a cleric represented the interests of private schools on the departmental educational council (*conseil départemental*) of the Loiret. Yet her link to *enseignement libre* did not make her unacceptable to republican educators, many of whom demanded a more thoroughgoing laicity for boys than for girls. Paris had dropped the *Tour de la France* from its book list by 1889 because of occasional references to the deity but kept three of Juranville's books with brief mentions of God and prayer.[38] However, Juranville's *Manuel d'éducation morale*, on forty-seven departmental lists in 1889, was not on that of Paris. By 1911 Larousse published fifteen editions which sold more than 150,000 copies, a respectable success but one surpassed by her *Premier livre des petites filles* (1873), which sold 808,500 copies by 1914; by *Le deuxième livre des petites filles* (1887), selling 686,000 copies; and by *Le Savoir faire et le savoir vivre* (1879), 364,000. Although none of Juranville's textbooks came anywhere near such record-breakers as Bruno's *Tour de la France* (eight million copies), Larive and Fleury's multivolume grammar course (twelve million), Pierre Foncin's three-volume *géographie* (eleven million), Pierre Leyssenne's arithmetic texts (six million), or Ernest Lavisse's history books (five million), they were very successful for the category of girls' books.[39] Sales figures available from the publishers Larousse, Hachette, Colin, Delagrave, Delaplane, and the Catholic firm of Vitte demonstrate that a printing of at least 100,000 copies placed a girls' textbook among the best sellers for the female primary school market, consisting each year of about 2,500,000 girls in public and private schools.

Unlike Gréville who never invoked the deity, Juranville joined Fénelon in attributing distinctive female traits to God's grand design. Motherly love was comparable to God's goodness, and woman's religious faith inspired others to belief in a future life. God made men and women "equal" but gave them different personalities and social functions. Lacking the "spirit of enterprise" and the ability to reason as well as a man, woman was destined to care for household and children. Her vocation was to give of herself and serve others. From this common "equal but separate" doctrine, it followed that women should not have the right to vote; woman's suffrage would disrupt the domestic tranquillity desired by God. Whereas Massy held out the possibility that a few women might obtain advanced educational credentials and professional positions, Juranville stated explicitly that for women intellectual endeavors were always less important than "manual works." Fénelon's words on the importance of sewing reinforced the point. Although Juranville noted that sewing abilities could provide an income for women, she valued sewing primarily for other reasons: it was economical for the family and gave women an excuse for not speaking when they had nothing to say and a pretext for not listening to or participating in a conversation. The motto, "silence is the ornament of women," well complemented Juranville's command to avoid anger and her profile of the feminine personality.[40]

Whereas Juranville portrayed the adult woman as a fulltime *maîtresse de maison*, Chalamet (1848–1925) realistically counseled girls of humble origin to expect to work after leaving school. Her *Première année d'économie domestique* discussed much more than homemaking, as the terms *morale, instruction civique,* and *droit usuel* in the subtitle indicated. A Protestant like Gréville, Chalamet was the daughter of a former prefect of the Ardèche, niece of a republican deputy with a special interest in education, and *directrice* of a private kindergarten in Paris until 1894. She wished to provide a girls' version of historian Ernest Lavisse's manual of moral and civic instruction for boys, one of the best selling textbooks published by Armand Colin. By 1914 her book had sold 185,000 copies; Lavisse's, 1,442,000. Warning girls that, like their brothers, they must know how to be self-sufficient, Chalamet discussed regulations on female apprenticeship and book-keeping details for shopkeepers. She also covered marriage contracts and noted that, by law, a husband could prevent his wife from becoming a "public merchant."[41]

Chalamet did not find her practical advice on work to be in conflict with the domestic ideal. "Nothing is more desirable for a young woman than to become the good and worthy wife of an honest man." Psychological subservience to the male was the rule for her married woman, as for Gréville's and Juranville's: the wife should please her mate with good grooming, attractive clothing, and an agreeable countenance; avoid anger and disrespect; and, if scolded unfairly by him, either reply calmly or keep silent. The teacher's manual accompanying the textbook also alerted *institutrices* to the importance of classroom discussions on how to please husbands. With such a future awaiting most schoolgirls, it was no wonder that Chalamet termed book-learning less useful than homemaking skills. Naming foreign countries would not amuse a husband and children at dinnertime, but "a good omelet" would always please the famished. Fourteen other textbooks were equally explicit in preaching that women's intellectual achievements were less important than domestic prowess, and the message was implicit in many more.[42]

How did the *morale* books by Gréville, Massy, Juranville, and Chalamet, all intended for "girls of the people," compare to presentations for girls from more comfortable homes who went to the elementary classes of a *lycée* or *collège?* Evidently these special classes, attended by less than 1 percent of public school girls aged six to thirteen in 1906 (Table 3), sometimes used the texts by Massy and Juranville, less proletarian in tone than those by Gréville and Chalamet.[43] Written especially for this select clientele was *Causeries de morale pratique* by Madame Thérèse Bentzon (1840–1907), a successful novelist and critic, and Mademoiselle A. Chevalier. First published in 1899 by Hachette and still available in a fifth edition in 1913, *Causeries* appeared in no more than 8,250 copies. Like girls' texts for regular primary schools, it destined woman to the foyer and gave her personality traits suited for domesticity. Granddaughter of the

Marquis de Vitry and daughter of the Comte de Solms, Bentzon did not make her own experience of marriage at sixteen and separation at nineteen the model for the traditional woman in this book.[44]

One sign of the special nature of the expected readers of *Causeries* was the authors' assumption that boredom might be a major problem. This possibility did not figure in ordinary primary school texts, presumably because girls of the people kept busy helping mothers and working in the interval between primary school and marriage. Bentzon and Chevalier expected their readers to remain at home during post-*lycée* years, although brothers of course began careers. Concerned that middle class girls often wasted too much time shopping or socializing, Bentzon and Chevalier recommended a series of time-fillers which would have been singularly out of place for working class girls. Apart from perfecting "son être moral"—something expected of all schoolgirls—a bourgeois girl should become adept at fine needlework and develop musical talents to help "break the monotony of family *soirées*." She could also learn from her mother how to "administer" a household and manage servants, who remained more available in France than in the United States.[45] Indeed, it was because domestic service was still such a common occupation for young French women that school texts for the regular primary school before World War I and even afterwards often included a section on proper behavior for both servants and their employers.[46]

Bentzon and Chevalier did advise bourgeois girls to think about a possible profession in case financial catastrophe ever struck, but their linking of woman's work outside the home to economic need mirrored the general belief that such employment was a sign of a family's poverty. Most middle class women preferred to be listed in the census as "sans profession" (without a profession).[47] Because paid employment was not a necessity for many young women at-

Table 3. Enrollments in the Special Primary Classes of Public Secondary Schools, 1896–1936

| | Enrollment in Special Primary Classes | | Special Primary Classes as % of Total Primary Enrollment | |
	Boys	Girls	Boys	Girls
1896	26,600	4,700	1.1	.3
1906	29,800	11,100	1.2	.5
1926	37,500	16,400	2.3	1.1
1936	55,900	25,800	2.4	1.2

SOURCE: *Annuaire statistique de la France* (1939). "Résumé rétrospectif," pp. 24, 28.

tending *lycées*, Bentzon and Chevalier also praised the value of study for the sake of study, stating that intellectual pursuits of this sort were vastly superior to those undertaken only with moneymaking in mind. Seekers of knowledge for its own sake formed "an elite capable of influencing all society." This perspective would have been totally inappropriate for primary schoolgirls from humble families. Educated middle class women were also expected to know how to direct social conversation, a skill women of the people could hardly be expected to develop when pedagogues like Juranville prescribed for them the virtues of keeping silent and not drawing attention to themselves.[48]

Discussion of woman's role outside the foyer allowed Bentzon and Chevalier to underscore the social values of the republican regime. Charitable obligations, another province of bourgeois women, were linked to pronouncements on "respect for property." At a time when the Third Republic provided comparatively few welfare programs, it was acceptable to state that only private charity could remedy inequities and that it was wrong for government to take money from one who works to give it to one who "cannot or does not want to work." Temperance societies were especially appropriate for women of "our bourgeoisie" to lead because drunken men in the "inferior classes" caused great suffering to women and children. "Girls of the people" read about helping the needy, too, but might find the message that telling beggars where to find work was better than a handout.[49]

The last section of *Causeries* devoted fully twenty pages to woman's religious duties, a much lengthier treatment than public school textbooks usually gave to the *morale* program's "duties to God." Nor, with the exception of Juranville, did most authors of primary texts for public schools say much about mothers' prayers setting a good example for children. Bentzon and Chevalier recognized the piety of many bourgeois women but also tried to accommodate this with the possible anticlericalism of a republican husband. Thus they stated that men could be moral and upright without practicing a religion. Whether the same was possible for women was left unsaid.

A separation of morality from religion was, of course, unthinkable in Catholic textbooks. Unlike Bentzon and Chevalier, Anne-Louise Masson's *Manuel de morale et d'instruction civique* (1909) for Catholic girls stated that one could not be a "perfect upright man" without religion. Masson duplicated many do's and don'ts for women in republican texts and reiterated the familiar dichotomy between woman's interior and man's exterior role, but she reinforced her behavioral commandments with religion. The Holy Family was the model for family life, demonstrating that "the husband is truly *le chef de la famille*." The father represented authority, force, and work; it was natural for him to command and for others to obey without question. By contrast, the mother exhibited *faiblesse* rather than force and *tendresse* rather than the imposing voice. Masson's ideal woman was like a clock, giving time only when one needed it. She tried to imitate Mary, the world's first Christian mother. Destined for a hidden interior life of service to others, woman should not "reverse roles" and behave like a man. Thus she must also shun the suffragettes' ridiculous campaign to usurp something naturally belonging only to men. Men make laws, women make customs, Masson pontificated. Although a young girl might earn money to assist parents, a Catholic married woman best served family, country, and church by remaining in the foyer. She would see to the religious upbringing of her children, send them to Catholic schools, and defend the church if she heard it attacked.[50]

How do feminine personalities and role models, similar in so many ways in republican and Catholic texts, compare to the masculine variety in moral instruction books for boys? Textbooks by Gabriel Compayré, Ernest Lavisse, and A. Mézières are a basis for comparisons. Appearing on sixty-eight departmental lists by 1889 and in at least 119 editions, Compayré's *Eléments d'instruction morale et civique* (1880), like Gréville's text, was placed on the Index in 1882. Its main characters were Georges, a good student, and his male teacher, from whom he sought advice after his father's death. The young boy's perception of his mother's place in the family was indicated by one of the first questions he asked his teacher after his loss: whom should he obey now? That the question was asked at all was as significant as the answer. The teacher counseled that the mother assumed the father's position in the family and then explained that women were no longer considered inferior to men. The wife was now "the associate and equal of the husband." Although a Catholic priest found this assertion of equality offensive,[51] Compayré added qualifications which significantly blunted its force. If father and mother disagreed, then the father's will must prevail. But such cases were judged rare in "well-run families," presumably because women heeded the Civil Code and textbooks and obeyed spouses. Like Compayré's manual, Lavisse's popular *Première année d'instruction civique* (1880), used in seventy-nine departments by 1889, advised in the chapter on the husband and father that parents should agree on the upbringing of children but made this point only after the standard reminder about legally required wifely submission to "le chef de la famille." Lavisse also characterized the father's authority as "plus forte" and the mother's as "plus douce."[52]

To outline proper behavior for Georges, Compayré's teacher reviewed the *morale* program's items on hard work and devotion to

duty. Like schoolgirls, Georges heard that one should be patient and
even resigned in the face of adversity. But he was also told to retain
his "independence of character," a trait not typically assigned to
girls.[53] Nor was Georges's life after leaving school identical to that
of Gréville's Jeanne or Cécile. He became a carpenter's apprentice
and then went on a *tour de France* to learn more about his chosen
trade, even though this journey was a dying custom by the late
nineteenth century. Rarely did textbooks advise girls to travel to
improve themselves professionally, although they often did so in
real life, at least to the extent of leaving rural areas to become
domestics, seamstresses, or workers in towns.[54] Instead, textbooks
warned girls about the dangers of traveling alone and working in
unfamiliar cities.[55] Returning to his native village, Georges married
a rich woman and prospered as the head of his own atelier. Georges's
eldest son would rise still farther on the social ladder, for he attended
a *lycée* and then studied at the Toulouse Faculty of Law. At the end
of the book, Georges had earned the respect of all who knew him
and was mayor of his commune, a political role of course closed to
women.

Compayré's Georges enjoyed wealth and public recognition rarely
accorded to women in primary school textbooks, but this Horatio
Alger story was not normative for all boys' textbooks. If republicans
agreed that students should view the current regime as one providing
opportunities for self-improvement and advancement, especially
through diligence in studies, many were nonetheless sensitive to the
dangers of arousing too lofty ambitions which, when unrealized, left
young men disappointed, angry, and *déracinés*. Thus Lavisse mixed
a majority of humble male workers with a few success stories and,
in a chapter on the achievements of one teacher's best pupils, noted
that while one was a farmer's son, three others were "children of
comfortable or rich families." The message that social immobility
was more likely than mobility predominated in A. Mézières's *Education morale et instruction civique* (1883), in use in fifty-seven departments in 1889. A deputy from Meurthe-et-Moselle, Mézières
advised that it was better to be a good worker or peasant than a
worthless bourgeois.[56] Lessons on social immobility for both boys
and girls were also prominent in the readers which told longer stories
about single characters than typical *morale* books.

The study of French received high priority in the primary school,
as at all levels of French education. Depending upon the grade,
moral and civic instruction occupied one and one quarter to two
hours per week, but reading, grammar, spelling, recitation, and composition were allocated ten hours.[57] In all grades pupils had a reader.

Some popular readers devoted unconnected chapters to aspects of proper behavior and the identification of everyday objects, but this didactic genre was less popular with students than *romans scolaires* about one or more central characters. Not surprisingly, readers for early grades often depicted youngsters as more genuinely childlike than did those for the *cours moyen* and *supérieur*. Nonetheless, few authors refrained as deliberately from moralizing as A. Eidenschenk-Patin, who described her *Premières* and *Deuxièmes lectures des petites filles* (1911, 1912) as "interesting stories, which are only *stories*." More typical of readers for six-to-nine-year-olds than Eidenschenk-Patin's collections of fairy tales and animal stories were Juranville's *Premier* and *Deuxième livre des petites filles* or A.-F. Cuir's *Petites écolières* (1893), all with chapters explicitly spelling out notions of right and wrong. Older students found gender roles added to the moralizing in school inspector Alcide Lemoine's *lectures* for *La jeune française* (1910) and *Le jeune français* (1914). In the former, coauthored with the head of a women's normal school, Fénelon's *femme au foyer* who gave joy to her husband was the model Frenchwoman; in the latter, coauthored with an *instituteur*, the mother's role and gentle sentimentality were contrasted with the father's work "outside the home" and his more reasonable and firm personality.[58]

The most popular *roman scolaire* was Bruno's *Tour de la France par deux enfants, devoir et patrie* (1877), which sold more than eight million copies for the publisher Belin and enjoyed its greatest success during the 1880s. With Bruno's classic schoolchildren followed the wanderings of two orphaned brothers, André and Julien Volden, and at the same time absorbed lessons on French history, geography, civic and moral instruction, and science. Moving from one part of France to another in search of an uncle, the boys learned about each region's economic resources and historical contributions. The text encapsulated the political, economic, moral, and cultural values of the republican elite, to which "Bruno" herself belonged as the wife of the noted philosopher Alfred Fouillée and the mother of another, Jean-Marie Guyau. Bruno's characters were extraordinarily resourceful, and the younger, Julien, was a model student who learned all that he could in "the very best school." But at age thirteen this very bright boy began adult life as a farmer; his brother was already a locksmith. *Francinet,* hero of another popular Bruno reader selling more than one million copies, became a factory worker.[59]

Although Francinet had the good fortune to be tutored with the grandchildren of his rich employer, that experience did not change his social position, just as similar friendships did not necessarily alter the fate of poor textbook heroines befriended by the rich.[60] Authors wrote about such friendships to show that harmony, rather than class struggle, prevailed in France and not to encourage unrealistic or dangerous aspirations toward social mobility. Like Bruno's heroes, many boys in pre-1914 textbooks grew up to be farmers and workers, not middle class professionals.[61] Authors sometimes told children about the availability of scholarships for secondary schools or less prestigious higher primary schools, but they presented recipients of state grants as exceptional cases. A single book might thus depict the life of peasant or artisan as the norm but also mention a success story attributable to educational opportunities.[62] The possibility of social mobility was addressed explicitly in only nine of the sixty prewar boys' or coeducational textbooks used in this study, and authors like Lavisse, Mézières, Bert, and Nicolas left no doubt about its rarity.[63] More representative were the sentiments in Jean Aicard's much used poem, "Les Métiers," which stated that there were no vile trades. The farmer, blacksmith, baker, woodcutter, mason, weaver, tailor, soldier, and mother—the latter Aicard's only feminine métier—all served France equally.[64]

If social immobility was often a striking theme in boys' books, it was even more prominent in girls' books. Not one of the girls in seventy-six pre-1914 republican and Catholic girls' textbooks went on from an ordinary primary school to secondary school, as did Georges's son in Compayré's text. In L. Leroux and J. C. Montillot's *Une Famille* (1893) son Pierre used the higher primary school as a stepping stone to greater things, but his family decided against post-primary schooling for his sister. Two girls in Marie Robert Halt's books went on from the primary to the higher primary school and became teachers, but they were exceptional cases in girls' textbooks.[65]

Self-sufficiency and strength of character were desirable traits for women, as girls' *morale* texts intoned, but strong women in textbooks always regarded employment as secondary to serving the family. The family, not the individual, was the basic unit of society in the social theories represented in both republican and Catholic textbooks. Republican pedagogue Charles Drouard wrote, "The true individual is neither man nor woman, it is man and woman. . . . The true social cell is the family."[66] Textbooks thus accurately mirrored a crucial fact about women's work recently underscored by historians Louise Tilly and Joan Scott: most nineteenth century women, single as well as married, valued earning money primarily as a way to contribute to the family economy.[67] However, girls' textbooks exhibited some variety in the social settings in which family-oriented women operated. There were heroines in urban, rural, Catholic, working class, and middle class milieus, and teachers could select those most suitable for their classes.

2. A textbook preparing girls for work and housework. Advertisement for
L. Ch.-Desmaisons, *Tu seras ouvrière* (Paris: A. Colin, 1892).

POURQUOI ALLEZ-VOUS A L'ÉCOLE ? 7

Arrivés à l'école, Jacques entra dans la grande classe des garçons, et Suzette dans celle des filles, après avoir mené François à la classe enfantine. [2]

3. — Pourquoi allez-vous à l'école?

La maîtresse, Mme Delorme, écrivit au tableau noir cette question : *Pourquoi allez-vous à l'école ?*

Chaque élève eut à donner la réponse sur son ardoise. La petite Zélie écrivit : « Je vais à l'é-

— Je vais à l'école pour apprendre les choses utiles que je ne sais pas.

cole parce que mes parents m'y obligent. »

[2] *CAUSERIE :* **Grammaire.** — Que veut dire le mot *aîné?* — Quel mot a servi à former *blondin?*

Histoire naturelle. — Qu'est-ce que le visage? — Quelles sont les parties qui le composent?

Comment appelle-t-on l'arbre qui donne les noix ? — Que tire-t-on de la noix?

Connaissances usuelles. — Qu'est-ce qu'une carriole ? — Quelle différence y a-t-il entre aller au pas, trotter et galoper?

3. Suzette's class comments on the utility of school. From Marie Robert Halt, *L'Enfance de Suzette*, 17th ed. (Paris: P. Delaplane, 1907), p. 7.

Madame L. C. Desmaisons's *Tu seras ouvrière* (1892) was the one girls' book in the publisher Colin's series of seven readers designed to orient children to adult roles, the others being *chef de famille*, citizen, soldier, merchant, farmer, and *prévoyant* artisan. The heroine of Desmaisons's tale (which sold only 31,000 copies) did something that women rarely did in textbooks: she not only survived but prospered in the world of work.[68] Through diligent performance of assigned tasks and help from benevolent employers, Jeanne, a seamstress, rose from rural poverty to urban comfort. Commencing work after leaving the primary school, this motherless girl left a backward area of southwestern France, moved to Paris, eventually became the head of one of the largest dressmaking establishments, married an agreeable merchant, and had two children. Because work in the textile and garment industry was the most important nonagricultural vocational possibility for French girls at the turn of the twentieth century, the heroine's occupational choice was not unrealistic. But Jeanne's financial success was unusual, as Jules Simon, onetime minister of education, insisted in a preface. Spelling out the message of social immobility and modest expectations often proffered to children of the people, Simon cautioned girls not to expect to duplicate Jeanne's record because the odds were "one hundred to one that *tu seras ouvrière*." He also warned that using marriage to gain status was ill-advised because a woman would suffer from ignorance of another class's style of life, never win acceptance from her husband's friends, and run the risk of losing his love as he perceived her unsuitability in his milieu. That Desmaisons herself also did not intend this heroine's success to deflect most girls from domesticity is indicated by her statement in a cookbook for girls' schools that "the true destination of woman is to be the careful and wise *directrice* of family life and the household." Nor did Desmaisons approve of the "militant feminists" of the late 1890s whose message about the rights of the individual woman seemed to her to threaten familial bonds.[69]

More typical of the public school's depiction of woman's life was Suzette, Marie Robert Halt's heroine in three popular volumes which followed a rural girl from age seven to middle age. The most successful girls' readers of the Third Republic, the *Suzette* books appeared between 1889 and 1895 and were still used during the 1930s. By 1920 1,535,000 copies of *Suzette* had been published and by 1932, 865,000 copies of *L'Enfance de Suzette*.[70] The daughter of a modestly successful farmer, Suzette learned early that girls' education should prepare them primarily to be good wives and mothers. At seven she already wrote dutifully on her slate that she went to school to learn to run a household later. When she was ten her mother died, an event not unusual either in real life or in schoolbooks, where parental deaths often forced children to behave like responsible adults. Pierre Jakez Hélias's mother, who began running a Breton household at age eleven, was one of many real-life counterparts of Bruno's heroes or Halt's Suzette. The mother's death plunged Suzette's father into despair, and he neglected farm and household for two years. Suzette, the only girl among four siblings, then realized that she must save the family. Aided by her teacher, she took on domestic chores, and readers learned how she cleaned house and budgeted. Suzette's transformation into a *ménagère* (housewife) lifted her family's spirits and motivated the males to save the farm from ruin. Eventually Suzette married a farmer and became a mother of three. At the close of *Le Ménage de Mme Sylvain*, the third volume, Suzette's father praised her domestic accomplishments in a fashion reminiscent of Fénelon: "Without a woman's providence, intelligence, and busy hands . . . , there is no household which can live and prosper."[71]

Suzette exemplified the industrious farm wife who served France by making men content with country life and thus disinclined to migrate to cities to swell the ranks of the urban unemployed or underemployed whose often marginal lifestyles threatened the social stability prized by middle class leaders. The most popular girls' reader in the Ain in 1909, *Suzette* was also long utilized in Paris schools, even though some school inspectors complained that paeans to country life were unrealistic for poor urban youngsters.[72] Halt (1849–1908), like Gréville, was a *femme de lettres* married to an author, Robert Vieu, a former *lycée* professor. She was also a member of the Comité des dames of the Ligue de l'enseignement, the important republican pressure group that grew out of Jean Macé's efforts to promote and secularize public schools since 1866.[73]

Like *Suzette*, Halt's *Droit chemin* (1902) endowed women with admirable fortitude within their distinctive sphere. An alcoholic's long-suffering wife saved herself and children from further misery by leaving him, a plot line never found in Catholic texts. The friendship between the woman's daughter and a bourgeois girl, whose father took an interest in the family's plight, permitted Halt to make the evidently controversial assertion that modern women demonstrated as much capacity for genuine friendship as men. Although a male's speech about woman's role across the centuries demonstrated that Halt did not really challenge the predominant domestic ideology for women, her textbooks illustrated how, within the domestic realm, a woman could be as strong as or stronger than a man. Professional activities were also possible for young, unmarried women in her stories. Suzette's daughter became an *institutrice*, as did the alcoholic's daughter in *Droit chemin*.[74]

While Suzette was a role model for girls in public schools, Elisabeth, the creation of Edmée de Kereven, and Elise, the heroine of Marie Thiéry, were exemplary Catholic girls. First published in 1909, the first two *Elisabeth* volumes had each sold more than 200,000 copies by 1934 and the third, 140,000. They and the *Elise* set were still used during the 1930s.[75] The most striking difference between the republican *Suzette* and the Catholic *Elisabeth* and *Elise* was the expected one—the treatment of religion. The first three chapters of *Le premier livre d'Elisabeth* were about "God," "The Holy Virgin," and "The Guardian Angel." *Lisette* included the texts of the Lord's Prayer, Apostles Creed, and Ave Maria; *La petite Elisabeth* contained several pages of prayers for memorization. Elisabeth and Elise eventually made first communions, and Elisabeth married in church, both ceremonies absent from Suzette's tale, although girls' public schools often experienced high rates of absenteeism when girls were preparing for first communions.[76]

It was the mothers of Elisabeth and Elise who taught them to pray, testimony to women's importance in preserving religious devotion within families in an increasingly secular age and at a time of renewed anticlerical attacks on the church. A law of 1904 prohibited members of religious orders from teaching even in private schools, and in 1905 church and state were separated. The introduction of the *Elisabeth* and *Elise* readers in 1909–1910 coincided with the church's launching of its second campaign against the lack of religious content in republican textbooks, fourteen of which were condemned by French bishops eager to enlist support from Catholic parents and obtain parental veto power over textbook choices for public schools.[77] Lyon publisher E. Vitte's boys' counterpart to *Elisabeth, Le premier livre* and *Le deuxième livre d'André*, gave religion an equally prominent place but, understandably, focused on the father's role as the "chef de famille" who toiled "away from home" in order to support his dependents.[78]

The family backgrounds of Elisabeth and Elise also revealed an important difference between many pupils in public schools and *écoles libres*. Unlike most republican textbook heroines, Elisabeth and Elise came from middle class homes, albeit modest ones. Elisabeth's father managed a paper factory in a small town in Champagne; Elise's Parisian family employed a devoted servant. Prosperous backgrounds made Catholic heroines more likely to have the leisure and money for charitable activities such as those undertaken by the real women of Lille's Catholic bourgeoisie, so well described by Bonnie Smith.[79] Young Elisabeth gave extra household money to a poor neighbor, and Elise made a dress for a poor friend's first communion. On a trip to Paris Elisabeth did visit a professional school where adolescent girls learned trades and office work, but it was unlikely that she would ever have to join the working women who made up about 37 percent of the French "active" population between the 1890s and World War II.[80] Elise also avoided the fate of two poor friends, one leaving school to become an apprentice in a flower shop and the other a servant.

Like Suzette, Elisabeth plunged into fulltime domesticity at age eleven when her mother died; Elise had a less unhappy experience in that she took over the household only temporarily while her mother was ill. Elisabeth's homemaking skills comforted her brother and father, especially when the father had to go through the travail of a strike at his factory. During this crisis women prayed, and a family friend inspired Elisabeth with stories about the courage of three saints, a nun, and three French military heroines (Jeanne d'Arc, Jeanne Hachette, and Jeanne de Montfort). The strike accurately mirrored mounting labor unrest in prewar France, but the author's sympathies lay with the employer, not the workers, whom she depicted as troublemakers or misinformed men who gained nothing from their foolish act. The third *Elisabeth* volume ended with a scene which signified not only the heroine's arrival at maturity but also the enduring importance of Catholic values and reestablishment of social harmony. At twenty-one Elisabeth married in church, and the factory workers came to wish her well.

The message that bourgeoisie and working class could coexist harmoniously was also dramatized in Alice Dereims's *Jeanne et Madeleine* (1902). Designed for both regular public primary schools and the *lycées'* elementary classes, it sold more than 100,000 copies by 1914.[81] The story was set in a suburb of a provincial industrial city on a street where, in the midst of many new and large houses, one worker's small dwelling remained. As the tale began, twelve-year-old Madeleine Renaud was on her way to the girls' *lycée*, followed by a maid whose presence indicated the bourgeoisie's distaste for letting young girls walk alone in the presumably dangerous world outside the home. Across the street walked Jeanne, not protected by a maid and in charge of two younger brothers as they all headed toward the primary school. At first sight the two girls disliked each other, Jeanne assuming that Madeleine felt superior to her poor neighbors. But the point of the story was that the daughters of a factory owner and a factory worker could be friends. Madeleine's mother took an interest in Jeanne's family and paid Jeanne to run daily errands. Madame Renaud's action conformed to the charitable model preferred by the republican middle class: one helped the poor with payment for work, not handouts. Her interest in Jeanne also brought the two girls together. Madeleine learned that workers were clean, honest, and hardworking and also realized that her own privileged position was no excuse for idleness. Ashamed at being unable to take care of her room as Jeanne could, Madeleine learned to clean. In turn, Jeanne's aesthetic sensibilities improved. Madeleine gave her a pretty Mediterranean scene to replace ugly pictures in her room and also lent books so that she could read something other than trashy stories in a popular newspaper. On a visit with Madeleine to the Renauds' factory, Jeanne heard Monsieur Renaud explain that because a worker spent most of his day at a factory job, his wife must provide "an agreeable interior, a foyer where he likes to rest during his leisure." Jeanne knew that his words were meant for her. At the end of the story, as the two girls continued on separate educational paths, they discussed the importance of solidarity among all citizens. Like Elisabeth, they had learned that women must help maintain a stable society free of class conflict.

While Jeanne was poised to start work after leaving school at thirteen, Madeleine would simply continue studies without, appar-

4. Bringing the daughters of the bourgeoisie and working class together: Madeleine lends Jeanne books. From Alice Dereims, *Jeanne et Madeleine* (Paris: A. Colin, 1892), p. 23.

5. Madeleine shows Jeanne that flowers and tasteful pictures beautify a simple room. From Alice Dereims, *Jeanne et Madeleine* (Paris: A. Colin, 1902), p. 41.

ently, having any vocational plans other than emulation of her mother, a model bourgeois wife. Some readers did teach, however, that because finances could become uncertain even for the well-to-do, middle class girls should prepare to be self-sufficient. *Le troisième livre de lecture à l'usage des jeunes filles* (1891) by Juranville and Pauline Berger was a girls' version of *Le Tour de la France*. Although not nearly as successful as Bruno's classic, 210,000 copies had been published by 1914.[82] It introduced two motherless girls whose father, once a prosperous factory owner in Dunkerque, suffered financial reverses and lost his business. So that the younger daughter, Madeleine, could learn embroidery, Monsieur Vieuville took her to his wife's friend in the Vosges. The older daughter Claire went to his sister, who ran a dressmaking business in Avignon. Significantly, neither girl traveled alone to reach the woman who could teach her the practical skills to make her self-sufficient. Later, when the father went on the road to represent his cousin's firm, the two girls joined him and thus, unlike André and Julien, did their *tour de France* with adult supervision.

Like Bruno, Juranville and Berger used the travelogue for lessons about each region's economic resources and notables. But unlike Bruno, they emphasized distinctly feminine crafts and occupations, such as lacemaking and embroidery in Lorraine or the perfume industry in Provence. They also included many famous French women, in addition to more familiar national heroes. Not surprisingly, their gallery of heroines featured Joan of Arc, the most common example of a celebrated French woman in Third Republic textbooks—she appeared in fourteen of the prewar girls' textbooks in this sample[83]— and already before canonization in 1920 more a patriotic symbol than mere mortal for republican as well as Catholic educators. Among the other distinguished women were the politically important Jeanne d'Albret and Madame Roland; writers like Eugénie de Guérin, Madame Recamier, and Madame de Stael; the painter Rosa Bonheur; and educators like Madame Pape-Carpantier and Elise Lemonnier.

Juranville and Berger were certainly not the first or only authors to place famous female role models in girls' textbooks.[84] Wirth's *Lectures* were an earlier example of the genre, although her royal and saintly heroines were chosen for service to others, not for creative endeavors. Saints were also the most common category of heroines described to the Catholic Elisabeth. Madame Fouillée ("Bruno") had made the point in one of her books for both sexes that little girls had "as much intelligence as little boys" and even included two examples of Old Regime women with impressive intellects: Sophie Germain and Madame Dacier. However, *Francinet*'s basic message was that most women would not gain renown for inventions or scholarship because their social role, although not less important than men's, was "exercised in an almost invisible fashion." Juranville and Berger permitted higher visibility for bright and active women, as did Eidenschenk-Patin in *Troisième lectures des petites filles* (1913). But just as most girls' textbooks and the boys' textbooks which bothered to mention female roles focused on how model housewives performed invaluable services for families, so Juranville and Berger took some pains to keep their attractive portraits of feminine high achievers from deflecting readers from service to others. "Studies must never make her [the female] forget her duties as daughter, spouse, mother." An educated woman could instruct her children, advise relatives, and add charm to "la vie d'intérieur."[85] *Le troisième livre* demonstrated more awareness of harsh economic realities than previous books written by Juranville alone, but at the end of the story, when the two girls had acquired substantial handicraft and commercial skills as well as historical, geographical, and scientific

d'Écouen où étaient élevées les orphelines des officiers de la Légion d'honneur¹.

Mme de Staël, fille du ministre de Louis XVI, Necker, la plus célèbre des femmes auteurs. Elle fut un *enfant prodigieux*. Dès l'âge de onze ans elle composait des portraits et des éloges suivant la mode d'alors. Dans ses ouvrages, on trouve une hauteur de génie et une profondeur rares chez son sexe. Elle n'avait pas de rivale dans la conversation ; son salon était rempli des hommes les plus illustres en tout genre. Napoléon ne l'aimait pas et la força de vivre en exil. C'est de là qu'elle répétait mélancoliquement en pensant à la patrie absente : « Rien ne vaut mon petit ruisseau de la rue du Bac. »

Mme CAMPAN, née à Paris.
(1752-1822.)

Mme Sophie Gay, romancière et poète à ses heures, et bonne musicienne, fut la mère de Mme de Girardin, Delphine Gay, un de nos plus gracieux et charmants écrivains. A dix-sept ans, elle écrivit une pièce de vers remarquable sur le dévouement des sœurs de Sainte-Camille pendant l'épidémie de Barcelone. Elle célébra plusieurs grands événements qui excitaient alors la sympathie générale et fut nommé la *Muse de la patrie*. Elle s'est peinte elle-même dans ce vers :

Naïve en sa gaîté, rieuse et point méchante.

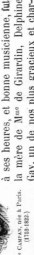

6. The presentation of distinguished role models. From Clarisse Juranville and Pauline Berger, *Le troisième livre de lecture à l'usage des jeunes filles*, 2d ed. (Paris: Larousse, 1892), p. 318.

7. Mme de Stäel. From Clarisse Juranville and Pauline Berger, *Le troisième livre de lecture à l'usage des jeunes filles*, 2d ed. (Paris: Larousse, 1892), p. 319.

knowledge, it was not clear just how self-sufficient they would have to be in the future. Through hard work and good luck, the father regained his business, thereby giving his daughters options other than assisting him financially for much of their adult lives.

Whatever the future of Claire and Madeleine, they had prepared for more than the homebound existence predominating for women in most readers and home economics books doubling as readers. The program of 1887 formally allocated time in girls' schools only for sewing (part of "manual works"), but official instructions also called for teaching other aspects of "économie domestique." In practice, teachers often combined domestic economy with such required subjects as science, hygiene, moral instruction, and reading. Departmental lists of approved textbooks of the 1880s and 1909 frequently classified home economics books as "livres de lectures," an indication that in girls' classes they might replace traditional readers since schools were required to use a reader but not a home economics book.[86] Among the popular tomes of this genre—which often included *morale* lessons, too—were Juranville's *Savoir faire et le savoir vivre* (1879), Chalamet's *Premier année d'économie domestique* (1887), Wirth's *Future ménagère* (1882), Alfred Hannedouche's *Livret d'enseignement ménager* (1903), and A. Leune and E. Demailly's *Cours d'enseignement ménager, science et morale* (1902), all selling well over 100,000 copies, and Julie Sévrette's *Jeune ménagère* (1904), which sold nearly 73,000 copies.[87] Sévrette's book and Halt's third *Suzette* volume, *Le Ménage de Mme Sylvain*, actually combined a skeletal plot with detailed chapters on domestic arts and sciences. Feminine personality profiles in home economics texts, republican and Catholic, duplicated those in *morale* books and readers. What was different was their lengthy instructions for cooking, cleaning, washing, sewing, gardening, and, sometimes, child care and nursing the sick.

There was nothing random about the organization of the house-wife's day in most home economics books. Appropriate morning, afternoon, and evening activities were delineated and accompanied by the injunction to keep busy at all times. The *ménagère's* work routine was thus quite comparable to the work discipline which schools wished to inculcate in boys. And while boys were asked to see the connection between modern science and technology and industrialization, girls learned that knowing chemistry was useful for meal planning and that Pasteur's work on microbes explained the dangers of household dirt, the removal of which was of prime importance to the health of their family and nation.[88]

Rural schools could utilize domestic economy manuals written especially for future farm wives, such as Senator Hector Raquet's

parents, fille soumise, pleine de bonne volonté pour
venir en aide à sa mère dans les travaux de la maison
(fig. 2) et du jardin.

A la basse-cour.   En course pour sa mère.

Fig. 2. — La jeune fille aide sa mère.

C'est ainsi qu'une jeune fille acquiert peu à peu les
qualités d'une bonne ménagère.

4. Qualités de la bonne ménagère. — La
bonne ménagère a de l'ordre; elle est propre et active, économe et prévoyante. C'est de plus une bonne
et honnête femme, instruite, obligeante et dévouée.

1° La bonne ménagère a de l'ordre. — Avoir de l'ordre,
c'est avoir une *place* pour chaque chose, un *temps* pour
chaque genre de travail; c'est mettre chaque chose à sa
place et se livrer en temps convenable aux différents travaux. L'ordre économise le temps.

2° La bonne ménagère est propre et active. — Être propre,
c'est n'avoir sur soi, ni autour de soi, aucune poussière,
aucune souillure. Grâce à la propreté, tout reluit dans la
maison; les meubles, si vieux qu'ils soient, semblent sortir
des mains de l'ouvrier; les vêtements sont lavés souvent
et raccommodés avec soin. Pour arriver à ce résultat, il
faut que la ménagère soit **active**. La ménagère active fait
vite et bien, cause peu et travaille beaucoup.

8. Domestic economy for the farm girl. From H. Raquet, *La première année
de ménage rural,* 13th ed. (Paris: A. Colin, 1908), p. 5.

Première année de ménage rural, 51,000 copies of which appeared between 1893 and 1920. These texts conveyed not only information about flower and vegetable gardening and the care of rabbits, chickens, and the dairy but also commandments to avoid heavy labor in the fields, supposedly the province of men.[89] In real life such advice was widely ignored, for over the centuries peasant women had of necessity worked alongside men and continued to do so during the Third Republic. Indeed, 43 percent of the women listed as "active" in the 1906 census were engaged in agriculture. A division between strenuous "exterior" work and less rigorous work in the courtyard or "interior" of the home was familiar to peasants in many parts of France, but in rural tradition the dichotomy was often not as rigid as the middle class norm presented by educators to the popular classes.[90]

Another ubiquitous prescription which generations of rural girls as well as boys often ignored was that of shunning urban areas in favor of allegedly superior rural life. Since the Second Empire, when some rural home economics books used during the Third Republic were first published, country girls had learned that cities were dangerous and that they could best serve France by making rural men happy down on the farm.[91] Yet in many cases women migrated to the city more readily than men, undoubtedly because they perceived fewer possibilities for economic survival or happiness in the countryside than did men. Unmarried women led a marginal existence in the countryside and might be turned into servants by married siblings.[92]

Clothing and feeding the nation's work force and restricting rural-urban migration were not the only social controls for which home economics books enlisted women and girls. Anti-alcoholism was also prominent, especially by the 1890s. Faced with the increasing consumption of alcoholic beverages in cafes—the number of which increased by 65 percent between 1855 and 1912[93]—and the fact that alcoholism reduced worker productivity and made alcoholics' families dependent upon public funds and private charity, the government added an anti-alcoholism campaign to the school curriculum in 1897. Although some authors encouraged French women to emulate the American and British temperance movement, the French educator's anti-alcoholism instruction would have raised many Anglo-American eyebrows. Home economics books distinguished between healthful drinks, which included wine and beer, and dangerous ones like hard liquor and absinthe.[94] Model women served only healthful alcoholic beverages and drank very little. Women who drank excessively sinned against their sex and wrecked their appearance, as one Catholic text showed graphically with an illustration of an old hag.[95] Wives and daughters should also realize that good housekeeping helped turn husbands, brothers, and fathers away from cabarets. Presumably men who had clean houses, decorated with white curtains, flowers, needle-work and a few inexpensive prints—all ubiquitous adornments in textbooks—found home a refuge after work and were less inclined to go drinking with other men. By not hiding the fact that troubled husbands squandered wages on drink and left wives and children destitute, pedagogues hoped to give women extra incentives for good housekeeping.[96] Textbook characters like Elisabeth dutifully showed interest in anti-alcohol instruction but, according to one teacher, real children found lessons and books on this painfully boring.[97]

Because home economics manuals dealt primarily with domestic tasks, their depictions of adult women were often even more restrictive than those in other texts which occasionally, as with Desmaisons's Jeanne or the aunt in Juranville and Berger's *Troisième livre*, permitted economic success for women. While authors of texts for girls from the laboring classes often admitted that many might need to earn money through work done at home or elsewhere, they usually kept employment expectations modest, even to the extent of discouraging girls from becoming teachers. The Third Republic certainly enhanced the status of women teachers, but in two popular home economics books for public schools mothers deliberately rejected teaching for daughters and directed them toward the more humble garment trades because they believed that honest manual labor afforded the greatest financial security and satisfaction for most women. Chalamet also intoned that it was preferable to be a skilled worker than a mediocre teacher.[98] At least three unhappy women teachers who responded to a survey on the situation of rural *institutrices* in 1897 voiced a comparable lack of ambition for their daughters, on the grounds that lower expectations than their own would minimize future disap-pointments.[99]

Most prewar *morale* textbooks, readers, and home economics man-uals presented similar views about what was distinctive in the fem-inine personality. The ideal French woman, republican and Catholic, was gentle, modest, self-sacrificing, and submissive to male au-thority.[100] The seven girls' books which stated that men and women were in some sense "equal" qualified that assertion by adding that the sexes had different roles and/or types of intelligence.[101] Some-times told that she was less reasonable than males or less able to perceive the "big picture," the girl was consoled with the thought that she was more intuitive about people and better able to handle small details—traits highly useful for caring for others and doing housework.[102] Like the ideal man of the people, *la femme du peuple* was also hardworking and respectful of parents, political leaders, and employers. But unlike the man, she performed her primary work at home, caring for husband and children and executing a variety of household chores. The Catholic woman also made religious practice an important part of family life. Leaving the interior world of the foyer for the exterior world of work was justified only by dire economic necessity.[103] Indeed, the middle classes often regarded women's paid employment as a public admission of familial poverty. What girls learned about the outside world of politics and government was of value primarily because of their later influence on husbands and sons who voted and served in the army. Although a few republican and Catholic texts, like those of Juranville and Masson, had criticized women agitating for the vote, most simply remained silent on the subject—an avoidance of heated controversy which one would expect of textbook writers.[104] Pointedly, Lemoine and Marie pronounced that woman "finds the greatest emancipation" in a close "intellectual and moral communion" with her husband.[105]

The life which textbooks presented to girls of the people before 1914 was rigorous. But precisely because girls from the popular classes were the audience for most primary schoolbooks, there was little indication that they would ever be threatened by the boredom and idleness sometimes plaguing their middle class sisters. The economic role that farm women performed by caring for animals and tending the garden and the household chores of cooking, cleaning, washing, and sewing—which most women executed without the aid of labor-saving devices or servants—were vitally important for the survival of families. So was management of the family budget by peasant or working class women, depicted in sixteen girls' textbooks as well as in Lavisse's important manual.[106] The activities which prewar textbooks presented to girls were very much in keeping with the multifaceted role of women in traditional, preindustrial societies. However, the importance attached to woman's place *inside* the home, so often contrasted explicitly to man's exterior role,[107] was indicative of the separation of home from work place that had become increasingly common during the nineteenth century, even if less widespread in France than in other more rapidly industrializing countries.

Not surprisingly, the textbooks of England, Germany, and the United States also provided abundant presentations of distinctly feminine personalities and domestic roles to schoolgirls.[108] But it has been argued that the French domestic ideology of the nineteenth century made French women happier than their English sisters by making the *maîtresse de maison* a more dignified and important figure than a mere housewife (*ménagère*) and thus able to command more respect from her family and society. One contemporary claimed that "in marrying, the French woman gains her freedom, the English woman loses it."[109] In the same vein, Emmeline Pankhurst explained that French women were less attracted to the suffragists' crusade than English women because they already possessed real power within their households.[110] As Patrick Bidelman and Karen Offen have pointed out, many middle class French feminists eager for support from republican politicians stressed the valued role of woman as the mother of republican children and agreed that the roles of husband and wife within the family were different but complementary.[111]

It was precisely this feminine domestic power that textbook writers attempted to mobilize when they ordered women to keep men happy in clean and peaceful households so that after a hard day's labor the virile sex would shun cafes, the cause of sad and costly drinking problems and a good locale for grumbling with others about working conditions and political issues. At least twenty-seven girls' textbooks stated explicitly that women must keep men at home and/or deter them from the evils of drink, and the message was implicit in plots in many other girls' books.[112] Republican and Catholic authors alike enlisted women's domestic talents to help preserve political and social stability. Although the school intended to reinforce women's commitment to domesticity, not to free them from it, the acquisition of literacy and disciplined work habits and the knowledge that financial need might make employment necessary did carry the potential for diverting some women from the foyer. Yet it was unlikely that many would doubt that familial obligations ranked first among women's priorities, for the school, like other major institutions, did not endow alternatives with comparable value.

CHAPTER THREE

The School's Dissemination of Feminine Images and Reactions to Them, 1880–1914

Morale textbooks, readers, and home economics manuals for girls contained many explicit messages about gender roles. How do we know that teachers actually transmitted textbook prescriptions on femininity to pupils? And what can be said about the reactions of girls and women teachers to the specifically feminine aspects of primary schooling? Three types of evidence suggest an appreciable dissemination of the school's version of a "feminine mystique": school inspectors' reports on teachers' classroom performance, notebooks (*cahiers*) kept by students, and special questions for girls on examinations for the certificate of primary studies.

The Third Republic's system for the annual inspection of public primary school classes was a legacy of the July Monarchy. Inspectors, nearly all of whom were male, visited classrooms to ensure that teachers followed the prescribed curriculum and made students behave and work in an orderly way. Teachers kept detailed records of what they taught each day and submitted these to inspectors for examination. Inspectors also looked at dictations and compositions in students' notebooks and evaluated their ability to write about assigned themes.

Although some recalcitrant teachers and teachers in one-room schools did not cover all items in the official program, many, if not most, conscientiously presented prescribed material.[1] Inspectors' reports from the department of the Seine, as elsewhere, usually listed topics covered on inspection day and included comments like "good," "satisfactory," or "need for improvement" after various lessons.[2] Thus we learn that in April 1899 Mme Louise Boquet used *Suzette* to teach reading in her *cours élémentaire* in the seventh arrondissement of Paris and that girls read with a "suitable intonation." Three years later, when her pupils utilized a Juranville reader in a *cours moyen*, the same inspector again praised their pronunciation.³ *Morale* lessons in Mme Jeanne Noterman's *cours supérieur* in the tenth arrondissement of Paris in 1905 and 1906 included duties of the father and mother and the servants.⁴ Whereas Inspector Belot praised Noterman's ability to accustom students to listening and obeying, Marguerite Ginier, one of four women inspectors in the Seine before World War I, often criticized teachers for requiring too much memorization, talking too much themselves, and not developing a sense of initiative in students.⁵

Many standardized reports on girls' classes differed little from those on boys' classes, but occasional notations were reminders of why the secular Republic maintained the Catholic tradition of separating the sexes. Women teachers were praised for ability to preside over a class in motherly fashion, the maternal role model being the one most prized for girls.⁶ Teachers also gave special lessons on the duties of girls and women, and textbooks used for this were sometimes named.⁷ One inspector wrote of a Tarascon teacher's treatment of "la vocation de la jeune fille":

> She knows how to choose simple and positive examples; she shows how the girl prepares for her future role by putting in order *un petit ménage*, buying at the store, and lavishing her attentions on a doll. She throws into relief how order and cleanliness are precious qualities and does not fear to say clearly, although in discreet fashion, that they [girls] will later be wives and mothers, and that they will keep their husbands at home through the elegance and poetry that they will introduce in their home.⁸

Because many schools long lacked special facilities for home economics instruction, teachers often treated topics other than sewing in a purely theoretical way.⁹ Those who managed to overcome material deficiencies in this area were applauded. The *Revue pédagogique* noted approvingly in 1885 that a teacher in the Lot simply took her class to a nearby stream for practice in washing clothes.¹⁰ *Institutrices* who related science lessons on such topics as the distillation of water to a girl's domestic destiny were commended for their instruction's practical thrust and criticized if this link to post-scholastic life was missing.¹¹

What can be said about girls' absorption of and reactions to the domestic and feminine values presented in primary schools? Were young girls conscious of receiving messages about woman's roles? The answer to the second question is an emphatic yes, testified to by entries in girls' *cahiers*, special questions for girls on examinations for the certificate of primary studies for which teachers drilled them extensively, girls' responses to surveys on schoolchildren's favorite subjects and attitudes toward the future, and evidence from teachers' conferences and memoirs.

Students recorded a variety of exercises in all subjects in their notebooks but with most entries had little opportunity for independent judgment. Dictations, spelling, arithmetic problems, and recording maxims from daily *morale* lessons left no room for originality. Even with compositions students frequently tried to write what was expected by the teacher. Typically a pupil first encountered an essay topic in a *morale* lesson or reader, heard a teacher's explication of it, and then responded, often in rote fashion, to oral questions about it. A dictation on it might follow and, finally, the pupil wrote a composition, most likely regurgitating previously absorbed details about the theme. Some material learned in this fashion would also be repeated on the examination for the certificate of primary studies.

Although largely unoriginal, *cahiers* well document the transfer of information from teacher and textbook to student. Girls' *cahiers* exhibit the many topics presented to both sexes and also the special lessons on femininity and domesticity. At Vieux-Rouen-sur-Bresle in the Seine-Maritime in 1886 a thirteen-year-old girl, later to become a seamstress, wrote a composition about how a girl her age could take on household chores. Noting that she straightened her room, helped in the kitchen, and assisted younger brothers and sisters with lessons, she concluded that by developing orderly habits now "we will become *bonnes ménagères.*"[12] Dictations about sewing reinforced both the domestic orientation and psychological acceptance of unquestioning devotion to duty. On 7 June 1886 she recorded that "from the age of six, seated near her mother, a girl must begin to use her needle an hour a day . . . for it is necessary to guard against the development in her of distaste for the most precise and consoling occupation of women." Another entry described a family evening where parents played the expected roles: the mother took up her mending and the father read aloud from a newspaper or book. Some twenty years later her daughter's class had a similar dose of domestic economy. In 1905, at age eleven, the daughter learned about storing eggs, washing clothes, and acquiring the essential pieces for a layette. The daugher also knew the value of the housewife for French society: "Often a woman can prevent her husband from going to the cabaret by providing him with the sight of a well-kept interior joined with the pleasure of partaking of meals prepared with care. She will succeed still more if she is orderly, if she economizes and looks ahead to the future by seeking insurance in the event of physical weakening in old age, sickness, or unemployment." Becoming a schoolteacher, the daughter would pass on such messages to the next generations.[13]

The notebooks of Marie C., a Catholic schoolgirl in the western department of Maine-et-Loire between 1904 and 1908, bore much resemblance to those of public school girls, for she, too, wrote compositions and dictations on such standard topics as the "atelier of a *couturière*," the qualities of the "good housekeeper," "economy and charity," and "the law of work." Her spelling lesson on the good housekeeper listed the essential feminine traits cited in text-books: "order, finesse, goodness, watchfulness, *douceur.*" Like the schoolgirls in the Seine-Maritime, Marie C. also knew about different gender roles. Her composition on "la veillée" noted that father spent his day at the office and then after dinner, while mother mended and grandmother knitted, father read a newspaper. But there was also a Catholic component in the evening activities. Left alone, the mother knelt before a crucifix and said a prayer. In a composition about her own activities on a day in May 1906, Marie wrote that she said prayers in the morning, went to mass, and then to catechism and vespers; in the evening she warmed up the soup, set the table, cleaned up, and prayed with other family members.[14] Although the Seine-Maritime public school girl of 1886 did write a composition about her religious observances in preparation for her first com-munion, her daughter in 1905 was not likely to write about such events for in that year of the separation of church and state the secularization of girls' schools was more thoroughgoing.[15] Both Cath-olic and public school girls recorded similar messages about the countryside's superiority to the city and the importance of thrift and hard work but, again, the Catholic exercises added a religious di-mension. Marie C.'s entry on "work" noted that all types of work pleased God but that "la morale catholique" attributed superiority to "un travail de l'esprit" which produced especially noble results.

Other students also heard pedagogues advise them to accept cheer-fully their lot in life and not to expect their efforts to yield great wealth or upward social mobility. A dictation on "love of one's station" in ten-year-old Ernestine Thomé's notebook from a school at Mériot in the Aube in 1883 included the observation that a person always "jealous of the fortune of others" can "never live" in the present because he is so preoccupied with the future. By contrast, "happy the man who . . . is content with what he is" and devotes all his energies to "the post that the country has confided to him; content to obey, it is for it that he struggles and not for himself." In Torteron in the Cher in 1913 twelve-year-old Fernande Debret dutifully observed in an essay on a wintertime "family evening" that "we are happy to think that in spite of our poverty, we are well warmed near a good fire, while many other unfortunates do not even have a roof to shelter them from the cold." Yet she did not always accept poverty and obscurity quite as passively as in that essay. In her 31 December 1913 "devoir" on New Year's resolutions Fernande promised to do more at home to help her tired mother and then added, "I wish for you dear parents less work; I should like to become very rich. I would give you all that you need and you would be happy, always, always! I cannot do that alas."[16] Strivings for something better than their parents' lives there certainly were, but there is evidence that a large majority of schoolchildren were well conditioned to expect no change.[17]

As French feminists became more active after 1900, unsympathetic schoolteachers were also in a position to indoctrinate pupils with antifeminist views and to shore up the domestic ideology. Hence in 1903 Marie Emonet, a schoolgirl in Le Mans, recorded a dictation that contained a man's warning that although the sexes had "common faculties," they did not share them equally. "Wherever woman values her rights, she has the advantage, wherever she wants to usurp ours she remains beneath us." Therefore, "to cultivate in woman the qualities of a man" was to create an unhappy being unable to reconcile masculine and feminine tendencies.[18]

Parisian girls of course learned the same precepts about femininity and duties as their provincial sisters. Indeed, one of the few women inspectors in prewar France counseled Parisian *institutrices* to present a distinctly feminine *morale* "de la douceur, de la bonté, de la retenue digne"—the very qualities textbooks designated as quintessentially feminine. Not surprisingly, in the special *cahiers de morale* kept by ten- and eleven-year-olds in one Paris school, a series of entries on the standard topics of good behavior, proper attitudes, and hard work included notions about gender roles. Three girls' answers to the question "why is it necessary to work" assigned different tasks to men and women. The woman must "bring up her children and take care of her household. The man must also work for his children and for his wife," wrote one pupil.[19]

Recording *morale* maxims in *cahiers* was one level of absorbing the school's ideology. Acting on them was another. Some Parisian *institutrices* eager to make pupils apply *morale* lessons to everyday life adopted the experiment of *cahiers de volonté*. At the start of each month a student wrote down a resolution to change or improve behavior, and at the end of the month a parent noted whether the resolution had been kept. An ungraded exercise, the *cahier de volonté* offered the student the reward of pleasing parents and teachers. Studying harder, helping mother with housework, making one's bed, and being "douce" with brothers and sisters were typical resolutions.

Although not all resolutions were kept, one teacher was encouraged that 49 percent of her girls kept resolutions faithfully, 37 percent kept them imperfectly, and only 15 percent ignored them completely. Another teacher in the fourteenth arrondissement, Mme J. Marie, boasted that of forty-nine girls, about fifteen had helped their mothers, some had tried to cook, three had stopped biting nails, and two or three had, according to their parents, noticeably improved their character. The *cahiers de volonté* were also intended to enlist parents in the school's good works, and many cooperated fully by frankly assessing youngsters' performance at home. Thus Germaine Borredon's mother wrote in December 1911 that Germaine had "imperfectly" kept her resolution to get up from the dinner table in place of her mother when something was needed. When Germaine stuck to her obligation in January, the mother changed her report and the teacher rewarded both daughter and mother by writing "victory" in the *cahier*. Another mother, whose daughter Madeleine promised to be "more useful" in the household, thanked the teacher for the special notebook because "Madeleine needed it especially for the house." Uncooperative parents ran the risk of displeasing teachers, as in the case of the mother of Jeanne. In January 1911 Jeanne had resolved to make her bed in the morning. At the end of the month the mother noted that Jeanne had not kept her promise but admitted, "I permit her not to do it." The teacher then scolded in red ink, "Madame, Jeanne can acquire will power (*la volonté*) only if she tries; it is very bad to abandon a resolution that one has not kept."[20]

Failures like Jeanne notwithstanding, Léon Bédorez, director of primary instruction for the Seine, was convinced in 1912 that a majority of teachers believed that *morale* lessons improved students' behavior. He discounted complaints that moral instruction often degenerated into the mindless repetition of maxims. Although the inspector of schools in the working class *quartiers* of the fourth and twentieth arrondissements reported pessimistically that changes in students' behavior were little in evidence, administrator Bédorez claimed significant results: "Schoolboys are less egotistical, less brutal, more polite, more sincere; schoolgirls have a better attitude, more discretion in speech, more refined manners, more frankness, more cordiality, a greater respect for society." Perhaps his list for girls was longer than for boys because primary inspectors tended to give women teachers higher ratings for effectiveness in the teaching of *morale*, sometimes explaining that feminine qualities especially suited them to teach the subject.[21]

To succeed in the primary school students of course had to do more than behave properly. For good students the climax of the primary school years was receiving the certificate of primary studies (*certificat d'études primaires* or *c.e.p.*). One obtained it by passing an oral and written examination testing retention of standard items in the curriculum. On the average, students took the exam at age twelve, and, if successful, fulfilled the compulsory education requirement, even if they were not yet thirteen. Only good students were encouraged to take the exam, and not all takers passed. Perhaps 25 percent of rural children passed the test at the turn of the century; by the 1930s, about 40 percent nationwide.[22] Those who passed received an educational credential comparable in importance during the Third Republic to that of an American high school diploma before World War II. The *c.e.p.* was also essential for entry into the lower levels of government service—for example, for jobs in the post office—and was the first degree required for those aspiring to be teachers. With the *c.e.p.* qualified girls could enter a *cours complémentaire* or *école primaire supérieure* and from there compete for a place in a normal school.

Although the basic structure of the examination for the *c.e.p.* was the same for boys and girls, girls often received questions about distinctly feminine topics. The written part of the exam consisted of one hour's worth of arithmetic problems, a dictation testing spelling ability and often lasting an hour, and a third hour for a composition on one of three categories of topics. The departmental inspector could select an essay on (1) moral or civic instruction, (2) history or geography, or (3) elementary science and its applications to agriculture, hygiene, or homemaking. For girls, questions on *morale* could readily encompass feminine virtues, and science could mean domestic economy. In addition, girls had to demonstrate sewing ability, a facet of the exam for which there was initially no counterpart for boys and which thus added, until 1897, five extra points to the total girls needed to pass it. The oral section of the test required the candidate to read and explain a passage, to recite one selection from a list of selections he or she had chosen in advance, and to respond to short questions on history, geography, and science.[23]

To drill their better students for the *c.e.p.* exam, teachers used collections of past questions which provided outlines for answers prized by examiners. Several collections of questions used in various departments before World War I reveal that for compositions and oral questions, girls had to repeat many statements about female roles and attributes found in readers and *morale* textbooks.[24] Students preparing for the exam memorized answers to many standard questions and also practiced writing compositions on them. For example, in 1893 girls in the *cours moyen* of a rural school in the Haute-Savoie wrote essays in their notebooks on "Why I love my mother," a topic also found on *c.e.p.* exams in the Tarn-et-Garonne. The format used by one girl to develop her answer followed closely the model in a book of sample exam questions, thus indicating that her class had been drilled on the topic before writing the essay.[25] Catholic girls desiring the *c.e.p.* had to take the state exams and so required similar indoctrination to succeed. Catholic pedagogical journals like *L'Ecole française* emulated republican ones like the *Manuel général de l'instruction primaire* and regularly published sample questions and answers in suggested class preparations for teachers.

Although girls might very well be asked to write compositions which had no distinctly feminine cast, many test questions touched on domesticity. To write about "the pleasure" and "utility" of sewing lessons, girls were expected to emphasize the moral and practical value of sewing. A sample answer by "Louise" recorded that girls found the four hours devoted to needlework two days a week at school a "great pleasure" and "agreeable relaxation after long hours of study." After leaving school, Louise expected that "we shall be happy to find in needlework a remedy against boredom and shall be able to be useful to our family." Later as housewives "we shall need constantly to apply what we learn now in school and we shall understand better that this instruction is indispensable to the education of the woman." Paeans to the importance of the needle—similar to the one entered in the *cahier* of the Seine-Maritime girl in 1886—also frequently appeared in dictations, as on an exam in the Vosges.[26]

Short questions about science on the oral part of the exam were often tailored to suit rural or urban environments as well as gender. Hence rural girls responded to queries about what rabbits ate and how to raise chickens. All over France schoolgirls recited the value of cold baths and simplicity of dress and knew that a mother's milk was the best nourishment for an infant. To explain how a wife could please a husband a girl should list neat attire, good housekeeping, and a cheerful and gracious demeanor. Other questions asked not only why it was a wife's duty to cook for her family but also why meals should be varied.[27]

Republican social and economic values and women's role in their defense figured in questions about work and patriotism. The inculcation of social immobility was explicit in a question on a Côte d'Or exam which asked whether a girl earning a low salary in the country should go to a nearby city for higher wages. The answer was "no in general" because higher urban wages were offset by a higher cost of living and because conditions in cities and workshops were "far from favorable to health."[28] To comment on the maxim, "It is not always good to have an important job," girls had to develop the point that people with prestigious métiers were "more exposed and often less happy than those with modest positions." The nobility of "manual labor" was also a common theme. Other typical questions with economic overtones called for writing about the virtues of thrift or composing letters to ask for a job or to appeal to a landlord for relief when a poor harvest made the payment of rent difficult.[29] The importance attached to the internalization of the economic values in the school's *morale* program is well illustrated by their prevalence on the 94 *c.e.p.* examinations given to primary students in the Seine between 1895 and 1915. Themes from the *morale* program figured in 62 dictations and 66 compositions on these exams; and of these 128 dictations and compositions, the largest group, 25 percent, related to economic issues: the work ethic, thrift, and contentment with one's lot in life.[30]

Since the importance of loving France was another predominant theme in the Third Republic's instruction, the nature of woman's patriotism was also a familiar topic for both classroom exercises and exams.[31] To discuss woman's patriotism for the *c.e.p.*, C. Wirth advised girls to develop four points: (1) the premise that women's patriotic duties differed from men's, (2) mothers' obligations to teach children love of France, (3) watchfulness to see that a husband fulfilled civic duties and that children learned to obey laws, and (4) bravery if the country called upon a son or husband to fight.[32] Young women mastering that question for the *c.e.p.* might then find it repeated on the competitive examination for scholarships for the higher primary school.[33]

Children's ability to parrot principles hammered in by teachers extended beyond the classroom or examination setting. In 1899 400 pupils aged nine to eleven from two boys' and two girls' schools in Lyon were asked to name their favorite subjects and give reasons for their choices. The survey listed five topics—*morale*, French, history, geography, arithmetic—and children could express preferences for one, two, or three. *Morale* was the favorite subject for both sexes with 210 votes; French was the least favored with 121. *Morale* received special emphasis from teachers at the start of each school day and was taught with a large number of stories and anecdotes, as Professor C. Chabot noted in his interpretation of students' answers. Pupils' reasons for preferring *morale* often echoed a teacher's words. Children identified *morale* as a subject preparing them for later life and cited the importance of such themes as fighting alcoholism and serving the *patrie*. Chabot found girls' answers more interesting than boys' because girls stressed that *morale* taught them respect for parents and masters, politeness, neatness, and *gentillesse*. One girl had grasped very well the kind of woman the school wished her to become: "I like *morale* which teaches me to be a model and virtuous young girl who will teach her children honesty, economy, work, and many other qualities. Without the good *morale* lessons of our teachers, prosperous France would fall into anarchy."[34]

Students' attitudes toward the school's offerings were also revealed in a more ambitious survey in the department of the Nord in 1899. Forty-one questions were posed to 37,012 pupils aged nine to eleven. For the question on favorite subjects about 25 percent of both boys and girls placed history first, and 14 percent of both sexes named arithmetic second. Girls ranked reading, geography, spelling, and drawing as their third, fourth, fifth, and sixth choices, respectively, while boys ranked drawing third, reading fourth, spelling fifth, and geography sixth. *Morale*, students' first choice in the much smaller Lyon survey, held the low place of eleventh with boys and tenth with girls. Of the subjects most related to domestic life, sewing was listed first by only 4 percent of girls and "domestic economy" by less than 1 percent.[35] The relatively low rank which girls assigned to sewing and home economics in 1899, like a comparably low sixth place received by sewing in an 1877 survey of Parisian girls' preferences for school subjects, suggests that the part of the curriculum which teachers told them was directly related to their future lives as homemakers or wage earners was by no means the most interesting to them.[36] In this regard, though, girls' attitudes were comparable to boys' lack of enthusiasm for the practical subjects offered them under the rubrics of manual works, agriculture, and maritime instruction. Only 1.5 percent of boys cited one of these as a favorite in 1899.

Why did students prefer academic subjects to practical ones? Was the public school, with its commitment to the goal of universal literacy and inculcation of the work ethic, really producing hordes of *déracinés*, as conservatives like Maurice Barrès charged? Admittedly, many teachers were less eager to give instruction in "manual works" than in academic subjects, and their neglect of and disinterest in the former probably influenced students' preferences.[37] There are also indications that the teaching of home economics and agriculture was more intensive in Catholic schools than in public schools.[38]

Yet children's low preference for topics directly related to future work lives in both 1877 and 1899 did not mean that they failed to perceive their importance or derive some enjoyment from them at school. In 1877 a large majority of Parisian girls taking the *c.e.p.* exam indicated that after leaving school they expected to work as seamstresses.[39] In 1899, when asked whether they liked or disliked "manual works," 73 percent of boys and 84 percent of girls indicated a liking, undoubtedly an expression of more enthusiasm than the unpopular anti-alcohol lessons could elicit. In the poll only eight girls and no boys rated anti-alcohol instruction the favorite subject. Acceptance of one's lot in life was also demonstrated by the high percentage of affirmative responses to the question of whether they would like to follow the profession of their father or mother: 66 percent of boys said yes, as did 78 percent of girls. That a higher percentage of girls than boys answered these two questions affirmatively might demonstrate more contentment with role models provided by the parent of the same sex or, alternatively, greater fatalism and a failure to perceive other options for the future. That the latter was sometimes the case is suggested by the difference between the way boys and girls responded to the question of whether they expected to be happier after leaving school than they were presently: 57 percent of boys said yes, as compared to 40 percent of girls.[40]

These statistical findings may also confirm the impression of at least two women teachers that elementary school girls were well aware of the drudgery in their mothers' lives at home and saw men as fortunate in managing to avoid routine domestic chores. "All the pain is for us [women] and the pleasure for them [men]," complained one ten-year-old girl who knew that women in her part of Burgundy did both field work and housework.[41] Sewing classes also had little appeal for both Jeanne Bouvier, a poor working class girl who became a labor activist, and the intellectually precocious Simone de Beauvoir, educated at a private school for middle class Catholic girls in the sixth arrondissement of Paris. The actress Germaine de Maulny, taught by nuns in provincial Limoges during the 1890s, complained that sewing and needlework received more attention during the school day than academic subjects. On the other hand, Marie Gasquet, daughter of a friend of the Provençal poet Frédéric Mistral, recalled with pleasure the lengthy sewing lessons in the Catholic school to which her father had sent her so that she might learn to smile and not be burdened by weighty thoughts.[42]

That bright and mischievous girls also mocked solemn moral values attached to domestic education is suggested by Claudine, the irrepressible heroine of Colette's novels based on her own childhood and coming of age in a Burgundian village. In *Claudine à Paris* the heroine recalled how she and a school friend had irreverently modified the maxims which they were supposed to memorize and take seriously in Louis-Eugène Bérillon's *Bonne ménagère agricole*. The sexual activities of Claudine and her friends,[43] like those of a few girls expelled from Paris schools, were also far removed from the primary school's program of moral instruction and hygiene, which ignored the topic of sex but did teach the importance of modesty, probably a veiled way of reminding thirteen-year-olds of certain taboos. The departmental regulation that a child's conduct in school should not endanger the morality of other pupils enabled teachers in prewar Paris to send thirteen-year-old girls home if their dresses were too short. School administrators also summarily dismissed adolescent girls who threatened the morality of classmates by bringing love letters or scandalous magazines to school or telling tales about amorous activities with boys.[44]

What do teachers tell us about their own reactions to the part of the school's offerings that was distinctly feminine? That most teachers of the Belle Epoque accepted many prevailing notions about femininity—even if they themselves had stepped from the "interior" to the "exterior" world—is suggested by a group of papers written in preparation for an international congress on primary education that was part of the extensive commemoration of the centennial of the French Revolution. The role of women as teachers, school principals, and inspectors was one of the three major topics discussed in August 1889 by an assembly of more than 1000 delegates, over 90 percent of whom were French.[45] Although women were not quite 11 percent of the French delegation of teachers, normal school professors, and inspectors, they were more prominently represented as authors of the position papers on women educators that were submitted in advance of the congress to Octave Gréard, vice-rector of the Academy of Paris and president of the committee organizing the congress. When assessing women's ability to function as *institutrices, directrices,* or *inspectrices,* authors often commented on the nature of womanhood, thus supplying a set of opinions which can be compared to the stereotypical personality traits and roles assigned to women in textbooks. With fifty position papers available, twenty-five by men and twenty-five by women, it is also possible to compare male and female opinions about the two aspects of women's pedagogical role which proved most controversial at the congress: (1) were women really suited to teach in *écoles mixtes,* as the law of 30 October 1886 directed, and (2) could women fulfill the duties of the authoritative primary school inspector, a position opened to them by article 22 of the law of 19 July 1889. Although some position papers represented the opinions of a group of both male and female colleagues, in only two instances did authors—both women—disagree with the majority of their group.[46]

Men and women differed noticeably in their handling of the two controversial questions, and professional rivalries undoubtedly contributed to this disparity. The expansion of women's role in the educational establishment threatened to reduce the number of jobs available for men. Of nineteen women who commented on whether women should teach in "mixed" schools where some pupils were eleven-to-thirteen-year-old boys, fifteen rated women able to do the job and four disagreed. Among twenty male opinions on the issue, seventeen preferred assigning men to coeducational schools, especially the larger ones, and thereby challenged the law which, while allowing for local exceptions, supposedly made the *écoles mixtes* the domain of *institutrices*. As Gréard noted, teachers were less liberal than the law, and the same was true for their reactions to the possible appointment of women to the primary school inspectorate. Previously women's role as inspectors had been limited to *écoles maternelles* or to the status of special delegate. Position papers by women were closely divided over whether women could be effective *inspectrices:* thirteen wanted women inspectors and ten did not. Only six reports by men recommended the regular appointment of women inspectors, and fifteen raised objections. The position papers foreshadowed the discussion of the controversial issues at the congress itself. The "second section" which considered women's role as educators resolved that primary school inspection should remain a male province and that "*écoles mixtes* should in principle be directed by male teachers," although in special cases the administration could appoint women principals.[47]

The marshaling of assumptions about the feminine personality to support stances on the controversial issues demonstrates that a majority of both sexes in the teaching corps of 1889 did not disagree with the depiction of women in textbooks. Both opponents and proponents of a feminine presence in coeducational schools and the inspectorate often cited presumably natural feminine qualities to buttress their arguments. The notions that women were physically weaker than men, more likely to be governed by sentiment than by reason, and less able to appear authoritative because of their naturally sweet and gentle natures figured prominently in objections to women inspectors or *directrices* of *écoles mixtes*. Ten men and nine women raised such objections in position papers, and at the congress others echoed the theme. M. Plazy, a primary inspector from Angoulême, asserted that a woman is "naturally *faible* and impressionable" and "will not be able to discover the truth as easily as the male inspector." Only the man possessed the "calm" nature and "impartiality" necessary for administrative roles. Mademoiselle Heurtefeu, head of the normal school for women in the Hautes-Pyrénées, echoed his opinion when, despite her conviction that it was "not suitable for women to speak in public," she decided to address the congress. Presumably the future teachers whom she regularly instructed did not constitute a public! After asserting that it was unsuitable for women to travel from town to town as an inspector must, Heurtefeu cited the psychological differences between men and women. "Man is generally directed by reason and good sense; woman, by the heart, by sensibility." Mademoiselle L. Gaudel, writing up the opinions of colleagues at the normal school in the Pyrénées-Orientales, rejected *inspectrices* on the grounds that, unlike men who were intended for "an active and almost always exterior life," woman "cannot occupy herself with public affairs, nor fill certain functions, she is made for family life." The factor of woman's religiosity was injected into the debate by a Parisian inspector, Delapierre, who predicted that if women took over the inspection of girls' schools, France would soon have "republican instruction, patriotic and neutral in regard to religious dogma in boys' schools, and probably the opposite in girls' schools."[48]

Significantly, those who argued that women were fully qualified to be inspectors and principals of *écoles mixtes* cited arguments about woman's special nature nearly as often as their adversaries. Nine women authors of position papers cited such qualities as woman's maternal nature, power of resignation, patience, *douceur*, and greater sensibility in order to argue that female inspectors would see to it that girls' schools fulfilled their mission of turning out young women endowed with such traits.[49] Madame Vilain-Philippe, directress of an *école primaire supérieure* in the Jura, was among those also arguing that woman's inherent maternal leanings made her better qualified than a man for a role in coeducational schools. Within a family a mother certainly reared boys as well as girls, but it was unnatural for a man to educate girls. Madame Bonnet, an *institutrice* representing colleagues in the Charente-Inférieure, recommended that the program for girls' schools and normal schools for women should contain less science and more emphasis on literature, domestic economy, and manual works.

Although advocates of removing barriers to women's advancement in the educational system did not typically reject prevailing notions about women's personality or natural domestic and maternal role, they sometimes expressed discomfort with restrictions on women's lives. Three women and two men demanded equal pay (not to be obtained by women teachers until 1918),[50] but so did two of their female adversaries.[51] Six women referred to the economic necessities which drove many women into the work force, insisting that precisely because employment opportunities for women were limited in many areas education ought to be one field where restrictions were eliminated.[52] Two, Madame Bonnet and Mademoiselle Hénocq, an *institutrice* from the Somme, wrote about the need to "emancipate" women, and Madame Mantoz-le-Gad, *inspectrice* of the *écoles ma-*

ternelles of Oran, was outraged that some women tried to limit other women's chances for professional advancement.

At the congress the most visible advocate of women inspectors was Madame Pauline Kergomard, a highly respected *inspectrice générale* of *écoles maternelles*. Claiming that a majority of the women attending the second section's debates on women educators did not share the opposition of the male majority to *inspectrices*, Kergomard combined a nod to domestic ideology with the argument that women should inspect primary schools, just as in certain departments they already inspected *écoles maternelles*. Woman was "the natural guardian of the foyer," and no woman would ever desert that role if she could avoid doing so. But for "an immense number of women," work was an "imperious necessity," as Kergomard herself well knew, her own husband's impecunious situation and the need to support two children having been cited by historian Gabriel Monod when he recommended to Ferry that she receive an educational post in 1879.[53] For women needing to work, "what work is more appropriate than that of the school?" Kergomard asked the congress. She rejected assumptions about female physical weakness and asserted that proper training could enable women to assume the same roles as male educators. Those who complained that women had too many ties to the church should realize that the best way to ensure that mothers spread the "republican idea" with "maternal milk" was to have a republican *institutrice* in each village—something possible if women ran the one-room *écoles mixtes* and were supervised by women inspectors.[54]

Despite the impassioned pleas for equal employment opportunities from Kergomard and Blanche Scordia, a Paris school principal, at the full session of the congress a majority of male delegates maintained reservations about the controversial roles for women colleagues. As president of the full session of the congress, Gréard succeeded in moderating the second section's preference for male teachers in coeducational schools by getting the full congress to vote that "*écoles mixtes* can be assigned to *instituteurs* or to *institutrices* depending upon particular cases and needs." However, the congress rejected his proposition that positions in the inspectorate could be assigned to women "aussi bien qu'à des hommes" and simply voted for a compromise that was less hostile to *inspectrices* than the second section: "on an experimental basis, some positions in the inspectorate can be assigned to women."[55]

The resistance of much of the educational establishment in 1889 to women teachers in *écoles mixtes* or to women inspectors indicates why women had difficulty obtaining these positions before 1914. As of 1907, two-thirds of *écoles mixtes* were still taught by men because many rural communes preferred them.[56] Furthermore, few departments appointed women inspectors, even though, in 1891, the education ministry spelled out different functions for *inspectrices* than for *inspecteurs*. According to a *décret* of 17 January 1891, only male inspectors would handle the potentially controversial matters related to the opening or functioning of private schools. Dealings with municipalities or the upper echelons of the educational bureaucracy were also the male inspectorate's preserve. Women inspectors would concentrate on supervising teachers and pay special attention to seeing that they presented a "morale" suitable for girls and gave adequate treatment to sewing and other domestic arts. By 1914 there were only five women in the national corps of 446 primary school inspectors: four were in the Seine and one in the Seine-et-Oise, both departments having appointed their first *inspectrices* during the early 1890s.[57]

Other writings by individual teachers do not significantly alter the impression from the 1889 conference that most prewar teachers accepted the assumptions behind the distinctly feminine component of girls' education. Few teachers' memoirs devoted much attention to isolating those features of girls' education differing from that of boys. Instead *institutrices* presented themselves as teaching general moral and patriotic values rather than feminine values.[58] Their dissatisfaction with the school itself tended to center on inadequate buildings and supplies or an inspector's harassment. Complaints about the perspective on women's lives offered by textbooks or pedagogoical manuals were far less common in available teachers' reminiscences than details about personal travails and problems with a sometimes hostile rural community.[59] Women teachers bemoaned their social isolation, although that was something which pedagogical leaders told them not only to tolerate but actively seek out so that within a community they would not lose their reputation for purity and objectivity.[60] One woman who keenly felt the perils of such a loss was once in charge of the demonstration school attached to the normal school at Chartres. In 1880 she had to seek a transfer because, her inspector noted, "the failure of the imprudent steps that she had taken to marry" had affected "her authority over students." For a Parisian teacher who became pregnant out of wedlock in 1883, the penalty was loss of her job and rejection of her repeated requests for reinstatement, despite her assertions that she had indeed learned a lesson and could promise exemplary conduct.[61]

The example of Marie Sandre well illustrates the continuing internalization of society's norms for women by *institutrices* whose education made them unique among the feminine role models most girls of the people encountered. Three generations of the Sandre family had been teachers before Marie entered the profession in 1900. Never married, she did not consider her career and single state to be superior to domesticity and motherhood. Surveyed in 1961 about her recollections on the nature of the profession and her part in it before World War I, Sandre stated that her mother, who had reared seven children, had been her model of ideal womanhood. Mothering had seemed to be the most important and "beautiful profession" for women. Sandre's views were thus no different from those of male colleagues or advice givers who repeatedly told women teachers to be motherly in dealing with students.[62] After all, this behavior generally earned the praise of school inspectors, male and female. Sandre had ignored feminism and remained aloof from teachers' unions and politics. In old age, though, she modified her views on woman's place in society, no longer believing that only single women should have careers. If given a second chance, she also thought that she might not remain so uninvolved in politics or teachers' organizations.[63]

Unlike Sandre, whose contented dedication to her profession and its rules of conduct were well described in fictionalized form by a nephew,[64] Marguerite Bodin complained about some aspects of republican schooling for girls. A feminist and socialist active in the teachers' *amicale* in the Yonne and elected by colleagues to the departmental educational council, Bodin championed coeducation and woman's suffrage at teachers' meetings and in *Les Surprises de l'école mixte* (1905). She criticized the low valuation society placed upon women's activities and had a class in an *école mixte* in rural Burgundy discuss society's unfair denial of votes to women and the fact that men suffered from keeping women in an inferior status. Women should view their education not only as something useful for rearing sons but also as a contributor to their own personal development, she taught. Women's intellectual abilities were demonstrated by their doing as well as males on exams. Nonetheless, Bodin still believed that each sex had "un esprit différent" which complemented that of the other.[65]

In reasserting an age-old dogma about innate differences between the sexes, Bodin resembled the less radical women teachers who had utilized such views in 1889 to argue for *institutrices'* professional advancement. A similar mixture of traditional beliefs about woman's nature and a protest against devaluing woman's abilities appeared in the complaint of a student at Fontenay-aux-Roses who disliked part of an address given at the school in 1888 by the distinguished classicist, Alfred Croiset. This young woman resented Croiset's suggestion that women's primary role was to please others and embellish private life. Yet she was not so rebellious as to doubt that men and women were intellectually different: "Vivacity and intellectual versatility, ease of assimilation, skill in hinting with the aid of sentiment what she cannot demonstrate with method, these are, in effect, the distinctive qualities of woman, who lacks that creative intelligence, capable of invention and of discoveries, that power of reasoning which seems reserved to man; the mind of woman is more sparkling than solid." Regrettably, the "superficial education" hitherto given to woman simply reinforced her intellectual deficiencies. What woman really needed, and what Croiset failed to recognize, she asserted, was a more rational "culture d'esprit."[66]

French *institutrices'* subscription to the existing wisdom that men and women had different natures should not seem surprising, for their pedagogical counterparts in other countries made comparable assertions. Women teachers in Germany used such premises in debate with male rivals to support the argument that women were the only proper teachers of girls. Additionally, English teachers and their allies who sought to extend educational and professional opportunities for middle class girls often, at the same time, relegated working class daughters to an inferior education strictly oriented toward preparation for domesticity. In Sara Delamont's judgment, it was only by not challenging the established gospel on woman's place in the family that ambitious English women were able to advance educational opportunities for their sex.[67] Similarly, contemporary feminists on both sides of the Atlantic often echoed familiar beliefs about male and female spheres. Whereas French feminists often argued that gender differences were complementary and compatible with doctrines of "equality" or "equivalence" of the sexes, some Anglo-American feminists asserted that woman was actually morally superior to man and thereby entitled to better treatment within and more influence over her society.[68]

How exceptional among teachers was Bodin's advocacy of woman's suffrage or coeducation? Admittedly, only a tiny minority of women teachers—probably no more than a few hundred—were radical enough to combine demands for full equality between the sexes with socialist positions, as did militant syndicalist *institutrices*.[69] Supporting coeducation or woman's suffrage was considerably less daring. Kergomard insisted that coeducation was actually good preparation for developing the personality traits distinctive to each sex in family life: boys would learn that "the duty of the stronger is to protect the weaker"; girls would begin learning the role of "adviser and comforter."[70] In 1905 a majority of the men and women delegates attending the fourth congress of teachers' *amicales* at Lille passed a resolution in favor of coeducation, calling it a means to integrate women more satisfactorily into society. Men would also benefit because coeducation was a way "to avoid unhappy unions and, in changing the mentality of women, to attenuate conflicts of opinion which exist in many households." In the same spirit, these activist teachers asked legislators to enact "civil and political equality" for women. Although the *amicales* represented a majority of teachers, the Lille congress, the fourth national *amicales'* congress since 1900, was controlled by syndicalists who eventually shunned the *amicales* as too establishment-oriented and, in defiance of the government ban on unions (*syndicats*) for public employees, formed the Fédération nationale des syndicats d'instituteurs in 1906. Significantly, even these activist teachers who wanted coeducational classes and recreation periods agreed that the common curriculum for both sexes should be supplemented with a practical "special education" addressed to the real differences in the lives of men and women. They also judged coeducation the best way to develop "the aptitudes which are natural to each sex." These arguments did not persuade the skeptical director of primary education for the Nord who asked sarcastically, in the quasiofficial *Revue pédagogique*, whether proponents of coeducation also intended to have women serve in the army.[71] The generalization of coeducation would have to await the Fifth Republic.

By the early twentieth century woman's suffrage had many respectable middle class French supporters. Indeed, French suffragettes have sometimes been chastised for an excessively bourgeois orientation.[72] In 1909 the staid *Manuel général de l'instruction primaire*, an adviser of teachers since the 1830s, had no qualms about airing both sides of the suffrage question. While Jeanne Roger-Lévy, a teacher at a higher primary school in Le Havre, based her opposition to the vote for women on the grounds that it would create discord between the sexes and thus disrupt society, the feminist Albertine Eidenschenk-Patin, *directrice* of the *école normale* at Douai, supported woman's suffrage. At Fontenay-aux-Roses Jeanne Adèle Dejean de la Bâtie, *directrice* from 1897 to 1917, permitted a leading suffragist, Cécile Brunschwig, to speak to her students.[73]

Eidenschenk-Patin had also issued complaints about certain aspects of the legal status of French women in *Variétés morales et pédagogiques, petits et grands secrets de bonheur* (1907), a book for teachers. She attacked, as well, at least a part of the prevailing pedagogical emphasis on domesticity for women by venting her dislike of Rousseau's educational model for Sophie, the female educated to please his hero *Emile*. She even charged that republican officialdom had been slow to enforce the secularization of girls' public schools because republican men preferred submissive women.[74] Such criticisms from republican educators were rare, however. They were more likely to come from particularly outspoken feminists or the fringes of the Left—from the anarchists rather than from the male socialist workers whose ideal was also *la femme au foyer*, supported by a higher wage for her worker husband.[75] Unlike the trade unionists who accepted middle class images of domesticity, some anarchists in 1897 criticized republican textbooks like those of Gréville and Chalamet for teaching female submissiveness to patriarchs and imposing extra duties upon woman which made *"la morale* much more difficult for her." In 1914 members of the Union française pour le suffrage de femmes, founded in 1909, resolved at their national congress to criticize feminine images in pedagogical reviews and textbooks that portrayed women as intellectually or socially inferior.[76]

If some women teachers protested against prevailing views on gender differences and sought greater equality between men and women, others complained that girls' education was actually insufficiently feminized. Ginier, one of the few primary *inspectrices*, argued in 1911 in the *Revue pédagogique* that the appointment of more women inspectors would better ensure that teachers properly prepared girls for expected adult roles. Like teachers who made this argument in 1889, Ginier tried to turn the teaching of prescriptions for feminine behavior into a weapon enabling women to gain a greater share in the power and prestige reserved to the largely male inspectorate. Her article provoked a rebuttal from a male inspector who asserted that girls' education was already sufficiently feminized, particularly in the case of the teaching of science where applications to domestic economy were stressed.[77]

That inspectors like Ginier had a strong commitment to seeing that schoolgirls learned about women's traditional duties of course posed another obstacle to individual teachers challenging the content of girls' textbooks. In 1908 a forty-year-old teacher in the fifth arrondissement of Paris was accused anonymously by a "père de famille" of teaching that "the husband is not the head of the household" and that "the wife should refuse to obey him" because she "is no longer his servant" or obliged to "take care of the interior of the house." Her inspector launched an investigation, during which he carefully read her daily plans for *morale* lessons. He then reported to the departmental director of primary instruction that he found nothing to reproach because she treated "the duties of spouses in the manner which is suitable" and simply discussed their "reciprocal duties." Presumably a deviation from the "duties" prescribed by the *morale* program would have aroused administrative as well as parental wrath.[78] In 1906 Ginier had chastised one teacher for failing to inject enough enthusiasm into her lesson on the qualities of the good housewife.[79]

It seems likely that Ginier and Sandre, who accepted the received wisdom about women's domestic roles, were more representative of pre-World War I women educators than the small number of feminist-syndicalist teachers who complained that the teaching of home economics was a way of perpetuating woman's "double burden" in life or who targeted the family as an oppressor of women.[80] The *institutrices* themselves, as professional women, had a prestigious position among women workers, but many probably agreed with Sandre that motherhood was woman's most important calling. The son of a prewar *institutrice* has recalled that although his parents were exceptional in their town in the Vendée in that they both worked and shunned the Catholic school, his mother was a docile wife who treated her husband, a *gendarme*, as the *chef* and later disapproved of her son's role in child care.[81] One Catholic teacher opined in 1912 that most women did not suffer from never experiencing "intellectual joys" and that unmarried teachers found these pleasures poor compensation for the family life they were missing.[82] If many women teachers felt this way, it is likely that they were emotionally convincing when they gave lessons on woman's natural roles of wife and mother. Indeed, by 1898 56 percent of *institutrices* were married.[83]

The official program of instruction, textbooks, reports by educational administrators, and teachers' memoirs depict the world of the prewar French primary school as an orderly one where pupils absorbed an encyclopedic array of information. Girls studied the same academic subjects as boys but often received lessons in reading, *morale*, civics, and science which had a distinctly feminine cast and were presumably accepted uncritically by most pupils and their teachers. Taught by women in separate classes in towns of more than five hundred, girls learned that they were destined for domesticity, to which they would devote the greatest part of their adult work lives, provided that they were fortunate enough to marry men whose incomes enabled them to remain in the foyer. As we shall see, that domestic ideal would retain an important place in girls' primary education as France moved from the trauma of World War I to the adjustments of the interwar period.

CHAPTER FOUR

From World War I to World War II: Continuity and Change in Curriculum and Textbooks

The program of 1887 remained the basic outline for primary school instruction until after World War II, but during the interwar period the education ministry made two curricular revisions, one in 1923 and the other in 1938. Neither altered the essential role of the primary school as the institution which made "le peuple" literate and prepared them for work and citizenship. Educational reformers like Marguerite Bodin noted the contrast between the general American respect for the public primary school and the French bourgeoisie's longstanding preference for sending children to private schools or the special elementary classes of public secondary schools.[1] In 1926 the primary program did become the basis for instruction in the elementary classes of *lycées* and *collèges*, a development which heartened reformers eager to abolish the social gap between primary and secondary education.[2] But at the end of the 1930s few educators had any illusions about the primary school's continuing role as the "school of the people." Girls' primary schooling of the interwar years must be viewed against a backdrop of reformers' attempts to democratize the public school system and the efforts of educators, progressive and conservative alike, to make schools better serve the needs of society.

The revised primary curriculum of 1923, sponsored by director of primary education Paul Lapie, attempted to simplify an encyclopedic program. Reaffirming that the primary school's purpose was to provide a general education rather than vocational preparation for the "children of the masses," the education ministry reduced the amount of time allotted to "manual works," the past teaching of which was judged inadequate anyway, especially in boys' schools. The 1887 program had dictated two to three hours per week for such practical instruction, but many teachers complained that this was excessive.

The 1923 program reduced the allocation by one-third to one-half and also recommended combining some required exercises in *travaux manuels* with science and drawing lessons. However, the revised curriculum still left more time for sewing and related tasks in girls' schools than for "manual works" in boys' schools. Henceforth in the *cours moyen* manual works occupied one hour for boys but two hours for girls; in the *cours supérieur*, one and one-half hours for boys and still two hours for girls. The hour's difference between the boys' and girls' schedule at the middle level was divided between extra instruction in French and science for boys; at the superior level boys still received an extra half hour of French. The official justification for the disparity was that "little girls learn to read with ease more quickly than do boys, and . . . consequently the reduction of hours in reading in the girls' schedule would not result in any real handicaps." Ministerial instructions on the importance of girls' manual works—sewing, knitting, and crocheting—stipulated that, ideally, girls should learn to darn "as our mothers did" and comprehend that the wearer of torn clothes lacked "self-respect." Thus, as in 1887, officialdom assumed that practical education produced moral improvement: a girl could acquire habits of "order, economy, pride in work well done; . . . taste . . . , power of concentration and perseverance."[3]

Manual works were not the only topic treated differently for boys and girls by the 1923 program. Girls' drawing lessons at middle and upper levels included more "decorative design" and the application of designs to "embroidery, crochet lace, and appliqué." "Geometrical drawing" was "more specially reserved for boys' schools" at middle and upper levels. For girls' physical education, teachers were "to select the games and movements best fitted to their sex, those which will give agility and grace rather than strength." Elementary science instruction was also geared to the different futures of girls and boys. Girls' science included a large chunk of home economics, to which a teacher might devote as much as half a day a week "by combining various prescribed exercises." "Theory" had "no place" in girls' science lessons unless it was "to justify practice," for above all, these lessons should "inspire girls with the love of home, making them feel that what appears to be the humblest of operations in domestic life is connected with the highest principles of natural science." Accordingly, girls' science courses and accompanying textbooks, especially for the superior level, contained home economics sections not offered to boys. Separate science books would remain in use until the 1960s and even into the 1970s. However, the emphasis on practical applications of science meant that not all boys' science lessons were identical either: "agricultural in the country, instruction in science will become industrial in the cities."[4]

As of 1923 two lessons a month on the care of infants (*puériculture*) were also added to the superior grade's science lessons for eleven-to-thirteen year-old girls. Intense postwar concern about "defense of the race," deemed in jeopardy because of the great wartime loss of life and the continuing low French birthrate, prompted this addition.[5] Three years earlier the legislature had passed a law banning the dissemination of propaganda in favor of contraception or abortion, and a presidential decree introduced three kinds of motherhood medals for women who had raised families of five or more. Yet concern about depopulation, while exacerbated by World War I, predated it.[6] During the 1890s such figures as the statistician Jacques Bertillon, a founder of the Alliance nationale pour l'accroissement de la population, had tried to create national alarm about the low birthrate. In December 1912 some of the Republic's medical and scientific leaders started the Société d'eugénique in the hopes of improving the population qualitatively as well as quantitatively. Women reformers, too, shared in these concerns, as is indicated by the presence of the name of Jeanne Schmahl, founder of the Union française pour le suffrage des femmes, on the list of the eugenics society's 104 original members.[7]

For at least a generation before its formal inclusion in the primary curriculum, influential educators, politicians, and women's leaders had promoted *puériculture* as an important way to increase the population and make it healthier. One of the leaders of this campaign was Adolphe Pinard, professor at the Paris Faculty of Medicine, a leading obstetrician, and an officer of the eugenics society. In 1902–1903 he gave a demonstration course on child care to girls aged ten to fourteen in a primary school in the seventeenth arrondissement of Paris. Such luminaries as Louis Liard, vice rector of the Academy of Paris, and Amédée Gasquet, director of primary instruction, observed and applauded his efforts. Subsequently *puériculture* was added to the curriculum of the *écoles normales* for women in 1905, at the same time that information on venereal disease was added to hygiene instruction in the *écoles normales* for men. By 1909 Pinard's textbook, *La Puériculture du premier age*, appeared on at least 30 percent of departmental lists of approved schoolbooks.[8] Prior to its inclusion in the official program, some Paris schools offered *puériculture* on an extracurricular basis, and Catholic educators also embraced it. *Puériculture* was a required subject in the last elementary grade of Paris diocesan schools by 1922.[9]

ÉDUCATION MORALE ET PRATIQUE
dans les Écoles de Filles

Dʳ A. PINARD
Professeur à la Faculté
Membre de l'Académie de Médecine

La
Puériculture
du Premier Age

NOURRITURE — VÊTEMENT — HYGIÈNE

Librairie Armand Colin
103, Boulevard Saint-Michel, **PARIS**

9. Education to combat depopulation. From Adolphe Pinard, *La Puériculture du premier age*, 6th ed. (Paris: A. Colin, 1913), cover.

Because of the preservation of a domestic emphasis in the special girls' subjects in the 1923 program, it is no surprise that feminine images in textbooks of the interwar period continued to differ from masculine ones. The denial of the vote to women in France after the war—unlike Great Britain, the United States, or Germany—meant that textbooks had little reason to recast women's relation to politics. Nor was it likely that depictions of family relationships would greatly change, for only in 1938 was the requirement of wifely obedience to husbands removed from the Civil Code. Indeed, the heightened concern about depopulation prompted a more explicit underscoring of the notion that woman's chief mission was maternal. But it is also important to ask whether textbooks and pedagogical manuals made any adjustments to feminine images in recognition of changes in woman's role in the workplace—changes which posed additional obstacles to the ability of real women to live according to textbooks' domestic ideal. A sample of forty-nine textbooks, nineteen specifically for girls, is the basis for discussion of depictions of women in textbooks first published after 1914.[10]

Morale books were as didactic as ever in setting forth students' duties to family, school, society, and country, the 1923 program having deleted only "duties to God" from the roster of the 1880s. Typical of enduring pedagogical faith in the efficacy of moral instruction were inspectors Miraton and Farges, authors of a popular new text, who believed that memorization and frequent repetition of textbook maxims (*pensées*) could raise the level of popular morality because schoolchildren would recite maxims at home and later, as parents, pass them on to offspring. Socialist teachers were more dubious about certain values transmitted in *morale* lessons. "Work" and "thrift" were the "inseparable deities" of "petty bourgeois" moralizing, complained *instituteur* Henri Chatreix.[11]

Chatreix's complaint at the end of the 1930s notwithstanding, many public school textbooks of the interwar years gave a less static picture of society and more often encouraged hopes for social mobility than did the prewar variety. Although glorifications of rural life remained common, sensible authors recognized the need to modernize the countryside and were less hostile to cities. Antonin and Léon Franchet treated city and country as equally important to the nation in *La Lecture vivante* (1926). In 1927 Kléber Seguin permitted a country boy to go to the city for better vocational training but still hoped that one day he would return to his country village, which already had running water and should soon acquire electricity.[12] Homages to Jean Jaurès and passages expressing discontent with the current distribution of wealth were a sign of socialism's growing appeal to underpaid educators, less eager to serve the Republic uncritically after World War I than before.[13] But as in prewar decades, most pedagogues demanded evolutionary rather than revolutionary change. Miraton and Farges combined Maurice Bouchor's call for redistributing wealth with Jaurès's criticism of the impatience of extreme revolutionaries.[14] Furthermore, books with bright children's success stories might still warn about the dangers of being uprooted (déraciné) and depict modest ambitions as more realistic for a majority of children.[15] In comparison, Catholic textbooks aimed at working class and peasant children were more traditional in their inculcation of social immobility, and Catholic texts with bourgeois heroes and heroines continued to condemn workers' strikes.[16]

Messages about women's roles were much less likely to show change than passages concerned with the plight of men from the laboring classes. Teachers perusing experts' advice on morale lessons still encountered explicit statements about gender roles and personality differences in pedagogical manuals. Citing the menace of depopulation, inspector Charles Ab der Halden and institutrice Marguerite Lavaut wrote in 1930 that children must understand the importance of founding a family and fulfilling parental roles. Woman was destined for home and motherhood, and her appropriate personality traits were "gentleness" and "tenderness," traits useful for comforting children or a spouse exhausted by his daily toils. The father, by contrast, must be "strong" (fort) and "masterful" (puissant). Charles Charrier's pedagogical manual, the teachers' "bible" of the interwar years, also declared that women discharged their primary duties at home.[17]

In comparison to prewar years, the morale text written for both sexes was more in favor than single-sex books.[18] Jules Payot's prewar Morale à l'école (1908) had designated material on one-sixth of its pages as especially for girls.[19] By the 1920s special girls' sections in morale texts for a coeducational audience were increasingly evident. Miraton and Farges concentrated messages for girls in a section on family life, about one-fifth of L'Education morale et civique par la suggestion artistique et littéraire (1920). In this section and the others they utilized selections from noted writers and reproductions of paintings, in conjunction with their own lessons, in the hopes that works with special aesthetic value would make more impact on the child than pedagogical prescriptions alone. Thus the first of thirteen lessons on the family opened with a picture of a mother nursing a child and concluded with five lines from Victor Hugo about motherly love. The lesson on "the sweetness of home" included a picture and a poem about a family's evening and the authors' own homily, "Happy the family which does not seek outside, in the noise and agitation of streets and cafes, a happiness which it knows how to find at home." Woman's role in keeping the family together was underscored by the reminder that mother was the first to rise and the last to go to bed, her entire day being filled with "the care of the household." Finally, pupils memorized two lines about how "l'épouse" and "la jeune fille" maintained the family abode.[20]

Miraton and Farges's treatment of "le travail de la femme" in the section on work was also consistent with their messages about the family. Five lessons depicted the male as peasant, factory worker, artisan, fisherman, scientist, explorer, and artist. The only lesson on woman's work was captioned "The housewife" and began with a picture of a laundress by a stream. A sixty-year-old selection from Jules Simon's *Ouvrière* (1861) did indicate realistically that when poor women had to earn money they were often pitifully overburdened because caring for children and spouse took what was left of their flagging energies after work. The typical linkage of good housekeeping and social order concluded the lesson: if a young wife kept her house clean, prepared meals on time, and was "always in good humor," her husband would not prefer the cabaret to home.[21]

The two volumes of *Morale pour la jeune française* (1923, 1926) by inspector Aimé Souché, a sermonizing Protestant who combined his post at Chatellerault in the Vienne with a prolific authorship of textbooks, also indicated that little had changed in girls' "duties" in *morale* lessons since Gréville's text of 1882. Indeed, Souché borrowed passages from such earlier pedagogues as Gréville and Lavisse and also displayed an endorsement from Buisson, director of primary education from 1879 to 1896, later a radical socialist republican deputy, and in the 1920s president of the Ligue de l'enseignement. Souché's *Second livre de morale* (1926) stated the familiar goal of teaching girls to be guardians of the foyer, good companions of husbands, and clear-sighted educators of children. They would learn about the feminine qualities of "informed intelligence, ordered activity, courageous and calm energy, smiling and effective goodness, and self-sacrifice" and also be reminded that the law required wifely "obedience" in return for the husband's "protection."[22]

Echoing Chalamet and Juranville, Souché rated lessons on housekeeping and childrearing more useful than any other knowledge. Heightened postwar natalism dictated his pronouncements that marriage and having a family were moral obligations and wishing to raise only one or two children was selfish. Because France needed to reduce infant mortality, he welcomed the addition of *puériculture* to the girls' program.[23] Although explicit injunctions to found families appeared in some prewar republican and Catholic texts and were certainly implicit in most lessons on the family,[24] the explicit message that national survival depended upon larger families became more prevalent after 1918.[25] In light of the urgency in textbooks' natalist passages, it is not surprising that when a militant syndicalist and feminist Breton teacher, Josette Cornec, persisted in writing articles about contraception, her inspector reprimanded her sharply.[26]

Although there was no novelty in Souché's discoursing on woman's domestic obligations or the joys presumably derived from sacrificing oneself to others, he did treat the two important issues of women's work and suffrage in a way indicative of gradual changes in attitudes toward woman's relationship to the world beyond the foyer. He praised women for demonstrating ability to combine earning a living with caring for children. But like predecessors, he also asserted that the best feminine métiers were those like sewing which permitted women to work at home all or most of the time so that children did not suffer. On women's suffrage Souché took no positive or negative stance, simply stating that the issue would likely recur. However bland, this statement at least recognized an important issue on which most other textbooks remained mute.[27]

The most notable change in Souché's depiction of woman's attitudes toward public issues was one equally characteristic of postwar boys' books, at least those for public schools. The prewar schoolgirl learned that woman's patriotism consisted of encouraging sons and husbands to fight for France if another nation attacked; the postwar girl, like her brother, learned more about the ideal of international solidarity and the new League of Nations' commitment to preventing war.[28]

A combination of traditional statements on gender roles and recognition that contemporaries sensed changes in roles also characterized *Devant la vie* (1936), a *morale* book for boys by Léon Emery, professor at the normal school of Lyon. He delineated two sides to current discussion of feminine roles: some believed that women were the equals of men and should have careers; others asserted that women's first obligation was to children. Although Emery did not explicitly support either side, his leanings were implicit. The idea that the child was a mother's "raison de vivre" seemed such an evident "law" that one need not discuss it. But if motherly love was powerful, the father's role in the family was "more complicated" because he must do more than simply love his offspring. Earning and managing money were his responsibilities. Assigning control of the family budget to men differed from earlier textbooks' assumption that among workers and peasants women managed household finances. Since women still held the pursestrings in a majority of working class households after World War II,[29] Emery was presumably trying to teach a middle class practice to children of the people, not mirroring a widespread change in behavior. He did state that the father was no longer "an absolute monarch" because women increasingly participated in directing the household and older children demanded a voice, too. However difficult the sharing of power, the ideal *père de famille* must use common sense and maintain a co-operative atmosphere when exercising "authority" over his family.[30] Although Emery denied that contemporary husbands were anything like patriarchs of antiquity, his depiction of the wife's role actually awarded her less power than older girls' books which assigned family finances to her and, for the good of society, asked her to use her wiles to control a spouse's behavior. The old image of a working class man subject to his wife's manipulation was not suitable for middle class males or for workers of the 1930s eager to emulate the middle class *père de famille*. Authors of the interwar period who still directed women to steer men away from the evils of drink and other undesirable pursuits were writing especially for "girls of the people."[31]

The treatment of woman's role in Catholic *morale* textbooks continued to resemble the public school's presentation in most ways but retained the expected religious foundation. Equally concerned about falling birthrates, Catholic pedagogues asserted that having children was a duty to God as well as a patriotic act. Discussions of the family were punctuated with reminders that divorce was not acceptable for believing Catholics. Some authors also cited religious reasons for rejecting undesirable political positions. Bellenoue's *Morale sociale* (1923) denounced socialism for its materialistic basis. Abbé E. Bourceau and Raymond Fabry's popular *Lectures littéraires expliquées avec enseignement moral et civique* (1933) insisted that most women did not desire the vote because they realized that it was inappropriate for their God-given role as "angel of the foyer."[32] This was the same antisuffragette position which Anne Masson had taken in a prewar *morale* manual still recommended for Catholic schools of the 1930s, although many Catholic legislators now believed that votes for women would widen their base of support.[33] Bourceau and Fabry did approve of women taking an interest in politics so that they could advise men against voting for unworthy candidates. More unusual was the Catholic home economics textbook that held out the hope in 1938 that some day women would receive the vote.[34] On the issue of women's work, Catholic educators advised professional preparation so that unmarried women could be self-sufficient and wives could augment the family budget. But work outside the home remained highly undesirable for the *mère de famille*.[35]

The public issue on which Catholic textbooks differed most noticeably from the public school variety during the interwar period was the perception of international relations. Catholic texts echoed conservatives' denunciations of antimilitarism and internationalism, finding it unrealistic to think that wars could be eliminated, as republican supporters of the League of Nations hoped.[36] Catholic texts were far more likely than republican ones to continue the pre-1914 examples of feminine bravery in wartime, and Bourceau and Fabry advised that in peacetime women should take courses on care of the wounded to prepare for war work.[37]

Like *morale* manuals, the somewhat less didactic readers of the interwar years still relegated males and females to different spheres. However, special girls' readers were less prevalent after 1918, those on the market during the 1930s being primarily prewar holdovers like *Suzette* (1889) or *Elisabeth* (1909). Of the twenty-three girls' readers advertised in the textbook supplement of the *Bibliographie de la France* in 1932, twenty were published before 1914. Catholic girls' books were as numerous as the public school variety in 1932, and the three volumes of the Catholic *Elisabeth* sold about as many copies between 1920 and 1932 as between 1909 and 1920.[38]

There were also changes in the format and content of readers. Illustrations were larger and more numerous, and children sometimes became more childlike and less like miniature adults.[39] Readers that were collections of excerpts (*morceaux choisis*) from works of great authors, past and present, gained more favor than the old *romans scolaires* about youthful heroes and heroines. The 1923 instructions for teaching reading stipulated that children should be exposed as soon as possible to the most outstanding French prose. Because compulsory schooling ended at thirteen, pedagogues deemed it essential, especially for the *cours supérieur*, to employ readers which would elevate pupils' tastes above a childish level.[40] Inspectors reinforced the new preference for excerpts from literary giants by criticizing teachers who utilized books now out of favor.[41] Although some teachers questioned whether children liked *morceaux choisis* as well as the *Tour de la France*, pedagogical reviews approved of the vogue for the former and dismissed the latter as too didactic.[42]

Contemporary disparaging of the preaching tone of pre-1914 textbooks[43] confirms the findings of a later scholar who found his sample of ten public school readers of 1931 to be less moralistic than Bruno's classic.[44] However, moral and social messages remained embedded in readers of the 1930s which, like predecessors, often glorified a simple rural world free of social, economic, and political problems. *La Vie des champs* (1930), a reader for rural public schools by two inspectors, grouped selections from great authors into four seasonal categories and attempted to make the ubiquitous theme of the virtues of rural life more palatable by indicating that the peasant is "no longer the slave of the earth: he is its master." Education and modern farm equipment presumably nullified reasons for emigrating to cities where rural youth might come to a bad end or fail and have to return home. "Why leave a village with modern comforts" and a "healthy" environment, asked Inspector Pierre Dudouit, when one could stay and collaborate with neighbors to modernize the countryside? Moreover, the school's improved home economics lessons now helped country girls make the "foyer rustique" attractive and comfortable.[45]

Competing with *morceaux choisis*, new *romans scolaires* often depicted heroes and heroines who were more childlike than Bruno's resourceful orphans or Halt's Suzette but still could be forced to mature quickly when misfortune struck. Newer "school novels" also tended to tell brother-and-sister stories instead of concentrating on just one sex. However, sharp distinctions between the destinies of brothers and sisters remained common, even if the importance of women's nondomestic labor was acknowledged. In *Jean et Lucie* (1920), set during World War I, Laetitia Dès paid tribute to women's wartime contribution of keeping farms and businesses running while men were absent. But children also learned that such activities were mainly for times of crisis. After the war, Jean entered a normal school to follow in his father's footsteps; sister Lucie learned housekeeping arts from their mother to prepare for "the best métier for a woman." As a wife and mother she could make her family one block in the foundation on which the nation's fortunes rested. Similarly, the heroine of part two of René Bazin and P. Dufrenne's *Il était quatre petits enfants*, published in 1923 by the Catholic firm of Mame, ran a farm while her husband and brothers went to war. Yet there had been nothing unfeminine about the socialization of this strong woman whom schoolchildren continued to read about until the 1940s. Heroine Jeanne learned from her pious mother that "the destiny of women" is to wait and that a wise woman lets her husband "believe that he is perfect." This strategy encouraged a husband to confide in his wife, thereby enabling her to function as a power behind the throne.[46]

Brother-and-sister stories published near the end of the Third Republic and still used during the Fourth Republic demonstrate that during the Depression decade educators did little to modify depictions of women's roles, despite changes in the job market for women.[47] Ab der Halden's *Hors du nid* (1934), which sold more than 200,000 copies, recounted the travails of Marguerite and Jacques Ligneul after their father's death. A schoolteacher, the father had been a strong man who inspired a bit of fear in his children, unlike their loving mother. The different parental personalities were a literary rendition of models for male and female personalities previously set down in the author's instructions for teaching *morale*. Marguerite, an older sister, was like a "little mother" in her concern for Jacques. When their widowed mother's earnings proved inadequate, Marguerite went to work in a pastry shop at the end of the school day. Becoming a governess in a private household, she unselfishly rejected a marriage offer a few years later because her mother and brother depended upon her for money. In the meantime, Jacques went on from primary to secondary school and became a writer. His coming of age and a new job for the mother eventually gave Marguerite freedom to marry. In comparison to pre-1914 textbook characters, both children enjoyed greater educational opportunities which enabled them, after early hardship, to lead more comfortable adult lives than those of typical farmers or workers. But Ab der Halden's tale required more self-sacrifice of the older sister than the younger brother.[48] The same disparity was in Kléber Seguin's popular *Histoire des trois enfants* (1927), still for sale in 1957. Grandmother and a family friend determined that the son of an impoverished widow should leave a country village to obtain vocational training in a city; they arranged for his sister to become a servant on a nearby farm.

André et Jacqueline, deux enfants de France (1940), a story by two clerics, focused on a comfortable middle class family more typical of Catholic than republican texts. Although this brother and sister enjoyed family outings together, the plot gave André the more exciting life. He went to camp and won a school prize enabling him to travel to the shrine at Lourdes. At the end of the story Jacques contemplated secondary studies and announced plans for a career in one of France's colonies. By contrast, Jacqueline looked ahead to a home economics course after primary school and promised parents that because André wanted to go far away, she would always stay close to home.[49]

Because most girls, unlike Jacqueline, came from families lacking the resources to send them to private homemaking courses, both public and private schools tried to improve home economics offerings in the primary school during the interwar years. The official instructions of 1887 had called for lessons on "domestic economy," but this item was often ignored, downgraded, or simply treated theoretically by prewar *institutrices*.[50] Teachers' disinterest in home economics stemmed from their preference for academic subjects and belief that "manual works" lowered the intellectual quality of their classes—a tendency certainly shared by male colleagues—and from the overloaded curriculum which was especially burdensome for teachers in one-room schools.[51]

Sewing, required as part of "manual works," received more attention than cooking, washing, and cleaning because it was often included in the exam for the certificate of primary studies and because, as of 1890, communes were ordered to provide sewing supplies.[52] Girls of seven or eight practiced stitches on scraps of cloth and sewed clothes for their own dolls or the class doll. To reinforce maternal instincts, teachers might have girls keep a special notebook, "Le Livre de ma poupée," with poems and songs about dolls. Older girls progressed to mending clothes and constructing simple items of clothing for themselves or to donate to the poor.[53]

Aspects of home economics other than sewing suffered from a lack of appropriate facilities and teachers' indifference. Whereas teaching sewing by hand required minimal supplies, teaching cooking necessitated an appreciable investment in equipment and foodstuffs which many communes could not or would not make. The separate room for home economics classes, found in some large urban schools, was simply absent from many small schools and certainly from one-room *écoles mixtes*. The instructions of 1887 had required a special room for manual works only in primary schools with four or more separate classes.[54]

Proposals to encourage the teaching of home economics surfaced at teachers' conferences after 1900, and the Ligue de l'enseignement also actively promoted it.[55] By 1914 some schools in the Seine had implemented a home economics program which became a model for all France. Fourteen girls' schools in St. Denis and Aubervilliers, working class suburbs north of Paris, launched the experiment of a homemaking day (*journée ménagère*) in 1913. Madame Fredel, *directrice* of a girls' school at Aubervilliers and author of a home economics textbook, was the driving force behind the innovation. Educators wanted the school to provide the domestic instruction for which working mothers lacked the time and perhaps even the knowledge. On homemaking day—possibly a Saturday—all lessons were organized around domestic themes. Girls not only tried out a menu or performed cleaning chores; they also had *morale*, arithmetic, hygiene, reading, and spelling lessons utilizing themes relevant to homemaking. On 15 November 1913 a pupil in a *cours moyen* in St. Denis recorded in her *cahier* an arithmetic lesson about calculating the cost of goods at the market, a *morale* lesson on solidarity within the family, a hygiene lesson about clean underwear, a *dictée* on the "kitchen of Jeanne," and the high points of a scintillating lesson about choosing kitchen utensils and washing dishes. Charles Dolidon, the school inspector who encouraged and publicized the St. Denis-Aubervilliers innovation, reported that parents praised teachers for this instruction, particularly because daughters became more helpful at home.[56]

The homemaking day soon appeared in other schools in the department of the Seine. Charrier's *Pédagogie vécue,* the teachers' "bible," also recommended it as the ideal format for domestic education. Although the official program of 1923 observed that a full day for home economics might be too much, the education ministry supported half a day for it and, as noted, specified that girls' science lessons should include practical applications to homemaking.[57] The city of Paris and its suburbs made the most extensive efforts to carry out ministerial dictates and by 1937 offered practical instruction in eighty-nine girls' primary schools, about 30% of the total. Elsewhere the record was far more sporadic, although concerned primary inspectors in rural areas sometimes encouraged teachers to use their own living quarters at the school to give cooking classes.[58]

Two types of textbooks reinforced homemaking education in the *cours moyen* and *supérieur:* science books and home economics manuals. Girls' science books were special adaptations of the basic boys' books; they duplicated sections on physical and natural sciences but, in place of lessons on farming or the repair and maintenance of equipment and appliances for home and farm, presented sections on menu planning, cooking, cleaning, care of the sick, and child care. Approximately 12 to 25 percent of the material in girls' science books had a domestic focus.[59] A few sentences on the feminine personality might also appear, although republican manuals now tended to be more prosaic about this than Catholic ones. The girls' edition of *Sciences physiques et naturelles* (1932), a popular text by A. Roudil, a primary inspector from the Seine, and Madame Bartoli, a teacher in a higher primary school in Marseilles, simply assigned the housewife the utilitarian traits of thrift and love of order and cleanliness. In comparison, the girls' edition of Chanoine C. Grill and P. Le Floch's successful Catholic science text (200,000 copies issued by 1937) gave *ménagères* not only these three practical qualities and love of work but also sweetness, gaiety, self-sacrifice, and piety. Such a personality was an appropriate accompaniment to the child care lessons designed to inculcate maternal devotion but not to explain how women became mothers. Reproductive organs were not discussed in lessons on the parts of the human body. The *puériculture* sections of both texts emphasized the importance of feeding infants at regular intervals, but the Catholic tome added that accustoming a child to a feeding schedule laid a sound basis for the "virile education" of a "man of character."[60] Presumably a female child fed regularly would nonetheless become *douce* rather than virile.

Puériculture lessons in home economics or science books or in separate manuals also spelled out the advantages of breastfeeding over bottle-feeding, described how to bathe an infant, and itemized the basic equipment and clothing needed for a new baby. Breast-feeding was proclaimed the ideal method because it was natural and

façon que sa bouche soit au niveau du sein.

FIG. 47. MAMAN COUCHÉE SUR LE CÔTÉ DROIT ET ALLAITANT SON BÉBÉ
(Bonne position des mains de la maman.)

FIG. 48. MAMAN COUCHÉE SUR LE CÔTÉ GAUCHE ET ALLAITANT SON BÉBÉ
(Bonne position des mains de la maman.)

10. The care and feeding of children. From Adolphe Pinard, *La Puériculture du premier age*, 6th ed. (Paris: A. Colin, 1913), p. 90.

best for the child.[61] Frequently drawings or even photographs of women nursing underscored the point, French educators here assuming that children appreciated the naturalness of nursing scenes and would not react with the adolescent giggles or smirks American educators might well expect. Indeed, such illustrations were also found in *morale* texts intended for boys as well as girls.[62] Authors explained that they included information on bottle-feeding primarily because a tiny minority of women in poor health might be unable to breastfeed.[63] The consideration that some working women found bottle-feeding a necessity was less common, and there was no room for bottle-feeding to be adopted because of personal preference.[64] Presumably those leaning toward that option would be dissuaded by statistics on the mortality of bottle-fed infants or assertions like "the mother's breast belongs to the child." That truism came from Dr. Pinard whose *puériculture* book, an early model of the genre for primary school girls, sold 94,500 copies between 1904 and 1938. Madame Foulon-Lefranc repeated the maxim in her home economics manuals and, as late as 1938, also echoed Pinard's denunciation of "mercenary" wet-nurses, widely employed by working mothers until the late nineteenth century when the Third Republic launched measures to discourage this.[65] Undeniably, political and pedagogical concern about infant mortality was both well intentioned and well founded, but the seriousness of the problem could have been conveyed without adopting a threatening tone toward women who, because of economic need or personal preference, replaced the procedures recommended in child-care manuals with alternate techniques of perhaps equal value for the welfare of the child. Although the French mortality rate for infants under age one remained nearly twice as high as that of the Netherlands or Norway in 1938, it had fallen from 160 per 1000 live births in 1900 to 102 in 1923 and to 70 in 1938.[66]

Like instruction in home economics, *puériculture* lessons were often more bookish than practical. Some *institutrices* also felt uncomfortable with the subject and questioned its impact on young girls' modesty.[67] However, teachers could not ignore a required topic likely to appear on girls' examinations for the certificate of primary studies.[68] On a minimal level, *puériculture* lessons were recorded in *cahiers*. Some Paris schools devoted a special notebook to the subject so that girls could take it home and thereby influence family members.[69] Apparently most teachers used dolls as substitutes for babies when they demonstrated techniques of child care. Only a few, usually in urban areas, found it convenient to follow the advice of educational authorities who recommended taking pupils to *crèches* a few times a year, if at all possible.[70] Yet rural areas lacking these public nurseries could still give schoolgirls contact with real babies if local cooperation was forthcoming. Even before the official addition of *puériculture* to the curriculum, a doctor in the Yonne welcomed the attendance of girls when he provided free treatment for infants of the poor. Schoolgirls in Appoigny and five neighboring communes observed and kept records on these infants.[71]

The techniques of homemaking and child care in Catholic home economics texts were indistinguishable from those in public school texts. Those written for girls from the popular classes assumed, like the public school variety, that mothers could not or would not instruct daughters in domestic arts because they did not know enough or lacked the time, owing to employment outside the home.[72] As with other types of schoolbooks, the expected religious content was the major difference between Catholic and secular tomes. Foulon-Lefranc's distinctly Catholic manual, *La Femme au foyer* (1938) included three pages on woman's religious obligations missing in her more secular *Ecole du bonheur* (1938), which did, however, present Sunday as a day of rest. The Virgin Mary remained the prototype of the ideal woman in *La Femme au foyer*, Foulon-Lefranc explaining that because motherly love was naturally so great, there was nothing blasphemous in calling a child "my Jesus."[73]

Submissiveness to men, a trait in harmony with the Civil Code's view of marital relationships until 1938, was also somewhat more exaggerated in certain Catholic textbooks than in republican ones. Because of prohibitions on divorce, Catholic women were not expected to escape from bad marriages.[74] If spouses made them suffer, they must bear this as a cross.[75] Whatever a husband's inconstancies, a wife must adapt to them, intoned the author of *Le Trésor de la ménagère*, 70,000 copies of which had been published by 1935. Moreover, women should consider whether they themselves bore any responsibility for bad treatment by a spouse. Foulon-Lefranc's texts even suggested that wifebeating was probably caused by bad housekeeping, a passage fortunately not retained in later editions.[76]

The orientation of girls toward domesticity and boys toward work was not one of the educational canons that the Popular Front called into question, despite socialist Léon Blum's unprecedented appointment of three women (one a former *institutrice*) to secondary positions in his cabinet. The recommendations of education minister Jean Zay for the girls' curriculum in primary schools demonstrated that a government dedicated to breaking down class barriers did not launch a comparable attack on inequalities based upon gender.

Democratization of the public school system was the major educational reform sought by the Popular Front, the unprecedented coalition of radical socialist republicans, socialists, and communists given a legislative majority in 1936 to combat the Depression and French fascism. For the first time, a socialist headed the government. Jean Zay, an exceptionally capable young radical socialist republican, became minister of education. Committed to knocking down the structural barriers which prevented gifted lower class youngsters from moving from the primary to the secondary school system, Zay took up the aims of those educational reformers who, since the end of World War I, had advocated a "single school" (école unique) for the public school system.[77] Zay remained in office until after the start of World War II, a tenure more impressive that that of the original Popular Front ministry which had frightened capitalists by legislating such benefits for workers as paid vacations and a forty-hour week. By the time Blum left office in June 1937, the Popular Front coalition was itself rent by disputes over economic issues and policy toward the Spanish Civil War. Although Blum returned briefly to office in April 1938, the Popular Front did not recover, and radical republicans headed the government until 1940.

Zay's moves toward an école unique illustrated the egalitarian aims of Popular Front educational policy. On the administrative level, the elementary classes of lycées and collèges were placed under the wing of primary education; at the same time, the écoles primaires supérieures were attached to the secondary school bureaucracy. To begin eliminating other structural barriers between primary and secondary schools, the government decreed in May 1937 that the classes of the higher primary schools and the corresponding classes of secondary schools (sixième through troisième) should, in principle, have similar programs. Zay also introduced the experiment of orientation classes to help bright students with the transition from primary to secondary school. A primary pupil who transferred to a secondary school often did so at age ten or eleven in order to start Latin with others of his or her age but thereby had to leave the primary school before obtaining the certificate of primary studies and thus risk having no degree if he or she later dropped out of school or did not obtain a baccalauréat. Although a secondary school program not requiring Latin had existed since 1902, beliefs "persisted that a baccalaureate obtained without the study of Latin was somehow not quite legitimate." Zay's project permitted children likely to enter secondary schools to take the exam for the c.e.p. before age twelve; they could then enter one of three types of orientation classes: one offering Latin, one with a modern foreign language, and one without a foreign language. Not surprisingly, Zay's orientation classes generated heated debate among educators concerned about protecting their professional turf. Secondary professors feared a dilution in the quality of the traditional secondary school, and primary teachers were not necessarily enthusiastic about a plan which, if widely applied, would take from under their wing the most academically talented pupils in the final primary grades.[78] Barely launched by the time Zay left office, his important and controversial orientation scheme foreshadowed reforms of the early Fifth Republic.

Of broader immediate impact on primary schools than orientation classes was the extension of the school-leaving age effected by the law of 9 August 1936. The requirement that children remain in school until age fourteen necessitated creation of a new primary grade, the *classe de fin d'études*. More than any other primary grade, the new "final" class was designed to prepare children to cope with the realities of life after school. Because during the 1930s, even before the Popular Front, more children were moving from primary schools to the now tuition-free secondary schools after the certificate of primary studies, those who remained in the primary school's last class were the ones destined to enter the world of work or apprenticeship once they left school.[79] According to a ministerial circular of October 1936, the extra year of primary school should (1) reinforce a student's understanding of material already learned; (2) give the student a taste for continuing the learning process on his or her own; and (3) help students find an economic activity best suited "to their family situation, aptitudes, and tastes and to the general interest."[80] The emphasis on adjusting students' vocational expectations to family background and the "general interest" permitted a distinctly conservative use of the policy; and the goal of adjusting vocational expectations to a student's aptitudes and tastes could mean advising a poor child to stay in his or her place just as readily as encouraging modest ambitions.

The girls' curriculum in the *classe de fin d'études* demonstrated that politicians and educators ostensibly committed to breaking down class barriers were not equally concerned about educational barriers to a woman's chances of equaling a man's income if she entered the work force after school. An *arrêté* of 23 March 1938 specified that in this final class, unlike other primary classes, all subjects should be related to problems of everyday life "in the family and in society, in the country and in the fields, in the city and in the factory." The ministry's proposal to help students find a suitable niche in life recognized that in 1938 only one out of seven thirteen-year-olds would go on to secondary school or the primary system's *cours complémentaire* or *école primaire supérieure*. While boys were to be directed toward traditional occupations available in their region, girls would receive additional domestic instruction to learn "the métier of housewife and mother."[81]

A comparison of the hours allocated to the most obvious parts of the practical education component in the old *cours supérieur* and the new *classe de fin d'études* underscores the novelty of the latter's vocational thrust. The 1923 schedule for the superior course projected 2½ hours for science, 1 hour for drawing, and 1½ hours for boys' manual works and 2 hours for girls', for a total of 5–5½ hours, out of 30 hours, for subjects with practical applications. The revised instructions of 23 March 1938 raised the time for these three topics to 7 hours for the superior course and to 9 hours for the new final course. Furthermore, science in the final course was retitled "elements of applied sciences," and "travaux manuels" became "travaux pratiques." Ideally, a school lacking a special room for "practical works" or "homemaking instruction" would create one to meet the goals of the final class.[82]

Zay denied that children in the *classe de fin d'études* were the dregs of the school population, but the denial was not convincing.[83] The class's vocational orientation was very different from the secondary school's presentation of a humanistic general culture to the nation's future leaders and professionals. Although some bright children from poor families unfortunately ended up in the "final" class because of parental opposition to further schooling, teachers' memoirs suggest that the class, especially in urban areas, often housed economically disadvantaged students and also the unmotivated who were simply marking time until they reached the school-leaving age.[84]

In the case of girls the public school system's discrimination between pupils in the final primary class and in secondary schools was perhaps in one respect less intentional than for boys. After a reform of 1924 finally made uniform the programs for boys' and girls' secondary schools, *lycées* and *collèges* prepared girls for the *baccalauréat* and university entrance. They were also staffed by many women professors dedicated to presenting girls with as many intellectual challenges as the boys' *lycées* offered, Simone de Beauvoir being one notable example. Yet Zay himself and other educational officials regretted that in girls' secondary schools there was not more instruction in home economics because this was so useful for the lives to which girls were destined.[85] Zay's concern did not mean, of course, that girls' secondary schools had become oriented strictly toward preparation for careers, even though some of their graduates embarked upon them. In 1932 the *directrice* of the Lycée Fénelon rebutted the charge that secondary schools interfered with girls' maternal destinies: she insisted that the *lycée*'s program of general culture corrected woman's "natural anarchism" by teaching a self-discipline applicable to running a household.[86]

As the Third Republic approached its demise in 1940, its political and educational leaders were, in general, as convinced that domesticity was, or ought to be, a girl's destiny as their predecessors had been at its outset. When the Ferry reforms for the primary school and Camille Sée's plan to create state secondary schools for girls were enacted during the early 1880s, anticlerical republicans wanted public schools to produce a young woman suitable as a wife and mother for the citizens of a democracy. One reason for laicizing primary schools and creating secular secondary schools for girls was to remove women from the influence of conservative religious teachers. By the late 1930s 23 percent of schoolgirls attended private primary schools, a big change from the pre-1880 decades when a majority were taught by nuns, although little different from the 1911 figure of 25 percent (tables 1, 2).[87] Yet many republican politicians of the 1930s apparently believed that several generations of republican schooling had done little to make women less politically conservative than men or less likely to follow the church's position on public issues. Although a majority in the Popular Front's Chamber of Deputies favored woman's suffrage, republican elders in the Senate remained hostile. Some announced that because women were more active churchgoers than men, a vote for votes for women might mean votes against themselves. By the end of the 1930s many republicans had long since toned down anticlerical rhetoric, as a rapprochement between Catholics and republicans—a "second Ralliement"—had been effected during the 1920s.[88] But antisuffragette republicans contended that on voting day—Sunday in France—women would, if enfranchised, leave mass and vote as instructed by priests.[89]

That antisuffrage argument assumed, of course, that women could not make independent judgments and were submissive to male authorities. It did not consider whether public schools bore any responsibility for turning out submissive females. In 1932 one prominent women educator recommended that schools attempt to make girls less passive, but she did not blame schools for encouraging passivity.[90] However, after the Liberation in 1944 a Paris school inspector, Mademoiselle Person, had no hesitation about raising this issue at a teachers' conference in the thirteenth arrondissement. She asserted that pre-1939 moral and civic instruction for girls had focused too exclusively on individual and domestic *morale*, thereby predisposing girls to "obedience and resignation" and not sufficiently developing their "sense of dignity." For the postwar era she recommended a more active and assertive model of womanhood, not only because women were to be enfranchised but also because their help was vital for the material and moral reconstruction of the nation.[91]

CHAPTER FIVE

The Feminine Image and Social and Economic Realities, 1880–1940

At the end of the Third Republic, as at the beginning, educators proclaimed the "interior" world of home and family more important for women than the "exterior" world of work. The differing prospects for the adult lives of brothers and sisters in the textbooks by Ab der Halden, Seguin, and Hamyon and Bragade were by no means exceptional. But while pedagogues assigned more importance to career planning for boys than for girls, some acknowledged the disparity between feminine images served up by the schools and the reality of the lives of many working class girls after age thirteen. In 1923 a woman school inspector estimated that 40,000 young women between the ages of thirteen and eighteen worked in "industry" in the Seine.[1] Recognition that women often did work outside the home led many educators to develop lessons about female employment.

Primary school textbooks, republican and Catholic, which addressed the issue of women's work tended to use part or all of the following four-point argument. (1) For young girls and single women from the laboring classes, paid employment outside the home or work on the family farm were the norm. Young girls were advised to learn a trade in order to contribute to their own support, help parents, and have a livelihood to fall back on should they remain unmarried or, once married, suddenly have to earn money because of a husband's illness or death.[2] (2) For most married women, however, the ideal was devotion to home and family. Work outside the home was labeled undesirable because it led to child neglect, bad housekeeping, the flight of husbands to cafes, and the overtiring of women who combined outside employment with housework.[3] Because work outside the home presumably affected families so adversely, educators counseled that thrift might produce as much financial advantage for the family as an outside job necessitating extra expenses for meals and clothing.[4] (3) Yet many pedagogues had to concede that if a husband's wages were low, there was no alternative to a wife's earning money. In that case it was most desirable for her to work at home, perhaps as a laundress or seamstress.[5] In light of the fact that fully 36 percent of women listed as "active" in the 1906 census worked at home, the primary school's teaching of sewing and the rudiments of home economics had a practical vocational thrust. These subjects met the economic needs of many of the women who wished to earn money primarily to contribute to the family economy.[6] However, home work was often poorly paid and so, some writers admitted, could prove inadequate for a family's needs.[7] (4) Thus in extreme cases there might be no alternative to a married woman's working outside the home. Discussion of this possibility became somewhat more common toward the end of the Third Republic, as changes occurred in women's patterns of employment.[8] Although there was little change in the percentage of French women at work during the first half of the twentieth century, jobs in home and sweatshop gave way to positions in stores and offices. Typically pedagogues taught that wives working outside the home must learn to combine jobs with a still efficient performance of household chores.[9] Daughters were instructed to assist overburdened mothers, but sons seldom received this message.[10]

Depicting cases where married as well as single women worked was a textbook concession to reality. Between 1870 and 1940 women made up at least one-third of the "active" population.[11] Predictably, the participation of single females, age fifteen and over, in the work force was greater than that of the married. Nonetheless, a higher percentage of married women worked in France than in any other major Western nation. In 1931 19 percent of French married women worked in nonagricultural jobs, usually outside the home, as compared to 10 percent of their British and 9 percent of their American counterparts. Since French per capita income in the 1930s was only half of the American and 56 percent of the British figures, it seems likely that economic necessity prompted many married women to work.[12] If the labor of farm wives is counted, then 44 percent of French married women worked in 1931, as compared to 61 percent of the single. Yet textbooks did not show women engaged in a wide range of occupations apart from homemaking. In schoolbooks, as in real life, women's work was usually of low status. Working women in school texts were most often *fermières*, dressmakers, laundresses, shopkeepers, shop clerks, and servants.[13] Jost and Braeunig's popular prewar *Lectures pratiques* (1882)—issued in 255,014 copies by 1911—depicted six ways for a girl to earn money: as a servant, ironer, seamstress, milliner, laundress, or teacher. More than fifty years later the selection of typical feminine métiers was no better in Félix Broutet and Marguerite Reynier's *Livre des métiers* (1938), for the authors enumerated twenty-two masculine activities (all workers or farmers) and only five feminine occupations: seamstress, grocery store owner, milkmaid-milkseller, laundress, and ironer. The most common profession for a well-educated woman was that of schoolteacher, the first occupation for women which enabled girls to rise above humble family origins.[14]

The textbook message that the main reward most women reaped from working was provision for basic individual and family needs and not an elevation in social status or sense of special accomplishment was simply one aspect of the lesson for both sexes that most children should expect adult lives comparable to those of their parents. Especially before 1914 boys were regularly advised to become diligent artisans, factory workers, or farmers, although bright boys were more likely to be encouraged to aspire to upward social mobility than girls. Pre-1914 republican schoolbooks often did no more to arouse such aspirations than Catholic ones. After World War I some republican authors presented a less static picture of society but still made farm, factory, or workshop the normal place of employment for many males.[15] Entering a profession required a post-elementary education that most French children would not have until after World War II. The number of higher primary schools, which provided working class and lower middle class children with a first step upward on the ladder of social mobility, was limited. Secondary schools, the avenue to prestigious professions, were not free until the 1930s, and only a small number of scholarships was available. Thus financial considerations plus the difficulty and risk associated with transferring from the primary to the secondary part of the school system were major obstacles for poor but bright boys and girls.[16]

Why did French pedagogues emphasize modest ambitions and often call on women to perform domestic duties as their patriotic contribution to social stability? Several answers previously alluded to—cultural traditions and economic, political, and demographic realities—may now be summarized. First, the rarity of American-style Horatio Alger models for males and females was in keeping with both French cultural values and economic realities. Making money was not viewed as an end in itself by the upper classes or intellectual elite. Thus Bentzon and Chevalier told middle class girls in the elementary sections of public secondary schools that intellectual endeavors undertaken without expectation of remuneration were especially ennobling. Nor were there unlimited opportunities for quickly acquiring large sums of money in a country whose late nineteenth-century rate of industrialization was less rapid than that of Germany or the United States. Like the rest of Europe, late nineteeenth-century France also suffered from an economic depression just as it was making compulsory a minimal level of schooling. For good reason, then, the Third Republic has been dubbed a relatively static or stalemated society.[17] Although studies of the Second Empire's secondary schools, public and private, and of the Third Republic's *cours complémentaires* demonstrate that education enabled some ambitious offspring of the lower middle classes or artisans to surpass their fathers on the social and educational ladder, only modest numbers of "children of the people" could reasonably expect such results.[18] Furthermore, there were more opportunities for boys than for girls, as is noted in more detail below.[19]

Before World War I primary school teachers—themselves frequently from humble peasant and working class backgrounds, although less often in the case of women than of men—cooperated with the country's political leaders in the inculcation of values and beliefs suitable for this sometimes static society.[20] They spread the gospel that hard work and intelligence could lead to social advancement, as their own career stories demonstrated, but that most children should be content with lower expectations. Indeed, the 1887 instructions for teaching *morale* had specified that children should learn the undesirability of too much love for money and profit.

Although France changed more slowly than major competitors, it did of course change. From the nineteenth century onward France experienced the social stresses accompanying industrialization and urbanization. Governmental reactions to such change supply a second reason for the image of a static society in much educational literature. The first year of the Third Republic coincided not only with the pain of military defeat but also with the cataclysm of the Paris Commune. In subsequent decades the socialist Left became an important element in political life, winning one-sixth of the vote in the last election before World War I. Communists entered the political arena after the Socialist Party split in late 1920. Although radical socialist republicans briefly joined hands with the Left in the unprecedented Popular Front coalition, republican leaders for decades had responded to workers' militancy and leftist politics by preaching the value of solidarity and social stability and trying to persuade younger generations that the regime, with its provision of universal manhood suffrage, was as just a political system as there could be.[21] Calling upon girls and women to keep men happy at home by providing clean and attractive surroundings and good meals was, despite its triteness, one aspect of efforts to dampen working class unrest and preserve social stability. Still ensconced in textbooks of the interwar period, this view of feminine roles presumably continued to be reinforced by many teachers.

However, the alliance of primary schoolteachers and republican politicans became less cozy after World War I. Teachers' unions lobbied for higher salaries and democratizing the public school system. Men found teaching less attractive financially and, by seeking other careers, increasingly opened the way for a feminization of primary school teaching ranks. Socialism also attracted many teachers who saw a disparity between the Republic's professions of equality and their own status, although the large Syndicat national des instituteurs (SNI) took more moderate stances than the minority Fédération unitaire d'enseignement.[22]

The teachers' movement leftward did not necessarily entail a change in basic attitudes toward women's traditional roles. As a group, teachers were more favorable to the enhancement of women's legal and professional status than other categories of workers, but probably no more than 4 percent of women teachers were truly feminists.[23] Furthermore, even the most radical women teachers of the interwar years, the minority who were feminist-syndicalists in the Fédération unitaire d'enseignement, often preserved the notion that men and women had different "faculties": men were judged more logical and women superior in qualities of imagination and assimilation.[24] Like other syndicalists, militant teachers, male and female, frequently viewed feminist issues as secondary in importance to the class struggle and the socialist cause, and by the mid-1930s the feminist current among syndicalist teachers had weakened considerably. Believing that equal employment opportunities for women could best be attained through socialism, feminist-syndicalist teachers had preferred, like French feminists from other social groups, to emphasize what brought the sexes together, not what divided them.[25]

Finally, the low French birthrate—lower than that of any other major Western nation from the early nineteenth century to 1914— haunted leaders of all political persuasions and colored thinking about women's roles.[26] Republican politicians worried that the low birthrate would not only place France at a disadvantage in a military confrontation with more populous Germany but also retard economic growth because of an inadequate pool of workers. The tragic loss of French lives in World War I exacerbated fears of depopulation, and the school mirrored these fears by adding injunctions to found large families to textbooks for both boys and girls and introducing *puériculture* lessons for girls. Thus the domestic emphasis in girls' education was an integral part of French leaders' response to social crises and fears of depopulation.

How did French girls and women react to pedagogical prescriptions for domesticity? Did they shun jobs or careers in favor of the care and feeding of large families? As employment statistics suggest, the answers are varied. We have seen that many prewar teachers—an elite among working women—professed that woman's place was in the foyer. Yet they often had an aversion to teaching home economics, and most of the girls they taught did not embrace home economics as the favorite subject. The continuation of the low French birthrate during the interwar period also demonstrates that as long as salaries were low and governmental financial incentives for large families limited, men and women alike were not noticeably swayed by natalist pronouncements from schools or politicians. Indeed, the birthrate hit an alltime low during the Depression years of 1937–1938.[27]

French women often did work outside the home. But in light of the school's presentation of women's work as a cause of problems for families or as a last resort for the single or impoverished— negative images also purveyed by other significant molders of values like the church, political parties, magazines, or movies—it is not surprising that girls frequently chose the most traditional feminine occupations and made choices haphazardly. In a primary school class of twenty-three Breton girls quizzed by an inspector about their attitudes toward work in 1925, twelve hoped to become seamstresses, four shopkeepers, one a farmer, and six teachers. Although the would- be teachers were probably more ambitious than classmates, the preponderance of *couture* suggests that little had changed since 1877 when a survey of the occupational expectations of 1754 Parisian girls leaving the primary school revealed that a majority expected to become seamstresses.[28] Reasons for occupational choice also remained largely traditional. In 1936 the review *Orientations* reported that only 29 percent of girls selected occupations because of personal interest in them. Family pressures were mentioned by fully 40 percent, of whom 32 percent cited the need to obey parents and 8 percent the influence of family traditions.[29] The weight of family considerations provides another parallel to the 1877 survey for which 40.5 percent of girls reported that their occupational choice was determined by parental needs or desires. The remainder of girls in the 1936 survey attributed occupational plans to factors apparently beyond their con- trol: 20 percent picked a job because there was nothing else to do and 11 percent cited the "force of circumstances."

However, many women did not overlook newer career opportu- nities made possible by the expansion of women's education. His- torians of education often note the paradox that while governments may intend to use the school as an instrument of social control, schooling itself may make individuals discontent with familial and social constraints and eager to use new skills to change and improve themselves, if not society.[30] The response of one girl to a question on an examination for the *certificat d'études primaires (c.e.p.)* in the early 1930s is instructive. Asked to describe the good and bad features of the profession of her father or mother and to indicate whether she would choose it, she wrote about her mother, a *couturière*. Aware that sewing could be done at home and thus was compatible with the roles of housewife and mother, this pupil nonetheless stated that she would not select it as a métier because it was tiring and unrewarding. That the answer appeared in a book of sample questions for the *c.e.p.* exam indicates that educators also found it acceptable for girls bright enough to be advised to take the exam.[31]

Although the primary school of the Third Republic did not endeavor to prepare most children for anything other than lives as farmers, workers, or housewives, the certificate of primary studies, obtained by better students, was a vehicle of limited upward social mobility. The importance of the *c.e.p.* during the Third Republic was comparable to that of the American high school diploma before World War II or, in the view of one French sociologist, to that of the secondary school *baccalauréat* in the 1970s.[32] The *c.e.p.* was especially prized in rural areas where opportunities to attend secondary or higher primary schools were more limited than in Paris and other cities and where education might supply the only hope for an exodus from local poverty.[33] However, the *c.e.p.* was also valued by urban working class families who perceived the primary school as the one route for economic improvement available to children. A woman who taught in Paris from 1914 to 1944 claimed that working class parents were often the most pleasant and cooperative with teachers precisely because they attached such expectations to schooling.[34] Although critics of the class-based nature of French schools have charged correctly that hopes for advancement often proved illusory for children of peasants and workers, James Marangé, head of the main teachers' union, the SNI, in 1966 remained convinced that public primary schools of the Third Republic had indeed been a key to social mobility for some bright children. There was, of course, always the danger that some parents might discourage children from pursuing further educational and occupational ambitions aroused by teachers. And there were no guarantees of success. One *institutrice* cited the case of a former pupil, a poor Marseilles girl, who became resentful toward her because after obtaining the *c.e.p.* she was unable to fulfill the raised expectations encouraged by the teacher.[35]

For girls, possession of the certificate of primary studies could lead to a low-level government job, such as a post office position, or to a higher primary school where one might obtain secretarial skills or follow a general course that provided preparation for entrance exams for a normal school. During the Third Republic girls increasingly took advantage of the chance to obtain the *c.e.p.*, although a somewhat lower percentage of girls than boys tried the examination for it. In 1877 girls obtained 29 percent of primary school certificates; in 1882, 42 percent; in 1902 and 1907, 46 percent; and in 1934, 48.4 percent (Table 4).[36] By the mid-1930s approximately half of all primary school students took the test for the *c.e.p.*, and 40 percent received it. In 1954, when women numbered 54 percent of the population aged fourteen and older—the generations born during the Third Republic— they constituted 52 percent of the group holding the *c.e.p.*. Admittedly, this primary credential was bypassed by many students in *lycées* and *collèges*, but women's eagerness for education by mid-century was also illustrated by the fact that in 1954 they numbered 49.4 percent of the adult population with an education beyond the level of the *c.e.p.* On the other hand, 50 percent of the female and 47 percent of the male population still had not attained the *c.e.p.* or a higher degree.[37]

How did girls from private schools fare on the *c.e.p.* exam in comparison to their public school sisters? In the case of Paris, Catholic school girls were less likely to take the exam and still more unlikely to pass it than public school girls. In July 1912 approximately 45 percent of eligible public school girls in Paris tried the test, as compared to 38 percent of private school girls; 52 percent of public school boys of the appropriate age and fully 87 percent of comparable private school boys tried the test.[38] Girls in private schools then numbered nearly 34 percent of the city's feminine primary school population but were only 23 percent of girls earning the *c.e.p.* (Table 5). Whereas 82 percent of public school girls taking the exam passed,

Table 4. Girls Earning the *Certificat d'Etudes Primaires*, 1877–1934

	Number of *c.e.p.* for girls	Percentage of total *c.e.p.*
1877	10,780	29
1882	38,000	42
1902	94,020	46
1907	100,310	46
1925	110,230	48.1
1934	156,610	48.4

SOURCE: Ministère de l'instruction publique, *Statistique de l'enseignement primaire* 3 (1884): 248–249; 8 (1909): 266–269; *Bulletin de la Statistique générale de la France* 25 (1936): 327.

the figure was 70 percent for private school girls. In comparison, boys in private primary schools fared better than their feminine counterparts; only 17 percent of the male primary school enrollment in Paris in 1912, they obtained 18.5 percent of the *c.e.p.*'s awarded to boys. An identical pattern for girls prevailed on the June 1929 exams, but private school boys' performance declined to 14 percent of the certificates for boys, although they remained 16 percent of the male school population.[39]

There were also some noticeable regional variations in girls' attainment of the *c.e.p.* by the early twentieth century. In 1907, when girls earned 46 percent of all *c.e.p.*'s there were eight departments where they earned only 40 percent or less (Table 6). Of these, five (Finistère, Ille-et-Vilaine, Morbihan, Mayenne, Vendée) were in heavily Catholic Brittany and the West, long noted for cultural variation from the national norm, as was the island of Corsica; the other two, Pyrénées-Orientales and Tarn-et-Garonne, were in the Southwest. Girls had the lowest percentage of departmental certificates in the Pyrénées-Orientales (34 percent) and the Vendée (35 percent).[40] Two of the departments at the extremities of France, Finistère (37 percent) and Corsica (38 percent), were among the seventeen departments which in 1863 were still almost totally non-French speaking, and four more were departments where the usage of patois was significant.[41] Forty years later four of the eight departments where girls obtained the lowest percentage of the *c.e.p.*'s ranked among the seven departments with the highest illiteracy rates for girls aged ten to fourteen. In 1906 the national average for illiteracy among girls ten to fourteen was 5 percent, but it was 10 percent in the Pyrénées-Orientales, 16 percent in Finistère, 19 percent in Morbihan, and a high 32 percent in Corsica. However, the other four departments were below the national illiteracy rates for girls ten to fourteen: Mayenne, 2.8 percent; Ille-et-Vilaine, 2.9 percent, Tarn-et-Garonne, 4 percent, and Vendée, 5 percent.[42]

The presence of five western departments in the group where girls' achievement of the *c.e.p.* was the lowest but where in three cases illiteracy for ten-to-fourteen-year-olds was below the national norm suggests that Catholic schooling played a role in girls' interest or disinterest in the *c.e.p.* The Breton departments and the Vendée were all Catholic strongholds. At a time when 23 percent of French girls attended private schools, more than half of all girls attended private schools in Morbihan, Vendée, and Ille-et-Vilaine, 45 percent did so in Mayenne, and 35 percent in Finistère (Table 6).[43] In light of the high literacy rates for schoolgirls in three of these western departments, the significance of the Catholic variable is less a case of truly poor academic preparation for Catholic schoolgirls than a matter of

Table 5. Pupils Earning the C.e.p. from Paris Public and Private Schools

| | Primary School Enrollment | | | | Number Trying C.e.p. | | | | Number Passing C.e.p. | | | |
| | Public | | Private | | Public | | Private | | Public | | Private | |
	Boys	Girls	Boys	Girls	Boys	Girls	Boys	Girls	Boys	Girls	Boys	Girls
July 1912	79,684	81,487	12,891	34,150	6,857	6,154	1,879	2,157	5,559	5,065	1,264	1,517
July 1929	61,278	65,619	11,622	24,423	4,850	4,830	1,151	1,364	3,491	3,474	549	693

SOURCE: Archives départementales de Paris D²T¹ 2, 17

Table 6. Primary School Statistics for Departments Where Girls Earned High and Low Percentages of the C.e.p. in 1907

	Girls' % of C.e.p.	% of Pupils in Private Schools		% of Women Teachers*	
		Boys	Girls	Public	Private
France	46	12	23	50.2	78
Basses-Alpes	58	2	4	62	82
Hautes-Alpes	56	1.5	2	67	75
Savoie	54	4	6	59.6	75
Cantal	53	10	19	60	76
Rhône	52.5	26	32	52	70
Alpes-Maritimes	52	9	22	56	83
Haute-Savoie	51.6	7	5	61	80
Isère	51.3	8	14	57	76
Vaucluse	51	15	23	53	72
Ille-et-Vilaine	40	33	50.2	52	72
Tarn-et-Garonne	40	11	29	51	82
Morbihan	39	37	52	53	66
Corse	38	2	6	55	92
Mayenne	37.5	12	45	50.7	86
Finistère	37	17	34	49	72
Vendée	35	19	56	46	81
Pyrénées-Orientales	34	5	10	48	83

SOURCE: Annuaire Statistique de la France (1909, 1910)

* (The inclusion of teachers of écoles maternelles, nearly all women, increases the percentage of women teachers in primary ranks.)

Catholic families and religious teachers being more inclined to shun a state educational credential for girls than for boys. Instituteur André Retail, born in the Vendée in 1909 and son of an institutrice, has commented on the resistance of early twentieth-century Catholic schools to preparing students for the c.e.p., even if parents desired this. Similarly, Pierre-Jakez Hélias, a Breton born in 1914, has confirmed that during the 1920s parents in his part of the Finistère sent daughters to public schools only if they wished them to obtain the c.e.p. and pursue careers; otherwise, they chose Catholic schools. Eventually parental and student demand for the c.e.p. led resistant Catholic schools to prepare girls as well as boys for it, but this happened more slowly in some departments than in others.[44]

Finally, the preponderance of agriculture in the eight departments where girls ranked the lowest in earning the c.e.p. probably also minimized the appeal of the certificate as something necessary for a job. In 1901, when 39 percent of the nation's female work force was engaged in the primary sector of the economy (agriculture, fishing, forestry), 56 percent to 66 percent of women workers were so engaged in seven of these eight departments. Women workers in the primary sector of the economy also had the highest illiteracy rates. Nationwide in 1901 28 percent of women in agriculture were illiterate, as compared to 18 percent of all women workers. Farm women in seven of the eight departments in question had illiteracy rates noticeably higher than the national average; in the Finistère and Morbihan, 47 percent were illiterate, as were 56 percent in Pyrénées-Orientales (Table 7).[45] That regional variations in women's educational achievements have had a *longue durée* is demonstrated by the 1954 census: 39 percent of all Frenchwomen then possessed the *c.e.p.*, but all eight departments still ranked below the national average, with the deviation ranging from three percentage points less for Ille-et-Vilaine to nearly eleven points for Morbihan (Table 8).[46]

A pronounced regional trend was also evident for the departments where girls obtained 51 percent or more of the certificates awarded in 1907 (Table 6). Eight were neighboring departments in the Southeast, and the other was the south central Cantal. In the Alps above average literacy rates were an Old Regime tradition, but primarily for men.[47] Evidently the rigors of the Alpine winter and the dearth of diversions enhanced the appeal of some seasonal instruction in reading and writing, and literate men from the mountains long served as itinerant teachers for much of the Southeast. Girls' success on exams in 1907 resulted from improvements in schools following the Ferry Laws and also demonstrated growing awareness of the link between educational credentials and employment opportunities. A generation earlier, in 1882, girls had obtained fewer certificates than boys in each of the nine departments in question (Table 8). In the Basses-Alpes at the turn of the century the 19 percent illiteracy rate among the female population over age fifteen was still significantly higher than the 13 percent rate for men, but for the population aged fifteen to nineteen female illiteracy (1.4 percent) was less than half of male illiteracy (3 percent). Girls did exceptionally well on the 1907 exam for the *c.e.p.* in the Basses-Alpes (58 percent) and Hautes-Alpes (56 percent). They also received 54 percent of the certificates in Savoie, 53 percent in Cantal, 52.5 percent in the Rhône, 52 percent in Alpes-Maritimes, 51.6 percent in Haute-Savoie, 51 percent in Isère, and 51 percent in Vaucluse. Although girls outnumbered boys in the primary school population in three of the nine departments, this was

Table 7. Women's Occupational Patterns and Illiteracy Rates in 1901 in Departments Where Girls Earned a Low Percentage of the *C.e.p.*

	Girls % of *c.e.p.*		Women as % of Workers 1901	% of Female Work Force in 1901 in					Women Workers' Illiteracy in 1901 in				
	1902	1907		Agric. Forest	Indust.	Comm.	Domes. Serv.	Prof'ns & Gov't.	Ag.	In.	Co.	DS	P/G
Ille-et-Vilaine	44	40	42	61	18.4	10.1	7.3	3.2	22	15	7	8	1.6
Tarn-et-Garonne	46	40	30	58.6	22.1	6.6	7.5	5.2	37	13	21	28	3.9
Morbihan	42	39	41.8	68.2	15.4	8	5.7	2.7	47	30	27	32	6
Corse	40	38	26	66.4	15.3	7	7.3	4	62	25	48	58	19
Mayenne	47	37.5	39	55.7	23	9	8.3	3.9	16	12	6	7	1.8
Finistère	35	37	38	64.5	17.6	8.6	6.8	2.5	47	29	27.7	28	2.5
Vendée	38	35	35	62	18.5	7.2	8.2	4	33	14	17	19	2.4
Pyrénées-Orientales	40	34	24	42	29.4	10.1	12.5	5.5	56	19	36	40	3.4
France	46	46	34.5	39.1	34.9	10.2	11.5	4.3	28	11.4	11.3	13	1.7

SOURCES: *Statistique de l'enseignement primaire* 8 (1909): 266–269; *Résultats du recensement de 1901.* (The 1901 census was utilized instead of the 1906 census because it provided illiteracy rates under occupational category.)

not the case in the four departments where girls' performances most strikingly surpassed that of boys.[48]

In comparison to the western region where girls received the lowest percentage of the c.e.p.'s, four of these nine southern departments (Basses-Alpes, Hautes-Alpes, Savoie, Haute-Savoie) had fewer than 6 percent of girls attending private schools, and only in the Rhône was the percentage of girls in private schools (32 percent) above the national average of 23 percent (Table 6). The preponderance of women teachers in these departments probably helped inspire girls' academic performance, too. At a time when women were about half of the public primary school teaching corps, women teachers constituted 56 percent to 66 percent of public school teachers in seven of these departments, and even in the Rhône, where they were the least numerous, were still 52 percent of public school teachers (Table 6).[49] That women made up 60 percent or more of the teaching corps in

Table 8. Educational Trends in Departments Where Girls Earned High and Low Percentages of the C.e.p. in 1907

	1882		1907		1954
	No. of c.e.p.	% of c.e.p.	No. of c.e.p.	% of c.e.p.	% of Women with c.e.p.
France	38,000	42	100,310	46	38.8
Basses-Alpes	104	46.4	340	58	41
Hautes-Alpes	105	43	384	56	42.5
Savoie	276	45.5	896	54	48
Cantal	284	49	638	53	35
Rhône	648	47	2138	52.5	47
Alpes-Maritimes	81	32	530	52	42.7
Haute-Savoie	227	37	949	51.6	49
Isère	749	46	1747	51.3	46.6
Vaucluse	125	36.8	550	51	37
Ille-et-Vilaine	367	40	1169	40	35.8
Tarn-et-Garonne	112	34	199	40	29
Morbihan	348	48	964	39	28
Corse	236	37	509	38	32
Mayenne	294	43	485	37.5	33
Finistére	356	45.6	1708	37	35.6
Vendée	165	35	443	35	31
Pyrénées-Orientales	44	15	355	34	35.6

SOURCE: Statistique de l'enseignement primaire 3 (1884): 248–249; 8 (1909): 266–269; Annuaire statistique de la France (1956), pp. xii–xxiii.

the Basses-Alpes, Hautes-Alpes, Haute-Savoie, Cantal, and Savoie is a sign that male teachers were better able to avoid or flee the remote hamlets in which many women taught. Indeed, these departments had experienced a decline in population since 1851, whereas the neighboring Rhône, Isère, and Alpes-Maritimes, with the lure of the cities of Lyon, Grenoble, and Nice, had gained population.[50]

Economic realities also spurred girls' performance in schools. Education and the *c.e.p.* offered the best hope for avoiding dire poverty in a region with many poor mountainous areas and limited employment opportunities for women. In the Basses-Alpes, for example, women were extremely underrepresented in the work force, constituting only 18 percent of the department's active population in 1901, as compared to 34.5 percent of the national work force. However, women who were teachers and civil servants—occupations where literacy was a must—were 10 percent of the department's female work force, whereas nationally only 4 percent of all women workers were so employed. In six of the other eight departments where girls outperformed boys on the *c.e.p.* exam, the percentage of working women in this high-literacy category of employment was also above the national average for women workers (Table 9). When jobs for women were relatively scarce, those requiring literacy became more important to would-be workers. In five of the nine departments under analysis, women's presence in the work force was below the national average of 34.5 percent (Table 9), but in three of these five departments (Cantal, Haute-Savoie, Vaucluse)—and in the more industrial Rhône—their participation in the total work force of professionals and civil servants exceeded the national average of 18 percent (Table 10).[51] In five of the nine departments women's rate of participation in the commercial sector, generally requiring literacy, was also above average. The low marriage rates in Basses-Alpes and Hautes-Alpes— where less than half of women aged fifteen to forty-nine married before 1901—must also have been a powerful incentive for girls to seek the *c.e.p.*, although comparable celibacy statistics for Corsica and the heavily Catholic Finistère, Morbihan, Ille-et-Vilaine, and Mayenne had not produced the same statistical results.[52] In 1954 seven of the nine departments in question still retained the tradition of women ranking above the national average for female possession of the *c.e.p.*, three of them (Rhône, Savoie, Haute-Savoie) being more than eight points above the average of 39 percent of women holding the *c.e.p.* (Table 8).[53]

Not surprisingly, the rates for possession of the *c.e.p.* also varied according to rural or urban locales. In 1954 among urban women aged twenty-five and over—most of whom had completed primary school by 1940—39 percent held the *c.e.p.*, as did 45 percent of

Table 9. Women's Occupational Patterns and Illiteracy Rates in 1901 in Departments Where Girls Earned a High Percentage of the C.e.p.

	Girls % of c.e.p.		Women as % of Workers 1901	% of Female Work Force in 1901 in						Women Workers' Illiteracy in 1901			
	1902	1907		Agric. Forest	Indus.	Commerce	Domest. Service	Prof'ns & Gov't.	Ag.	In.	Co.	DS	P/G
Basses-Alpes	52.1	58	18.4	43	26	11.8	9.5	9.7	25	3	8	13	0.4
Hautes-Alpes	52	56	30.4	69.2	13.7	6.8	4.7	5.6	15	5	6	9	0.1
Savoie	51	54	38	72	13.7	5.7	4.8	3.8	17	5	5	6	0.6
Cantal	52.4	53	33	63.2	13.9	8.7	8.7	5.5	18	13	11	13	1.5
Rhône	54	52.5	39	13.2	57.3	9.6	14.5	5.4	12	8.8	8.7	8.9	0.9
Alpes-Maritimes	44	52	36	29	29.6	13.9	22.7	4.8	49	29	18	17	1.8
Haute-Savoie	49	51.6	31	64.4	17.5	7.1	5.9	5.1	12	4.7	4.9	6	1.3
Isère	48	51.3	35	33	48.9	8	5.9	4.2	17	6.6	6.7	8	1
Vaucluse	47	51	26	24.9	44.7	12.5	11	6.9	33	13	16	20	2.2
France	46	46	34.5	39.1	34.9	10.2	11.5	4.3	28	11.4	11.3	13	1.7

SOURCES: Statistique de l'enseignement primaire 8 (1909): 266–269; Résultats du recensement de 1901. (The 1901 census was utilized instead of the 1906 census because it provided illiteracy rates under occupational category.)

urban men. In the countryside, where the *c.e.p.* was less important for those in agriculture but highly important for those wishing to leave it, the percentage of both men and women with the *c.e.p.* was lower, but there was also less difference between the sexes: 29 percent of men and 28 percent of women had it.[54] Of course, the census does not indicate how many urban men and women with the *c.e.p.* had obtained it initially in a rural area and then were emboldened to try to improve their fortunes by moving to a town or city, as so many had done since the mid-nineteenth century. The school was clearly one agent promoting the exodus from rural poverty and boredom, for one study done in Brittany in the 1950s revealed that 42 percent of those migrating had decided to do so, or considered doing so, before age fourteen. By then women had long been more numerous than men in this rural to urban migration.[55]

As departmental statistics suggest, girls' educational achievements may sometimes be correlated with changes in women's employment patterns, which included an increase in the number of women in government service and professions. But because women's increased representation in white-collar jobs by the end of the Third Republic was also due to the fact that more and more girls were obtaining education beyond the level of the primary school and the *c.e.p.*, further discussion of women's employment will be preceded by consideration of what girls earning the *c.e.p.* encountered if they

Table 10. Women's Representation in Different Economic Sectors in South-eastern France, 1901

| Department | Percentage of Work Force That Was Female in | | | | |
| | | | | Domestic | Government/ |
	Agriculture	Industry	Commerce	Service	Professions
Basses-Alpes	13	25	33	*88*	16
Hautes-Alpes	*34*	33	*40*	*84*	10
Savoie	*41*	30	*49*	*87*	24
Cantal	32	27	*44*	*87*	25
Rhône	28	*41*	28	*86*	25
Alpes-Maritimes	*35*	25	33	81	14
Haute-Savoie	30	26	*42*	*84*	21
Isère	28	*43*	*38*	80	18
Vaucluse	14	35	31	82	20
France	32	34	37	82	18

Above-average rates of participation are in italics.
SOURCE: *Résultats du recensement de 1901.*

continued schooling at the next levels of the primary system, the *cours complémentaire* or *école primaire supérieure*.

Before 1940 girls more often obtained post-elementary education in the primary sector of the public school system than in the secondary. The *cours complémentaires* and *écoles primaires supérieures*, the so-called "secondary schools for *le peuple*," accommodated more girls than the *lycées* and *collèges* (Table 11). In 1891, a decade after the creation of public secondary schools for girls, 4,600 were enrolled in *lycées* and *collèges* or *cours secondaires* but 11,800 attended *cours complémentaires* and *écoles primaires supérieures*. While 2.5 times as many girls attended post-elementary classes in the primary as in the secondary part of the school system, boys attending post-elementary classes were twice as numerous in secondary schools (60,300) as in higher primary schools (31,700). By 1906, after the creation of more higher primary schools and complementary courses for both sexes and the assignment of the *écoles pratiques du commerce et d'industrie* to the Ministry of Industry and Commerce in 1892, girls remained less likely to receive post-primary instruction than boys, and boys were still less numerous in higher primary classes than in secondary schools (Table 11). Although the number of girls in all types of post-elementary courses in 1906 was only 47 percent of the number of boys, this was a marked gain over 1891 when the comparable figure was just 22 percent. During the interwar period this gap between the sexes was narrowed further, with the ratio of girls to boys in all types of public post-elementary schooling becoming .72 by 1938. In the post-elementary classes of the primary school system near parity had then been achieved between boys and girls, for 137,600 girls were in such classes in 1938, as compared to 148,300 boys.[56] However, the more significant difference between the educational opportunities offered to girls and boys by the Third Republic remained the imbalance in secondary schools. Girls constituted only 33 percent of the enrollment in public secondary schools in 1938, although they were over 40 percent of the enrollment in private secondary schools, whose academic standards generally commanded less respect than the *lycées*.[57]

Because public complementary courses and higher primary schools long educated noticeably more girls than secondary schools, the type of instruction and professional orientation they offered is of interest. A detailed investigation of post-primary "primary" classes is beyond the scope of this study, but it is essential to note that they mirrored the values of the primary school system in which they were encased and that some offerings for girls differed from those for boys.

Both *cours complémentaires* and *écoles primaires supérieures* provided "higher" primary instruction, but they differed in structure and set-

Table 11. Enrollments in Public Post-Primary Education, 1881–1938

	Cours Complémentaires		Ecoles Primaires Supérieures		Ecoles pratiques du Commerce et d'industrie		Lycées and Collèges	
	Boys	Girls	Boys	Girls	Boys	Girls	Boys	Girls*
1881	4,600	2,300	13,200	4,200			73,200	4,600
1891	9,900	4,000	20,500	7,400			60,300	8,200
1906	16,500	13,500	26,900	18,500	8,700	2,200	67,100	21,500
1926	26,100	32,100	37,900	36,700	24,400	8,900	79,800	36,800
1938	56,900	67,600	50,800	54,500	40,600	15,500	133,900	66,600

(*Includes Cours secondaires de jeunes filles, founded in 1867)

SOURCE: Annuaire statistique de la France (1966), pp. 137, 139; Antoine Prost, Histoire de l'enseignement en France, p. 346.

ting. The *cours complémentaire*, one or two years in length, was located in a primary school and supervised by that school's principal. Its curriculum mixed repetiton of the *cours supérieur* of the primary school with segments of the program for the *école primaire supérieure*, the academic portion of which was also to a large extent an in-depth version of the primary school curriculum.[58] Housed in a separate building, the *école primaire supérieure* lasted for a minimum of three years. It also had a more urban orientation than the *cours complémentaire*, which was added to primary schools in rural towns whose population was too small to justify creating a separate higher primary school. The *c.e.p.* was required for admission to both levels of primary schooling.

The relationship of the complementary courses and higher primary schools to the secondary schools was described precisely by the education ministry in September 1920. Referring to the likely occupations of male graduates, the ministry stated that advanced primary schooling formed "men who, under the direction of *chefs* graduating from the universities and *grandes écoles*, will constitute the cadres of the economic army and the administrative army." This vision of the higher primary school's mission thus continued that of Guizot, its creator in 1833. Whereas the higher primary school could turn out "overseers, head foremen, [and] clerks for various administrative offices," the less ambitious complementary course would produce "educated workers" or, "at the most extreme limits of its proper domain," students qualified for the normal schools.[59]

Traditionally regarding higher primary school instruction as more practical than theoretical, educators did not assign it the same role in disseminating a humanistic "general culture" that the secondary school received. However, before World War I there was less difference between the secondary school and the higher primary school for girls than for boys because both could serve as finishing schools and both attracted many lower middle class students, the bourgeoisie not having been as eager to send daughters to public secondary schools as their creators had hoped.[60] After secondary school girls received the option of taking the same program as boys in 1924—an option that quickly became the most popular because it led to the *baccalauréat*—the differences between the two post-primary public schools for girls became more apparent. One woman who in 1939–1940 attended a provincial complementary course preparing girls for the entry examination for the normal school later complained bitterly about the contrast between secondary instruction, intended to "form minds," and the boring higher primary school program that required repetition of much subject matter already encountered by students in the primary school.[61] Yet if higher primary schools were less intellectually stimulating than secondary classes, there is evidence that students and parents able to choose between the two often opted for the former precisely because they seemed to offer better job preparation than the "general culture" of the secondary schools.[62] While girls' secondary schools attracted a new clientele after their creation in 1880, the enrollment in boys' secondary schools stagnated until the 1930s (Table 11).

Girls attending higher primary schools received not only a program different from that of girls' secondary schools but also a vocational orientation somewhat different from that provided by boys' higher primary schools. All students, male and female, studied the same academic subjects during the first year. However, girls' moral instruction included a special section on duties of the girl and woman, prescribed in 1893 (and previously discussed), and science lessons included *puériculture*, added in 1909. In addition, the first year differed for boys and girls in practical subjects; girls received domestic instruction and boys learned more about crafts and agriculture. Beyond the first year, students still spent at least half the week on academic subjects but also elected a specialization. Girls had three options: general, commercial, and homemaking, the latter two introduced in 1909. With the commercial option, girls received five hours of instruction per week in shorthand and typing during the second and third years and no longer had to take home economics. Girls in the general program—the most popular and the one recommended for would-be teachers or post office employees—took six hours of home economics during the second and third years. Those in the homemaking section took twelve hours of home economics, did not take the four hours of foreign language required of the other two sections, and received an hour less of French and of mathematics.[63]

As late as 1936 the education ministry described the homemaking section as the one which ought to have the largest number of students because it was ideal preparation for "excellent *maîtresses de maison*" and "*bonnes ménagères*."[64] The combination of general courses and home economics suited girls whose parents simply wanted a type of finishing school for them. However, the homemaking option was not the most popular with pupils. At the girls' higher primary school in Toulouse in 1913, 71 percent of 211 students were inscribed in the general section, 10 percent in commercial courses, and 19 percent in "feminine arts," some of the latter anticipating work as *couturières*.[65] Students hoping to become teachers at the end of the 1930s also had the distinct impression that sewing, home economics, and drawing were less important than their academic subjects because the former were worth only a few points on the entrance examination for the normal school.[66] Evidently many educators had recognized by 1920, if not earlier, that most girls sought professional preparation at the higher primary school, just as many young women desired the same from the public secondary school.[67]

Preparing for a career was not, of course, tantamount to great eagerness to be engaged in it, but increasingly the daughters of all social classes recognized that education was the key to supporting themselves if they remained single or suddenly faced financial exigencies. Secondary school professor Amélie Gayraud reported in 1914 that the majority of a small group of *lycée* graduates aged eighteen to twenty-five whom she had surveyed regarded preparation for careers as a practical necessity but did not expect to work once married. Nonetheless, middle class girls eager for careers could be very annoyed by secondary school teachers who treated academic study simply as an embellishment for a cultivated lady. Such was the reaction of the future feminist Louise Weiss to the Lycée Molière in Paris before 1914 and of Ménie Grègoire, author and television personality, to the Catholic Cours Jeanne d'Arc in the Vendée during the 1930s.[68]

Boys attending higher primary schools could choose from up to five options: a general section or a commercial section, like those available for girls; and also an industrial section, an agricultural section, and, in certain areas, a maritime section. The boys' curriculum for the two advanced years of the general section differed from the girls' only in the traditional area of "manual works." In the commercial section boys received one more hour per week of accounting than did girls. The industrial section, requiring twelve hours a week of manual works and five hours of geometrical drawing and design, trained skilled craftsmen, foremen, and managers.[69]

Textbooks for complementary courses and higher primary classes, like those for primary schools, mirrored the different vocational paths demarcated for males and females. *A nos jeunes filles* (1893), a textbook for reading and moral instruction by Mathilde Salomon, energetic director of the private but secular Collège Sévigné, conformed to the official instructions that girls must learn about duties unique to their sex. Thus Salomon expected all women, regardless of social status, to practice the métier of *ménagère* and realize that they set the tone of households. The working woman forced to leave her home to earn money should perform her household chores as diligently as any other woman. She must rise first, prepare breakfast for the family, and supervise her children's departure for school. Presumably she could expect help only from older daughters who, aware of the mother's burden, assumed cleaning and cooking duties so that both parents would find it a joy to return home. Except for this example of a working mother, whose precise employment was not named,

Salomon did not depict women in nondomestic roles. Yet her text was more than a narrow glorification of domesticity, for she was addressing a group that was not destined for the lowest echelons of French society. Indeed, some secondary schools also used her book. Salomon counseled girls to avoid letting family obligations blind them to responsibilities to the rest of humanity. She also showed more understanding of the psychological subtleties in relationships between family members than did many textbook authors. Whereas a child's unquestioning obedience to parents was the norm in primary textbooks—sometimes even to the point of accepting unjust punishments from parents rather than disrespectfully challenging their authority[70]—Salomon recognized that an adolescent girl could feel constrained at times by her mother's demands. She reminded *adolescentes* that a child and a mother were not equals and that a mother had a right to expect deference, but she also wrote sympathetically about a young woman's desire to create her own life.[71]

Whatever career a female student in a higher primary school might have in mind, she was not allowed to forget that as a woman her position in society was different from a man's. In a *Cours de morale* intended for both boys and girls Albert Pierre, a school inspector, and Mlle A. Martin, a teacher, counseled wifely submission in arguments not only because the husband was legally head of the family but also because he was more logical and had better judgment. The husband should protect his wife from "the temptations of ignorance or laziness," as well as from boredom and suffering. Pierre and Martin also broached a topic ignored in elementary school texts but deemed appropriate for adolescents: chastity. Recommended for unmarried males as well as for females, chastity was included in a chapter on selecting a spouse. To enjoy conjugal harmony, one should, ideally, marry a person similar in social position, age, education, and "esprit." Good health was important, too, for the "future of the race" depended on families.[72]

Despite the predominance of traditional domestic images in turn-of-the-century textbooks for girls in higher primary schools and complementary courses, many girls and their families saw the advanced primary school as the avenue to better jobs and not simply as a finishing school for a clientele from a lower social stratum than that of the secondary school. Yet most analyses of the relationship between higher primary schools and social mobility have tended to focus on the family backgrounds and career choices of male graduates. Admittedly, boys were more likely than girls to enter the work force right after graduation and less likely to leave it after marriage or the birth of children. Nonetheless, more than 40 percent of married women and about 60 percent of the single were in the work force during the first half of the twentieth century.[73] Thus it is regrettable that there are no reliable measures of how many young women several generations ago might have been interested in the kind of longterm professional success desired by young men. Available statistics tell more about what girls had to settle for than about what they actually desired after leaving school.

Contemporary interest in the linkage between schooling and social status prompted the education ministry to publish a chart comparing the professions of parents and all the male graduates of *écoles primaires supérieures* between 1889 and 1898. It did not add a companion one for girls, even though some data on their parents had been gathered, but it did present tables comparing the initial post-scholastic activities of boys and girls leaving the *cours complémentaires* and *écoles primaires supérieures* throughout France between 1898 and 1907. These tables demonstrate girls' greater difficulties in entering the work force and probably also a lesser inclination to do so. Between 1903 and 1907, 24,630 girls left post-primary "primary" classes. Of these, about two-thirds were destined for the work force or additional schooling (Table 12). Teaching was their most common career choice: 17 percent went to normal schools and 12 percent were going on for additional primary or secondary schooling, after which some would also opt for teaching. Those going directly to work had occupational possibilities that were varied but distinctly more limited than for boys: 9 percent of female graduates would help with family enterprises, 8 percent became workers or apprentices, 5 percent had jobs in education, 6 percent went to stores and offices, 4 percent to public administration, and a negligible number to railroads and banks. An additional 1.5 percent planned to attend specialized schools. However, fully 35 percent had no immediate career plans, usually because of a lack of job possibilities or because parents expected assistance at home. In comparison, only 8 percent of 52,308 boys leaving advanced primary schooling between 1903 and 1907 were so classified. Male graduates were about five times more likely to attend special schools for advanced training or work in stores and offices, eight times more likely to work for banks, four times more likely to work for railroads, twice as likely to be destined for a family business, but only half as likely to attend a normal school.[74]

Like the national statistics published for female graduates of the years 1898–1907, those available for students leaving the *cours complémentaires* a few years earlier confirm the pattern of a high percentage of fourteen-to-seventeen-year-old girls going back home rather than to work. In the most useful study of this data so far available, Robert Gildea devoted only a few lines to the discrepancy between

Table 12. Future Activities of Pupils Leaving *Ecoles Primaires Supérieures* and Public *Cours Complémentaires*, 1898–1907 (% of Pupils)

Future Activities	Girls		Boys	
	1898–1902	1903–1907	1898–1902	1903–1907
Help Family at Home	21	20		
Normal Schools	17	17	8	8
Workers/Apprentices	14	8	14	11
Family Business/Farm	10	9	19	19
2dry School or E.p.s.	8	12	8	9
Stores & Offices	5	6	22	23
Jobs in Schools	4	5	1	2
Government Jobs	3	4	5	5
Special Schools	2	2	8	7
Banks & Finance	.5	.3	2	3
Railroads	.4	.4	2	2
Unable to Find Work	4	7		
Future Unknown	9	8	9	8
Deceased	1	1	1	1
Other	1.1	.3	1	2
Number Leaving Schools	17,389	24,630	41,153	52,308

SOURCE: *Statistique de l'enseignement primaire* 8 (1909): cii–civ.

male and female plans and instead concentrated on comparing the professions of parents and male graduates in three very different departments. Gildea found mobility greatest in the department of the Gard in the South, middling in the industrial Nord, and lowest in the agricultural Ille-et-Vilaine in Brittany. He also confirmed, like the education ministry's aforementioned chart, that the children of farmers were very underrepresented in post-primary education. The prospects of boys from white-collar backgrounds were the most promising. The offspring of tradesmen and artisans were more likely to continue the activity of their fathers than those of industrial workers, but this was often because the former found their fathers' situation somewhat attractive. Mobility was demonstrated by the fact that between 29 percent and 36 percent of the sons of artisans, tradesmen, and workers were destined for normal schools or white-collar jobs and that some of the 10 percent headed to secondary or specialized schools would also achieve a rise in status.[75]

Because the statistics on those leaving the *cours complémentaires* during the late 1890s also contain information on the occupations of girls' parents (usually only their fathers), an analysis was undertaken of the plans of nearly five hundred girls leaving these courses between 1896 and 1898 in six of the southern departments where their success on the *c.e.p.* (Table 8) was so notable a decade later. As Table 13 indicates, one-third returned to their family's home or farm, often to help with housework, and another 7 percent were slated to work in a family shop or business. In addition, one-fourth would become workers, with nearly two-thirds of them destined to become seamstresses or apprentices doing needlework or laundry. Mobility was thus not likely for this particular working group, which was actually 5 percent larger for the girls than for their fathers. On the other hand, additional education held out brighter prospects for another one-fourth of the girls, evenly divided between those heading immediately to normal schools and those heading to a secondary school, another higher primary school, or to private schools. Here again, however, one must qualify the notion that such girls were often able to do more than simply "reproduce" parental status. Although the number of girls going to normal schools was 50 percent greater than the number of parents who were teachers, girls do not fare quite as well as fathers if the combined total of normal school students and future employees of Postes, Téléphones, et Télégraphes (PTT) is matched with fathers in these or other government jobs.[76]

The aggregate figures testifying to girls' difficulties in surpassing parental status do not mean, however, that individual success stories in the world of work after school cannot be told, even though they were more rare for girls than for boys. Of the sixty-two future teachers in the sample, 40 percent were the daughters of teachers (sixteen) or government workers (eight), but one-third were the children of farmers—the size of whose holdings was, admittedly, not indicated—and another 17 percent were the offspring of artisans, workers, or shopkeepers, or were orphans. Data on the mothers of sixty girls in Vienne in the Isère show that only two of their mothers were teachers but that seven of them were heading to an *école normale* (Table 14). The special valuation of education for girls in poor departments—seen in girls' particularly high rates of earning the *c.e.p.* in the Basses-Alpes and Hautes-Alpes—is also borne out in the choices of girls leaving higher primary education in these departments. Of fifty-nine girls leaving the *cours complémentaire* in Sisteron (Basses-Alpes) between 1894 and 1898, thirteen (22 percent) were headed to the normal school and eleven (19 percent) to secondary schools or other advanced primary schools. Six of the future teachers had parents already working in education or for the government; five came from modest circumstances. Of seventy-one leaving the *cours complémentaires* in Gap and Embrun (Hautes-Alpes) between 1896 and 1898, fully 24 percent were going to the normal school but twice as many, 48 percent, were returning to their families with no future employ-

Table 13. Future Activities of Girls Leaving *Cours Complèmentaires* in Six Southern Departments, 1896–1898, and Occupations of Parent

Destination/Occupation	Girls in 6 Depts.* No.	%	Parents** No.	%	French Girls in E.P.S. and C.C., 1898–1902 (% in Occupation)
Normal School/Teacher	62	(13)	41	(8)	17
E.p.s. or 2dry School	62	(13)			8
Workers/Apprentices	118	(24)	93	(19)	14
Stores & Offices	8	(2)	7	(1)	5
Family Business/Shop	36	(7)	97	(20)	8
Family Farm	21	(4)	144	(29)	2
Family Home	71	(14)			21
Family, Future unknown	63	(13)			9
Gov't Jobs (& PTT)	21	(4)	49	(10)	3
Jobs in Schools	6	(1)			4
Vocational Schools	1				2
Unable to Find Work	17	(3)			4
Other	8	(2)			3
	494	(100)			100%

			(Parents):		
*Departments:		Railroad	31	(6)	** Parental
Basses-Alpes, Cantal,		*Rentiers*	8	(2)	Occupations
Haute-Savoie, Isère,		Other	9	(2)	are largely
Savoie, Vaculuse		Unemp.	4	(1)	those of
		Dead	11	(2)	fathers
			494	(100)	

SOURCE: Archives Nationales F[17] 11688–11690; Ministère de l'instruction publique, *Statistique de l'enseignement primaire* 8 (1909).

ment specified.[77] An *institutrice* born in the Hautes-Alpes later reminisced that without the encouragement of a teacher and the primary inspector, who persuaded her father to send her to a normal school, she probably would have become a laundress.[78] Urban girls of course had more options for employment. Furthermore, additional opportunities for females in white-collar jobs in government, private offices, or banks would open up during the first decades of the twentieth century. Of young women in *cours complémentaires* in the thirteenth arrondissement of Paris in 1917, one-third were preparing for teaching, one-third for commerce, and one-sixth for public administration and banking.[79]

Statistics on girls' educational achievements in primary, higher primary, and secondary schools may be correlated with changes in types of women's work and an increase in the number of women in government service and professions. Admittedly, most working women remained in low-status jobs at the end of the Third Republic, and their wages averaged only about 58 percent of men's wages.[80] But as jobs in stores and offices opened up to women, fewer entered the agricultural and industrial sectors of the economy and more turned to the tertiary or commercial and service sector. Between 1906 and 1936 the percentage of women workers who were in agriculture declined from 43 percent to 40 percent, and in the nonagricultural work force 8 percent fewer women were working in industry (including home production) in 1936 than in 1906 (Table 15). In turn, the tertiary sector employed 53 percent of nonfarm women workers in 1906 and 61 percent in 1936, and within that sector domestic service suffered a well-known decline in popularity.[81] Although the representation of women in the work force during these three decades was essentially static, at about 37 percent, a significant number left

Table 14. Future Activities of Girls Leaving *Cours Complémentaires* in Vienne (Isère), 1896–1898, and Occupations of Fathers and Mothers

Destination of Girls or Parental Professions	Girls	Fathers	Mothers
Normal School/Teaching	7	4	2
E.p.s. or 2dry School	5		
Workers/Apprentices	20	18	18
Stores & Offices	1	2	
Family Business/Shop	10	16	
Family Farm	1	5	5
Family Home (Housewife)	4		33
Family, Future Unknown	7		
Gov't. Jobs (PTT)	4 (all PTT)	4	
Other	1	2	1
Railroads		3	
Deceased		6	1
	60	60	60

SOURCE: AN F[17] 11689

the home to work at another location. In 1906, 36 percent of nonfarm working women—about 1.5 million—worked at home; by 1936, there were 700,000 fewer working women in this category.[82]

In government service and the professions, women registered significant gains. Whereas in 1866 only 164,000 of the nonagricultural female workers were so employed, by 1906 the figure was 315,000 (7 percent of nonfarm women workers) and in 1936, 647,000 (14 percent).[83] Teaching, a traditional profession for women, increasingly became more feminized. In 1906 women were 49 percent of public school personnel; in 1926 they were 59 percent, and in 1934, 66 percent. Women teachers were also 71 percent of private school staffs in 1926. Nursing had become another popular "feminine" occupation. In public administration the number of women approximately doubled between 1906 and 1926, when 185,000 were so employed. Within the public sector other than teaching, women who were clerks, secretaries, and functionaries rose from 2 percent of those employed in "public authorities and controllers' offices" in 1906 to 36 percent in 1926; from 2 percent to 11 percent in departmental and municipal services; from 22 percent to 31 percent in the postal service; and from 1 percent to 13 percent in "registration, taxes, and customs."[84]

Table 15. Evolution of Women's Work, 1896–1936

Area of Occupation	1896	1906	1926	1936
Agriculture, Fishing, Forest	2,760,000	3,330,000	3,391,000	2,922,000
Manufacturing (Factory & Home)	1,716,000	2,058,000	1,998,000	1,689,000
Mines, Construction, Utils.	9,000	8,000	24,000	22,000
Commerce, Banks, Insurance	510,000	642,000	780,000	859,000
Transport, Communications	161,000	241,000	160,000	132,000
Services, consisting of:	*1,219,000*	*1,422,000*	*1,487,000*	*1,698,000*
Gov't & teaching	88,000	107,000	201,000	247,000
Armed Forces	1,000	1,000		
Liberal Professions	202,000	208,000	302,000	400,000
Hotels, Cafes	236,000	326,000	296,000	338,000
Personal Services (e.g., Nurses, Concierges, Beauticians), Domestics	692,000	781,000	688,000	713,000
Total	6,375,000	7,701,000	7,840,000	7,321,000

SOURCE: Paul Bairoch et al, *La Population active et sa structure* (Brussels: Institut de l'université libre, 1968), pp. 172–174.

Earning educational credentials was not, of course, the only explanation for the growing representation of women in white-collar work. Economic change increased the demand for those with such credentials. The tertiary sector of the economy expanded during the first decades of the twentieth century, while agriculture declined slightly and industry remained relatively static. Thus there were more positions for men as well as women in commerce, banking, government service, and the professions, but the statistical changes for men were less striking. Men working in industry represented 53 percent of nonagricultural male workers in 1906 and 51 percent in 1936, while those in commerce, banking, and insurance increased from 40 percent of male nonfarm workers in 1906 to 44 percent in 1936. The increase in the number of male professionals and public servants from 845,000 in 1906 to 1,081,000 in 1936 was, again, a much less noticeable increase than the doubling of the number of women in these occupational categories.[85]

Despite the high percentage of women in the work force, higher primary school textbooks at the end of the Third Republic, like regular primary texts, still placed most women in domestic settings, and they presented natalist views far more explicitly than before World War I. Félicien Challaye and Marguerite Reynier, secondary school teachers whose socialist sympathies were apparent in praise for Jean Jaurès and Lucien Herr, in no way gave a revolutionary view of woman's roles in *Cours de morale* (1939). They designated founding a family a duty which no one should shirk unless in bad health. To prefer vain personal pleasures to fecundity was both immoral and absurd. Large families presumably had the added advantage that children acquire a sense of solidarity with others, something denied to the only child. Workers had bigger families than the selfish bourgeoisie, they remarked. However, the authors' leftist leanings did not prevent the assignment of stereotypical personality traits to men and women: men were protectors and women were "gentle" beings who softened the rough edges of men and added grace to family life. Now that wifely obedience had been removed from article 213 of the Civil Code in 1938, the obligations of spouses could be defined simply as mutual assistance, fidelity, and devotion.[86]

Challaye and Reynier did expect women to prepare for a métier, but they stressed that the one chosen should be neither too physically strenuous nor demanding of large amounts of time away from home, where woman fulfilled her most important role—maternity. Despite these restrictions on occupational choice, the authors insisted that a young woman could find something suiting her aptitudes, tastes, and resources and at the same time enabling her to develop "all the

riches of her nature." For collateral reading they referred girls to
Nouvelles lectures professionnelles (1928) by their colleagues Rogie,
Bornecque, and Madame Levesque. If students and teachers picked
up this other textbook for the higher primary school, they discovered
a chapter on "Feminine Professions." It opened with the encouraging
assertion that women were not only housewives but also store clerks,
factory workers, typists, government employees, and even lawyers
and doctors. But after this progressive introduction to the myriad
professional possibilities for women, the authors announced that the
rest of the chapter (twenty-eight pages) would discuss woman's
"natural role in the family" and, secondarily, the humble professions
of servant and worker. The ten excerpts which followed all glorified
woman's domestic role. The one example of a wage earner was an
embroiderer.[87] Such were the role models presented to young women
at a level of schooling which, for their brothers, was intended to
bring "children of the people" into the ranks of the lower middle
class in low-level or middle-level supervisory, business, and administrative positions.

Although young women graduating from higher primary schools
were by the 1930s more likely to opt for teaching, government jobs,
or office work than embroidery, the messages in school texts about
women's work outside the home did not give a very positive image
of such employment. Enjoined to remember that women's professions
should always take second place to familial responsibilities, they were
primed to experience that familiar double bind of conflict between
work and family roles. Feminists, socialists, and other reformers
have drawn attention to the plight of women caught in this conflict.
No society has yet eliminated it. During the Third Republic educators
simply counseled women to adapt to the demands of both work and
family life and never to forget that it was more desirable for them
to remain at home as full-time mothers if the family's financial
position permitted it.

Textbooks for the primary school and the higher primary school
thus perpetuated the gap between the image of an ideal woman
ensconced at home and the reality of many women's everyday
working lives. If educators perceived and drew attention to this gap
at all, as did a woman inspector for girls' professional education in
the Seine in 1923 (cited above), they often did so in order to plead
for the creation of more jobs which women could perform at home
rather than in an office.[88] When the longtime *directrice* of the Seine's
normal school for women recommended in 1933 that women needing
to earn money work at home, she was clearly not holding out her
own career history as a viable model for all women.[89]

Chapter Six

From Vichy through the Fourth Republic

The collaborationist Vichy Regime did not need to import an ideology of *Kinder, Küche,* und *Kirche* from the conquering Nazis. The belief that "children" and "kitchen" were essential in a woman's life was a Third Republic legacy already familiar to secular educators. Although public school teachers could not officially assign comparable value to "church," Catholic pedagogues naturally accepted all of this feminine trinity. Vichy merely underlined the desirability of devotion to the foyer a bit more explicitly than the Third Republic. For a short time Marshal Pétain's traditionalist regime attempted to drive married women from the government work force through legislation in October 1940 and April 1941 but then rescinded it in September 1942.[1]

Vichy's educational policy, in effect in both the occupied and unoccupied zones, sought to inculcate the credo of "work, family, country" that replaced the republican trinity of "liberty, equality, fraternity." Because antidemocratic values were attached to the new national motto, civic instruction differed, in theory, from that of the Third Republic. Vichy civics texts expounded unquestioning obedience to a national leader and denounced the Third Republic for weakening the nation and spreading the "false idea of the natural equality of men."[2] In practice, claimed a postwar leader of the major teachers' union, many teachers omitted the ideology of Pétain's "National Revolution" from their classrooms, especially when no inspector was present."[3]

Although Vichy revised the civics program of the Third Republic, there was really nothing in previous moral instruction, already emphasizing devotion to family, country, and work, which need have upset the Pétainistes. But new regimes which come to power after assisting in the demise of predecessors tend to seek legitimacy for themselves by exaggerating the predecessor's faults. Pétain accused the primary schools of the Third Republic of deracinating youth and announced a new program for implanting traditional values in the next generation.[4] To the Third Republic's "duties to the family" in the official program for *morale* Vichy added the obligation "to found a family." Minister of education Emile Mireaux also lifted the 1904 prohibition on teaching in private schools by members of religious orders, and the next minister, Georges Ripert, yielded to the urgings of his assistant and successor, Jacques Chevalier, and made religious instruction an optional subject in public schools as of 6 December 1940. Although religious lessons were soon abandoned after the classicist Jérôme Carcopino took over the education ministry, the 1941 program did require connecting moral ideals to the nation's "Christian" heritage. This item could lend itself to anti-Semitism, but the program also called for teaching the importance of "tolerance," defined as "respect for the ideas and religious beliefs of others."[5]

Vichy's reorganization of the primary school aimed to reduce the "encyclopedic and theoretical character" of the curriculum and provide a larger place for "manual works." Ideally most students would leave school prepared to take up eagerly the traditional occupations of farmer or artisan. The pace of industrialization would be halted or even reduced, a realistic design in light of German control over French destinies at the moment but also one expressing the conservatism of Pétain and many associates who, like Barrès and other right-wing theorists since the late nineteenth century, believed that the solution to national problems lay in firmly rerooting Frenchmen "in the soil of France."[6]

In August 1941 two primary school "cycles" were created, the first for ages six to eleven, the second for ages eleven to fourteen. The second, intended for students not going on to more advanced schooling, stressed practical education. In effect, the Vichy program for the second cycle extended Zay's plan for the *classe de fin d'études* to a slightly younger age group. The general education segment of the second cycle thus retained an emphasis on local and regional culture, and vocational preparation continued to orient rural boys toward agriculture, urban boys toward commerce and industry, and girls toward homemaking.[7]

The higher primary schools, which prepared adolescents for more prestigious métiers than those envisioned for the *classes de fin d'études*, had been placed by Zay under the secondary school administrative structure, and were now renamed "collèges modernes." Although this was another step toward coordination of the different segments of post-primary schooling sought by reformers of the interwar period, Vichy intended it to perpetuate elites, not to promote Zay's democratization of the school. Nonetheless, the reform would endure in the postwar period.[8]

Under the short-lived Vichy regime most schoolbooks were carryovers from the Third Republic. The education ministry's twenty-three page list of acceptable texts, issued on 21 October 1940, included old public school classics like *Le Tour de la France* and Catholic books like Thiéry's *Elise*. Textbooks with anti-German statements were banned. Vichy appended a short list of unacceptable books to its list of October 1940, by which time German occupation authorities had also issued the first of several lists of forbidden texts. As of 31 July 1943 ninety-five titles had been banned.[9]

In light of previous emphasis on woman's role as wife and mother, especially as natalism intensified during the interwar years, it is not surprising that a sample of eleven textbooks published or reprinted during the war showed no significant changes in images of women.[10] L. P. Renaud's statement in *Notre morale "servir"* (1944) that the mother was the "soul" of the family and the father the "force" was no more striking a dichotomy between male and female than that in Ab der Halden's popular *Hors du nid*, still on Vichy's recommended book list.[11] However, in keeping with the new official instructions, *morale* texts added "le devoir de fonder une famille."[12] Not surprisingly, when teachers solemnly read population propaganda to their classes, adolescents, if not younger pupils, easily found something to ridicule. The sociologist Evelyne Sullerot has recalled that her class in a *collège mixte* responded to the pronouncement, "It is at the *collège* that we must learn to become parents," with laughter and the cry, "Oh, yes! immediately, immediately."[13]

Promoters of home economics instruction were pleased that Vichy's emphasis on vocational preparation for children aged eleven to fourteen finally gave their subject the importance they believed it had long deserved.[14] Appreciating greater interest in domestic education, Madame Foulon-Lefranc expanded her manuals *Ecole du bonheur* (1938) and *La Femme au foyer* (1938) by more than one-fourth. The enlarged *Ecole du bonheur* (1943) included sample questions and answers on homemaking from examinations for the certificate of primary studies, and some of these, virtually unchanged since the late nineteenth century, reinforced the regime's emphasis on woman's role at home. If asked to respond to a misinformed young woman who wished to work in a factory or office because staying at home was boring, girls should explain how one could spend a day "joyously" on "le travail de la maison." In the more distinctly Catholic *Femme au foyer* Mary remained the model homemaker whose performance of routine housekeeping tasks like washing and cleaning presumably showed the nobility in even the most humble work.[15]

Both Catholic and secular versions of Foulon-Lefranc's text had first appeared during the late Third Republic and remained in use after Vichy's collapse, for formal political changes had little effect on lessons on woman's familial obligations. The significant differences between republican textbooks and Vichy creations concerned political concepts and religious values which, unlike homemaking lessons, could not be transferred readily to the postwar republic. Vichy's civics lessons about the naturalness of social hierarchy and elitist rule rejected "false" democratic ideas, and *morale* texts reintroduced the word "God" and religious obligations.[16] After the Liberation, a few cosmetic changes left some textbooks of the Vichy era suitable for another republican regime. The 1948 edition of the *morale* book of Renaud, a normal school director, differed from the 1944 version only in the excision of a reference to religion as one source of morality, the change of the title from *Notre morale "servir"* to *La Vie morale de l'enfant*, and the related rewording of a section heading from "Servir la patrie" to "Les Devoirs envers la patrie." "Servir," once a respectable word to connect with patriotic obligations in the 1930s, was used in Vichy texts to teach unquestioning obedience to Pétain's regime.[17]

After World War II a coalition of leftist, centrist and Catholic groups active in the Resistance assumed political power, led until January 1946 by Charles DeGaulle, provisional president. The tripartite coalition of socialists, communists, and Catholic republicans affiliated with the new "Popular Republican Movement" (MRP) was reminiscent of the composition of the Popular Front, except that the MRP had replaced the anticlerical radical socialists as the dominant republican party in the coalition. The first ministries of the Fourth Republic launched a series of significant social and economic reforms, including nationalization of important sectors of the economy. Women benefited from the urge to remake society after the trauma of military defeat and the moral ambiguity of Vichy. DeGaulle awarded the right to vote to women in 1944, expecting their religious leanings to provide a moderate voting bloc to counteract the Left, stronger than ever after the war. The constitution of the Fourth Republic, adopted in 1946, stipulated that "the law guarantees to the woman, in all domains, rights equal to those of the man," and civics textbooks quickly incorporated this important statement.[18]

Women's participation in the first postwar parliament also demonstrated that at last French women were assuming an active role in public life. By 1956, however, the number of women in the National Assembly had dropped from the high of thirty-nine in 1946 to nineteen. Further declining to six in 1958, the number of female deputies was still only ten in 1972; in 1981 there would be twenty-six.[19] The dwindling number of women in highly visible political positions in the 1950s and the documentation of much less interest in politics on the part of women and girls than of men and boys were but one sign of the strength in postwar France of the ideas about woman's place which an American feminist in 1963 aptly dubbed the "feminine mystique."[20] Despite the enfranchisement of women, the director general of primary education stated in 1952 that the duty of the male teacher was to form "the man and the citizen," whereas the woman teacher formed "the housewife and mother."[21]

The school was but one of a group of institutions advocating renewed feminine devotion to domesticity. Also in the forefront in calling for "la femme au foyer" was the church. In 1948 Pope Pius XII asked for new policies and institutions "to bring back the wife and mother to her proper vocation in the heart of the domestic foyer."[22] One Catholic textbook identified the Communist party and the Communist labor union, the Confédération générale du travail, as the major opponents of the church's teachings about women's roles.[23]

Public school textbooks as well as Catholic ones glorified "la femme au foyer." And in postwar France, poised for an unprecedented level of prosperity, there was a better economic basis for believing that woman's place was at home. Many Third Republic textbooks, especially before 1914, had been adapted to the realities of a traditional economy of scarcity where both men and women of the rural and urban laboring classes had to work very hard for sheer survival. Repeated injunctions to stay in the country, included in many schoolbooks even in the 1920s and 1930s, had been an effort by educators to shore up an old way of rural life that men and women were, in fact, abandoning in droves in the hopes of finding something more profitable and satisfying in towns and cities. After World War II the lesson on staying in the country, the virtues of which had been trumpeted by Vichy, was often dropped in favor of teaching adaptation to urban life and discussing the availability of jobs in the industrial and service sectors of the economy.[24] Nonetheless, textbook authors remained cautious about encouraging expectations of social mobility and continued to depict many humble occupations.[25] The curriculum for applied science in the last grades, separated into rural and urban components for boys in 1923, was similarly divided for girls in 1953.[26] However, homemaking still predominated in the special girls' sections of science textbooks, for presentations on women's roles underwent less change than treatment of the relative merits of rural and urban life. Once again, economic considerations contributed to the prevalence of certain textbook images of women because in postwar France it was more possible than ever before for a worker to earn enough money so that his wife would not need to work. During the 1950s, for the first time since the late nineteenth century, the percentage of women in the "active" population actually dropped and did not rise again until the late 1960s.[27]

The state's social policies also provided economic incentives for a wife to stay home. The Fourth Republic expanded the system of family allowances initiated by the Third Republic, codified in 1939, and further promoted by the Vichy regime. Households with only one wage earner received special supplements, and financial rewards were offered for the birth of the second and each additional child. Women who began childbearing at an early age and then had additional children within three years of a previous birth received maternity benefits. Allowances for children continued so long as they were enrolled in a primary or secondary school, but there was also a special incentive for keeping adolescent girls home to help their mothers. If girls who finished primary school then assisted with the care of at least two children, their parents received an allowance for them until they were twenty.[28]

A sampling of thirty-seven textbooks from the Fourth Republic revealed that, as during the Third Republic, educators often advised girls to prepare for some type of work in case they needed to support themselves.[29] But married women were still much less likely to appear in textbooks as part of the work force, and explicit statements that married women should not work remained standard fare.[30] Inspector Souché's post-World War II morale texts, like his earlier ones, made domestic duties the most valued occupation for women. Although he praised women's role in businesses and on farms during the wartime absence of men, he left no doubt in Nouvelles leçons de morale (1945) that in peacetime the schoolgirl should expect to become a "ménagère and maîtresse de maison." "Domestic chores" had as much merit as work "outside the home," and childrearing was an essential national service. Judging the "peril of depopulation" the "greatest that France has ever known," Souché advised each couple to have at least three or four offspring.[31]

In January 1949 the education ministry added force to the natalist message conveyed by Souché and many others since the interwar years; it required adding demography lessons to morale.[32] Children would learn that a low birthrate had weakened France before 1939 and presumably would not repeat that error as adults. Textbooks for moral and civic instruction underscored the natalist message by including details about the state's family allowances and incentives for women not to work.[33] Science books, especially in puériculture sections, also referred to family subsidies and portrayed childrearing as a "duty" to oneself and the nation and "an assurance of happiness" for a couple.[34] In 1954, when the population was 42,781,000, one textbook put the ideal size for the French population at 60,000,000.[35] But despite natalist propaganda in the schools and financial incentives, the postwar increase in the birthrate was not large enough to reach that textbook goal or DeGaulle's target in 1962 of 100,000,000. The birthrate did rise from 148 per 10,000 citizens in 1936–1938 to 209 per 10,000 in 1949. In 1950 it began dropping slightly but as of 1958 still remained at 181, well above the historic lows of the Depression era.[36]

In keeping with papal emphasis on woman's natural maternal role, many Catholic textbooks not only reiterated old injunctions against women working outside the home but made them stronger. In 1947 Abbé Gaston Lecordier added to the usual reasons why women should not work—neglect of children and household—the point that feminine employment damaged the male ego. His outrage that an unemployed man might end up as a *ménagère* while his wife worked was a remarkable handling of economic realities. Lecordier favored women's occupations that could be pursued at home and, not wishing to encourage would-be emulators of Marie Curie, judged women's employment in scientific fields the most incompatible with family life.[37]

Although readers of the Fourth Republic were less didactic than contemporary *morale* texts or readers of an earlier era and also more likely to offer stories with purely imaginary rather than real-life settings,[38] many still relegated boys and girls, men and women to traditional gender roles. The postwar version of the Catholic *André et Jacqueline* had three new chapters, two dealing with women's domestic roles. One was a lesson on washing clothes; the other was about "Mother's Day," first recognized as a special occasion in France during the 1920s and much promoted by Pétain. The text did mirror the greater likelihood after 1945 that girls would attend secondary school, for heroine Jacqueline was now destined to try for the *bac*, like her brother.[39] But whether additional education would lead her to a career was in doubt, for Jacqueline would still take a private homemaking course and presumably heed her father's advice, added in the postwar version, that even as a schoolgirl she could start preparing for the maternal role to be assumed in ten or fifteen years. Dad recommended learning to sacrifice herself for others as excellent training for what lay ahead.[40]

In contrast to the predominantly domestic orientation in lessons about girls' futures in many textbooks, secular and Catholic, *Pour nos filles* (1957), a reader for eleven-year-olds by Jeanne Séguin and Pauline Millett, presented a remarkable variety of adult role models. The publisher Larousse advertised *Pour nos filles* as part of its long tradition of girls' books, epitomized by Juranville's volumes of the

Third Republic. However, the range of nondomestic options offered by Séguin, a school inspector for the Seine, and Millett, a teacher, differed greatly from the confining prescriptions on domesticity characteristic of all Juranville's books except *Le troisième livre de lecture*.

While identifying many family obligations as woman's special responsibility, Séguin and Millett demonstrated that occupational possibilities had expanded significantly for women. Half the book consisted of stories that followed the feminine life cycle through infancy, girlhood, adolescence, marriage, motherhood, aunthood, and grandmotherhood and depicted women in domestic activities. The other half presented women at work. Traditional occupations were not absent: farm wife, laundress, seamstress, embroiderer, lacemaker, salesclerk, secretary. But there were also stories about women in the professions—not only the familiar *institutrice*, secondary school *professeur*, and nurse but also a lawyer and a doctor. One selection on Marie Curie showed her discrediting the "prejudice" which had long made "people consider the sciences inaccessible for female intellects." Rosa Bonheur, Marie Laurencin, Sarah Bernhardt, and Colette represented women's achievements in the arts and letters. Other selections portrayed women in unexpected activities: mountain climbing in Asia, exploring (with a husband) in Africa, and flying airplanes. Finally, there were women valiant in wartime—a group more traditionally found in girls' textbooks than professionals, scholars, artists, and writers. Joan of Arc, Jeanne Hachette, Madame Roland, and Florence Nightingale, all in this gallery of heroines, had been familiar examples of women's patriotism in textbooks of the Third Repubic. To update the list, Séguin and Millett added two women from the Resistance, two aviatrixes noted for "independence" and "ambition," and a final selection on Madame Curie at work.[41]

Although half the book dealt with women's domestic roles, no other textbook of the Third or Fourth Republics showed women engaged in such a wide range of activities. That Larousse printed only 30,000 copies and withdrew it from the market after five years was probably more a sign of the disfavor into which special girls' textbooks other than science and home economics manuals had fallen on the eve of the era of coeducation than an indication that many teachers completely rejected its images of women achievers, however exceptional such women were. Members of the educational establishment writing a textbook for an old firm like Larousse were not likely to have views unacceptable to most colleagues. Indeed, Séguin has indicated that the large number of examples of women at work was included primarily because the book would be read by working class girls who were more likely than their middle class sisters to need to earn a living.[42]

Less realistic than Séguin and Millett were the many educators, male and female, who did not emulate *Pour nos filles'* special efforts to make girls aspire to combining domesticity with careers, some traditionally male. When Hélène Sourgen, an *inspectrice générale* of national education, wrote on women's civic education for a UNESCO publication in 1954, she began with the old assumption that men and women had different types of minds well suited to their distinctive social roles. Women were generally concerned with "concrete situations" and "rarely" rose to the level of "metaphysical speculations." They were capable of "conscientious and methodical" attention to "well-defined tasks," but "personal creations" by them were rare. Woman's attentiveness to detail and warm, intuitive approach to learning and living made her the ideal "guardian of life" in the foyer. From the different natures and destinies of males and females it followed, Sourgen intoned, that girls and boys should not have identical educations. Even if they studied the same subjects, they required a different orientation. Girls' civic education should emphasize the social value of woman's role in the family. Hence future homemakers needed to know about (1) economical use of household funds, (2) the responsibility to bear children, (3) the obligation to teach children respect for laws and country, and (4) ways to function as "chef de famille" in the event of widowhood or divorce. All four points were reminiscent of standard lessons on woman's patriotism conveyed in the Third Republic's textbooks and examination questions. Although Sourgen was well aware that many French women (including married women) worked outside the home, she insisted that their civic education be oriented not toward active participation in political life but rather toward what they most valued: foyer and children.[43] Little wonder that when researchers surveyed the knowledge of politics possessed by elementary school boys and girls in 1961, a striking disparity between the sexes was already apparent at ages eleven and twelve. Girls were less inclined than boys to affirm that a country should be run by a representative assembly rather than by a single man (52 percent of girls vs. 65 percent of boys), and they were also more dubious about the value of the Revolution of 1789 (39 percent of girls rated it a good thing vs. 63 percent of boys).[44]

The traditional perspective on woman's place also appeared in an educational encyclopedia published in 1960 by the Institut pédagogique national. Writing on "l'enseignement ménager," Henriette Sourgen asserted that "parents and girls know with certainty today that, whatever girls undertake to earn their living, whatever they can try in the domain of science, arts, commerce, whatever be their profession, employment, métier, it is undeniable that marriage and maternity are their essential vocation." She blamed feminists for misleading women about the true nature of personal happiness and causing misguided searches for situations women could not attain. Sourgen's views were not simply special pleading for the importance of home economics, long neglected by many colleagues. In the article on post-primary technical education for girls Marthe Broussin wrote that a "professional formation" for a trade also enabled a young woman to enhance the quality of family life. "To create, in her house and around her, thanks to the artistic formation received, the good habits acquired, [and] the qualities developed by the discipline of *travaux manuels*, this atmosphere of order, simplicity, equilibrium, sober elegance"—this was how a woman produced the "moral and physical comfort" important not only to her own family but for the well-being of society.[45]

Thus during the Fourth and early Fifth Republics many educators, female and male, still stated explicitly that a woman's most important role was domestic. Praised for the moral and material comforts that she brought her family and reassured that her role was important for the nation as well, the French woman who was "queen" or "angel" of the foyer[46] paid the price of restrictions in spheres of life beyond that foyer. Because a majority of teachers, like other social and professional groups, believed during the 1950s and early 1960s that woman's place was at home, they often gave girls the impression that woman's paid employment was generally a temporary activity ended when marriage and children made the primary claims on one's time.[47] Even educators who argued that girls should take their professional "formation" as seriously as boys and view their chosen métier as a lifetime activity, rather than something transient, imposed limits on feminine aspirations so that women's work would not interfere with their natural role in the family.[48]

The uncompromising nature of so many educators' pronouncements on a woman's place undoubtedly represented an effort to establish a firm position on an issue about which there was actually much debate and uncertainty. Textbooks of the Third Republic had stated repeatedly that solidarity between social classes prevailed in France, despite political and economic crises which often indicated that the opposite was true. Similarly, assertions after World War II that woman's place was at home frequently seemed an effort to alter what was already the common reality of many working women exiting from the home for at least part of the day. Some textbooks recommended classroom debate over whether woman's place was in the foyer, and teachers tried such discussion, sometimes in the hope that it would stir up special interest in a passive class.[49] Although the percentage of the active population that was female dropped after World War II, the percentage of women workers engaged in nonagricultural employment actually rose.[50]

Surveys on attitudes toward women's work, parents' occupational aspirations for girls, and girls' own ambitions during the Fourth and early Fifth Republics indicate that many parents and daughters subscribed to the "feminine mystique" promoted by the school and other institutions. A poll conducted in 1946 by the French Institute of Public Opinion (IFOP) recorded that 71 percent of respondents preferred that women remain at home rather than work. Only 10 percent named the second option, while another 18 percent answered "it depends."[51] During the 1950s "la femme au foyer" remained the ideal of many teachers as well as the general public, although women teachers were significantly more sympathetic to women's careers than men. In 1953–1954 51 percent of male teachers and 35 percent of female teachers interviewed in the department of the Seine thought that women belonged at home; 28 percent of men and 40 percent of women favored female employment; and the rest answered, "it depends." Since 67 percent of the male teachers' wives worked, it is clear that the expressed ideal often conflicted with economic necessity or women's own preferences.[52]

Differences between male and female views of women's work also appeared in a detailed study of contemporary attitudes toward women conducted in the Paris region in 1958. Equal numbers of working class, middle class, and upper class married couples—360 men and women in all—were interviewed. All groups divided on the general question, "should women work?": 41.6 percent said yes and 41.3 percent said no. But 57 percent of women responded affirmatively, as compared to only 27 percent of men. Of the 56 percent of men who expressed hostility to jobs for women, upper class men were the least hostile (48 percent), middle class men more hostile (55 percent), and working class men, most likely to have wives in the work force, the most hostile (65 percent). Among women, 18 percent of middle class wives, 27 percent of working class wives, and 35 percent of upper class wives opposed jobs for women. Yet when interviewers asked specifically whether single women or childless married women should work, respondents significantly adjusted their idealized images of women. Fully 97.5 percent of both sexes approved of work for the single and 75 percent for married women without children. However, the overwhelming majority (87.5 percent) disapproved of work for women with pre-school age children, and a substantial majority (68 percent) of work by those with children in school. Middle class women were more likely than upper class or working class women to question the image of a woman bound to home, not only because they realized that a wife's salary could provide a higher standard of living and extra benefits for children but also because their above average education opened the way to satisfying careers. Nonetheless, most of these middle class women believed that home should be the central focus for married women and so, like most nineteenth-century women and contemporary working class women, still viewed women's employment within the context of the family economy. Polled about the importance of eight possible reasons for women to work, the men and women, most of whom had been schooled during the Third Republic, ranked financial need and providing educational benefits for children far ahead of the next two reasons, which were more directly related to meeting a woman's own needs: namely, her interest in a career and avoiding boredom at home.[53]

For comparative purposes, the views of one hundred university students on women's activities were also tabulated by the sociologists conducting this 1958 study. Although the young people schooled during the Fourth Republic favored work for women more than did other adults, a striking disparity between male and female views remained. Among women students, 82 percent believed that women should work; among men, only 46 percent.[54] Clearly, young women were not insensitive to differences between their own views of what they wished to be and their male counterparts' attitudes. In a survey whose results were published in 1960, 68 percent of young women aged seventeen to twenty selected as the most desirable of three models of young women the one who prepared for a métier, expected to marry, but would not need to depend on a man to assure her existence. However, only 8 percent of those surveyed also thought that males their age currently preferred such a companion, and only 38 percent thought that males, once more mature, would prefer to marry this independent woman instead of a more traditional woman who, although a serious student, intended, once married, to devote herself to the foyer.[55]

That teenage girls' attitudes toward work also varied according to social class was borne out by two studies of apprentices and lycée students. Asked to rank the importance of some thirty-six characteristics for adolescentes and adult women, the two groups of young women agreed that feminine personalities were marked by such traditional traits as the predominance of "sentiments" over "reason," the "desire to please," "generosity," and "self-sacrifice." However, the apprentices ranked the desire for success at work much higher in importance (fifteenth place) than did lycéennes, who saw this as the least important of all traits evaluated. Apprentices' responses to additional questions on woman's roles nonetheless indicated that their higher valuation of work was not tantamount to believing that work would "liberate" women but rather confirmed that they saw work as an unavoidable financial necessity. About two-thirds of both apprentices and *lycéennes* agreed that "equality" between the sexes existed but that this equality was "moral" rather than "professional" because "the normal and natural role of women is to stay at home; the normal and natural role of man is to work, to earn money." Although both groups, like their elders, subscribed to the ideal of "la femme au foyer," *lycéennes* had a better developed perception of women's "rights." Nearly twice as many *lycéennes* (35 percent) as apprentices (19 percent) agreed that "in order for equality truly to exist" between the sexes, "woman must be able to choose her profession and earn her living like men." In turn, apprentices were eight times more likely than secondary students (16 percent versus 2 percent) to adopt the distinctly minority viewpoint that the idea of "equality" between the sexes is "false and dangerous" and threatens to destroy the family because a "wife owes obedience to her husband."[56]

Differences between bourgeois and working class *Weltanschauungen* were also confirmed by a second study which asked young men and women to indicate how they defined "success" in life. Not surprisingly, the males valued material and professional success more than women, but both male and female working class adolescents rated material success as more important than did the middle class students of either sex (Table 16). In turn, realization of one's human potential (*réalisation de soi-même*) was much more a bourgeois than a working class ideal. Among young women, it was clear that material gain occupied in working class notions of achievement about the same place that self-realization occupied for the middle classes, who probably often took material comfort for granted. Material gain was ranked as the chief sign of success by 30 percent of working class girls, as compared to 13 percent of *lycéennes*; and self-realization came first for 35 percent of *lycéennes* and only 13 percent of their working class counterparts.[57]

Since the young female apprentices in the first study also believed that work was less important for married women than for themselves, they, like the adults polled in 1958, demonstrated that general attitudes toward work for single women and for the married continued to differ. However, the likelihood that young working class women would have to support themselves for a while or help with family finances meant that parents as well as daughters appreciated the links between education and jobs. After World War II, as before, working class and farm families continued to find the primary school certificate useful for their children's futures, although it was not

Table 16. Adolescents' Criteria for Success in Life

| | Boys | | Girls | |
Criteria	Group I* (142 answers)	Group II* (114 answers)	Group I* (183 answers)	Group II* (132 answers)
I. Social Success				
A. Material Success	27%	41%	13%	30%
B. Professional Success	27%	18%	22%	19%
Total	54%	59%	35%	49%
II. Emotional Success (Family, Friends)	20%	29%	31%	37%
III. Self-Realization	26%	11%	35%	13%

* Group I: secondary school students; Group II: primary school graduates, either apprentices or salaried workers

SOURCE: Bianka Zazzo, "La Représentation de la réussite chez les adolescents," L'Enfance 15 (1962): 279.

essential for the increasing numbers going on to secondary schools. In a 1950 poll three-fourths of parents rated the *c.e.p.* as necessary to their children's futures; only one-third assigned that importance to the *bac*.[58] By 1952 girls received 49.2 percent of the primary certificates.[59] Examinations for the *c.e.p.* tested ability to memorize as much as ever, and, as Laurence Wylie observed in a village in the Vaucluse during the early 1950s, teachers still drilled only good students for them. Memorization was, of course, not tantamount to comprehension. Thus a Paris school inspector noted with some amusement that on the oral section of the exam one girl, when asked what she knew about Joan of Arc, replied that when she grew up she hoped to become a *pucelle* (virgin) just like Joan, even though she had heard her parents say that this was difficult to achieve. Most girls presumably associated other ambitions with earning the *c.e.p.* Jeannette Roussel reported that although the girls she taught in a *classe de fin d'études* in Paris showed little enthusiasm for learning, many were determined to get the *c.e.p.* in order to obtain a good job.[60] Those with a certificate in hand were in a more competitive position than the one-third of the school population which at the end of the Fourth Republic left school without it or any secondary education.[61] The 1962 census indicated that among the general female population 40 percent had an educational credential; among women workers 49.6 percent possessed the *c.e.p.* or something better.[62]

What girls actually went on to do immediately after primary schooling during the Fourth Republic often depended on their families' social position, something also true for boys. Although material and professional success was as important, and sometimes more important, to working class as to middle class teenagers, the former were much less likely to choose (or be able to choose) to pursue this goal through post-primary education during the 1950s. Daughters as well as sons of farmers and workers were much less numerous than offspring of the middle classes among the 30 percent of boys and girls who in 1953 left the primary school at age eleven or twelve for a more advanced type of school. And few children from poor backgrounds were among the 5 percent of schoolchildren who attended the special elementary classes attached to *lycées* and *collèges* and nearly always began secondary studies. In 1953, 83 percent of the daughters of the upper class (bourgeoisie) left the primary school at age eleven or twelve to begin advanced studies; for the middle class, the figure was 37 percent; for the working class, 20 percent; and for peasants, 15 percent. Both girls and boys were also much less likely to go on to secondary schools of either the academic or technical variety if they stayed in the primary school until age 14, the limit for compulsory schooling, for fully 90 percent of those who obtained any post-primary schooling during the 1950s had changed schools at age eleven.[63]

The vocational objectives of girls attending post-primary schools were often less clearly developed than those of boys, but their exposure to advanced schooling did make it more likely that they would enter and remain in the work force. As compared to boys who left primary school at age eleven or twelve for another type of school, girls were slightly less likely to choose secondary schools (50 percent girls, 54 percent boys), less likely to choose technical instruction (3 percent girls, 8 percent boys), and more likely to opt for the *cours complémentaire* (39 percent girls, 30 percent boys).[64] The census of 1954 indicated that among women aged fifteen to sixty-five, 41 percent of those without any educational credential worked but that 65 percent of those with the *baccalauréat* or *brevet supérieur* and 75 percent of those with a university degree worked.[65] Women who had received post-primary vocational training in métiers other than the low-paying couture were also more likely to remain in the work force than those who had not.[66]

Just as girls going on to post-primary studies often chose programs with somewhat less clearly defined career objectives than boys, so, too, girls who left school at age fourteen often opted for activities indicating less expectation of the need to work for a living over the course of a lifetime. Parents—and especially mothers—tended to have less ambitious career plans for girls than for boys, and girls' educational choices often reflected adjustment to these reduced expectations, which other individuals and institutions beyond the family reinforced.[67] The number of girls neither in school nor at work at age fourteen in 1954 was noticeably higher than that of boys. Whereas 11 percent of girls had "no activity" after leaving school and another 12 percent received some homemaking training, only 3 percent of boys were without work.[68] Of the other girls leaving school at age fourteen, 18 percent of middle class and 33 percent of workers' daughters went directly to work; and 11 percent of middle class, 18 percent of working class, and 4 percent of farm girls began apprenticeships. Most likely to remain at home, perhaps eventually taking a homemaking course, were farmers' daughters, three-fourths of whom presumably helped their parents with household and farm chores after age fourteen. In comparison, about one-sixth of workers' and middle class girls, and 7 percent of bourgeois girls remained at home after age fourteen.[69] The difference between the choices of rural and urban girls leaving school at an early age was thus far more striking than the differences between urban girls from different social backgrounds in this group.

Table 17. Enrollments in Post-Primary Education, 1938–1958

| | Public Schools | | | | | | Private Schools | | | |
| | Cours Complémentaires | | Ecoles Primaires Supérieures | | Lycées and Collèges | | Cours Complémentaires | | Lycées and Collèges | |
	Boys	Girls	Boys	Girls	Boys	Girls	Boys	Girls	Boys	Girls
1938	56,900	67,600	50,800	54,500	133,900	66,600	8,400	34,600		
1941	58,700	70,900	41,100	41,900	126,000	69,700	13,200	35,700	95,700*†	71,500*†
1948	80,200	100,700	(included as		192,500*	158,500*	18,500	41,900	88,800*†	93,300*†
1953	107,400	132,400	collèges as		224,600*	207,500*	23,300	46,100	98,700*	107,900*
1958	185,600	224,700	of 1942)		327,200*	332,500*	37,800	66,200	131,800*	141,100*

(* Estimated figures. Available public secondary school totals for 1943–1958 and private secondary totals for 1920–1958 include special primary classes in the secondary enrollments for each sex. Figures above were obtained by subtracting the estimated primary class enrollment from the published totals.

† Estimated from statistics for years 1942 and 1949.)

SOURCE: *Annuaire statistique de la France* (1966), pp. 137–142.

Of special concern to researchers disturbed during the Fourth Republic by the relative lack of scholastic achievement for lower class children, in comparison to middle and upper class offspring, were those who received good grades but still left school at age fourteen. One 1955 study estimated that 15 percent of pupils with "excellent" or "good" marks did not go beyond the primary school, although this happened much less often in urban areas such as the Seine, where only 5 percent of bright children did not continue studies. The most noticeable difference between reasons cited by bright boys and by girls to explain discontinuing school was in attitudes toward work. For boys the wish to work was the most common reason for leaving school early; 31 percent of boys but only 15 percent of girls cited this explanation. Typically girls mentioned the lack of financial resources to continue school (25 percent) or the need to help parent (25 percent), reasons also given, respectively, by 22 percent and 20 percent of boys.[70] Another explanation which the authors of this study might have addressed but did not was the lack of encouragement from teachers concerned about the social maladjustment which bright but poor children might experience if they tried to rise too far above humble family origins. Even in the Paris region, where one might expect teachers to view social mobility as a more realistic possibility than in rural areas, a majority of teachers during the 1950s feared, in a fashion reminiscent of Barrès's classic novel of 1897, that poor but bright children would suffer from "déracination" if their occupational and educational expectations were raised too far.[71]

These studies of girls' attitudes and educational choices were conducted at a time when the primary school was losing the place in the preparation of a majority of French children for adult life that it had held during the Third Republic. By 1958 the number of children attending some type of public post-primary school was 2.2 times what it had been in 1938, a sign that nearly one out of every three children now went beyond the primary school. In secondary education girls had also become as numerous as boys, their enrollment slightly exceeding that of boys for the first time in 1958 (Table 17). At the university level women had also risen from 27 percent of the student body in 1936 to 37 percent in 1957.[72] Soaring post-primary enrollments after World War II demonstrated that both students and parents were more likely to view additional education as necessary for obtaining a well-paying position. Employers, in turn, wanted a better educated work force. Reforms to "democratize" and expand secondary education were, therefore, much discussed during the Fourth Republic, but they were not launched until 1959.

CHAPTER SEVEN

The Fifth Republic: Educational Reforms and Reevaluations of Girls' Schooling

During the Fifth Republic the secondary school, especially in its less prestigious form of the *collège d'enseignement secondaire* or *collège d'enseignement général*, assumed much of the role in the preparation for work and citizenship that the primary school had played for parents and grandparents during the Third Republic.[1] Now limited to ages six to eleven, primary school was gradually shorn of the "superior" classes and "classes de fin d'études" that previously had helped equip twelve-to-fourteen-year-olds for life after school.

Efforts to make post-primary education less elitist and more democratic began with some important reforms in January 1959, a few months after an impressive majority had approved de Gaulle's constitution for the new Fifth Republic. The age for compulsory schooling was raised from fourteen to sixteen, but because this statute did not apply to children who had entered school before 1959, its real effects would be felt only in 1967, by which time more badly needed secondary facilities were to be in place. In the meantime, classes for twelve-to-fourteen-year-olds in existing primary and secondary schools were to become a transitional "observation cycle" that, ideally, would channel students toward the type of post-primary school most appropriate for their talents and needs.[2] The former *cours complémentaires* that would participate in this process were rebaptized *collèges d'enseignement général*. Not surprisingly, the special elementary classes in secondary school were judged incompatible with the presumably egalitarian thrust of the observation cycle. Technically abolished by an *ordonnance* of 3 March 1945, these classes had in fact subsequently experienced an increase in enrollment that peaked in 1956; they finally disappeared from the institutional scene during the 1960s. Accompanying their demise was another new institution, the *collège d'enseignement secondaire*, a French version of the American junior

151

high school. Originated in 1963, this institution was intended to function as a genuine *école unique* that would overcome an obvious problem with the original implementation of the observation cycle—namely, that only 1 percent of students "oriented" in classes housed in primary schools were making the transition to academic secondary schools.[3]

Public school teachers, who had long called for "democratizing" the school system, at last saw the results of two generations of pressuring for such change. However, they were not enthusiastic about a different educational benchmark of 1959, the Loi Debré of 31 December that created a mechanism for state financing of private schools which provided far more funds than the allocation already instituted by the Loi Barangé of 1951. Nearly eleven million signatures protesting the Loi Debré were collected in 1960, but by 1966, 62 percent of those polled in one survey supported aid to private schools, a sign that outside the ranks of the political Left the heated anticlerical passions of the Third Republic had cooled considerably.[4] Members of the Fédération de l'éducation nationale (FEN) who found the Loi Debré's breach of separation of church and state hard to accept were in the difficult position of having their hostility perceived as a case of their acting primarily to serve their own professional self-interest.

Changes in the primary school curriculum that accompanied the restructuring of the educational system at the end of the 1950s also testified to the altered role of the primary school. As more children headed for secondary schools, the primary school continued to emphasize reading, writing, and arithmetic but gave less attention to other subjects useful for inculcating work discipline and appropriate civic behavior. In 1956, in the interests of helping working class children whose parents were presumably less able to assist with school assignments, the education ministry had formally eliminated homework for primary students and reallocated five hours of the thirty-hour school week to "devoirs" which previously would have been homework. In practice, many parents and teachers were appalled by this breach with tradition and so both groups have often conspired to ignore this still extant ban on home assignments.[5] But as a result of the 1956 regulation, there remained in the school week for the *cours moyen* only six hours for *morale*, history and geography, *exercices d'observation*, manual works, drawing, and singing. Similarly, between 1969 and 1978 fifteen hours of the school week, now reduced to twenty-seven hours, were devoted to French and mathematics, six to physical education and recreation, and six to "disciplines d'éveil," a rubric for what remained of social studies and sciences as well as drawing and singing. By contrast, a student in a *cours moyen* of the 1920s would have found 9¾ to 10¼ hours of a thirty-hour week devoted to academic and practical subjects other than the 3 Rs or physical education.[6] Paralleling curricular changes, readers of the early Fifth Republic became much less didactic in tone and presented more purely imaginary tales and depictions of children at play rather than at work.[7]

Curricular reform and nearly universal advancement to secondary schools for those entering school in 1959 or later would not bring an end to well-founded criticism that the public primary school "divides" French children according to social origins instead of equalizing chances for success in later life. Once secondary schooling became universal, the problem of children having to repeat primary school grades drew increasing attention. Using statistics from 1965 to 1970, Christian Baudelot and Roger Establet demonstrated that among six-year-olds in the *cours préparatoire*, the offspring of workers and farmers were four to five times more likely to have to repeat this "first" grade than children of professionals. Fully 26 to 30 percent of workers' and farmers' children had to repeat it (*redouble*), and these repeaters were also more likely to repeat later grades. Of workers' children born in 1959, only 36 percent would avoid repeating a class and be ready to leave the last primary grade (*cours moyen-2*) at the "normal" age of eleven. In comparison, 77 percent of professionals' children born in 1959 would have an uninterrupted progression through the primary school.[8] American-style policies of "social" promotion of virtually all students in an age group were thus not a French norm.

By the early 1980s *redoublement* was more in the educational limelight than ever, for 1979–1980 statistics indicated that despite attention to the problem during the 1970s, only 60 percent of children who had entered school in 1975 had reached the second year of the *cours moyen* at the normal age of ten.[9] Although girls were less likely to repeat grades than boys—10 percent less often, according to one 1973 study[10]—both sexes were much affected. Those concerned about the dilemma focused attention not only on the curriculum but also on the nature of teacher-student relationships and suggested that the social origins of teachers, less modest than during the Third Republic, sometimes produced a cultural gap between themselves and their charges. There was also speculation that the feminization of the teaching corps (67 percent female at the primary level in 1979), coupled with the fact that the social background of women teachers was more middle class than that of male colleagues, contributed to the somewhat greater difficulties of boys in primary schools.[11] However, such charges needed to be counterbalanced by the consideration that attending pre-primary *écoles maternelles*— as virtually all four- and five-year-olds did by 1982—seemed to be the most important factor enabling children from disadvantaged backgrounds to progress normally through primary school and that 99 percent of all teachers in *écoles maternelles* were women.[12]

The breakdown of segregation by gender in schools accompanied other educational reforms of the Fifth Republic. In 1959 the education ministry decreed that all newly created secondary schools should be "mixed" and in 1966 mandated coeducation for the primary school, too.[13] Whereas in the mid-1960s 66 percent of public school primary classes were separate ones for boys and girls, by the mid-1970s coeducation was nearly universal (Table 18).[14] At the same time, coeducation increasingly became the norm in private schools; in 1966 only 15 percent of private elementary classes were mixed; in 1973, 63 percent.[15] Long traditional in small country towns, *mixité* came to urban areas in the 1960s and 1970s, in some cases over the objections of concerned parents. One principal of a public primary school in the fifth arrondissement of Paris reported that the introduction of coeducation in his school in 1975 had prompted objections from mothers that their sons would be deflected from serious study by the presence of girls and that mixing the sexes at the ages of nine or ten could have dubious moral consequences.[16] In general, however, parental attitudes toward coeducation had evolved considerably from a majority hostile to it in 1952 to a majority in favor of it by the mid-1960s.[17] For private schools, too, there had been a noticeable change of attitude since the condemnation of coeducation by Pope Pius XI in 1929 and the insistence of Pius XII in 1951 that if mixed classes were necessary, boys and girls must sit on separate sides of the room.[18] As for children's reactions, one eleven-year-old Parisian girl whose school became *mixte* only in 1975 wrote during that first year, "A girls' school or a boys' school is less complete than an *école mixte*. A boys' school has a brutal aspect with fights and violent games, a girls' school gives instead an impression of a calmer life, which always has the same routine. . . . The ideal would be to mix all schools so that boy-girl relationships are no longer remarked upon and become natural."[19]

Coeducation did not end the conveying of different messages about adult roles to boys and girls, and both sexes continued to be influenced by such presentations. During the late 1960s the sociologist Marie José Chombart de Lauwe drew attention to the differences between images of male and female activities in textbooks, television programs, and films and argued that these differences helped determine boys' and girls' expectations for themselves. Children at the *cours moyen* level were asked, first, to select the child character whom they most admired in a book, film, or television program. Boys were chosen by 94 percent of boys but also by 50 percent of girls. A second

Table 18. Coeducation in Primary Schools

	Number of Schools				Number of Classes	
	Total	One-Room Schools	Mixed Schools	Boys' or Girls'	Mixed	Boys' or Girls'
Public						
1958	73,059	19,522	2,339	51,198		
1966	61,069	20,237	17,794	23,038	63,321	122,030
1971	53,549	16,261	28,413	8,875	128,137	62,652
Private						
1966					4,377	24,621
1973					21,891	13,025

SOURCES: Ministère de l'éducation nationale, *Informations statistiques*, no. 101 (March 1968); *Statistique des enseignements*, no. 1 (1972), no. 1 (1975); Antoine Prost, "Quand l'école de Jules Ferry est-elle morte?" *Histoire de l'éducation*, no. 14 (1982), p. 30. (As of 1972–73, official statistics no longer classified public schools by sex.)

question about whom they would most like to resemble as adults elicited a selection of male role models from 99 percent of boys but also from 33 percent of girls.[20] The findings confirmed that masculine activities often seemed more exciting, varied, and productive than traditionally female ones. Textbook efforts to glorify the role of the mother evidently could not counteract the perceptions of schoolgirls in a remote mountainous section of the Alpes-Maritimes who responded in 1966 to their teacher's question, "What is a mother?" with the less than flattering answers, she's the one who does dishes, washes clothes, cares for the rabbits and chickens, and cries when papa drinks too much.[21]

Although Simone de Beauvoir's important feminist treatise, *The Second Sex*, appeared in 1949, France, like the United States or Great Britain, was not ready for a renascence of feminism before the late 1960s. The Conseil National des Femmes, the creation of leaders of republican women's groups in 1901, remained in existence, but more militant feminist organizations were to appear. The Mouvement Démocratique Féminin (MDF), roughly comparable to the American National Organization of Women (NOW), was founded in 1964, and the more radical Mouvement de Libération des Femmes (MLF) in 1968.[22] During the 1970s the school's role in the promotion of *sexisme* became an important element in feminist social critiques.

Concerned educators as well as feminists increasingly drew attention to the disparity between textbook images of women basking in domesticity and the actual activities of many women in the workplace. In 1970 Suzanne Mollo included this theme in a larger study which indicted schools for allowing their interest in preserving their own institutional traditions and values to interfere with the adaptation of pedagogy to the contemporary world. Such verdicts were to be aired frequently as France fumbled for explanations of the university upheaval that had triggered a general crisis in May 1968. Judging that there was a gap of two generations between the society described in primary textbooks and the one in which children now lived, Mollo's *Ecole et la société* demonstrated that textbooks were more than three times more likely to depict peaceful rural scenes than urban ones and twice as likely to present women in the foyer as at work. The most common image of a housewife and mother was that of a woman "liberated from all material contingency" and incarnating "an idealized conception of femininity."[23]

In 1974 *sexisme* in schoolbooks was treated in *Les Temps modernes*, a review created by Jean Paul Sartre and long a favorite with intellectuals of the Left. Dissecting several popular primary textbooks, a study group of the Ligue du Droit des Femmes blasted *Daniel et*

Valérie (1970), one of the best-selling readers of the 1970s, for its stereotypical rendition of parental personalities. Although a historical comparison was not made, the *mère* and *père* in question could have been comfortably ensconced in such Third Republic readers as Ab der Halden's *Hors du nid*. Whereas the mother of Daniel and Valérie hoped to shield them from harsh reality, "papa finds, on the contrary, that children should know, very young, that life is not easy for all the children in the world."[24]

By the mid-1970s public pressure on both sides of the Atlantic had prompted governments to recognize the general problem of discrimination on the basis of sex and also to note the way in which schools contributed to maintaining outmoded gender stereotypes. In the United States, legislation passed in 1972 prohibited discrimination in employment on the basis of sex (as well as race, color, religion, and national origin) and also banned discrimination in salaries and fringe benefits. Title IX of the Education Amendments of 1972 prohibited discrimination against students or others on the basis of sex in all federally assisted education programs. The goal of the Women's Educational Equity Act of 1974 was equity for girls and women at all levels of the American educational system; it authorized "the Secretary of Health, Education, and Welfare to make grants to conduct special educational programs and activities designed to achieve educational equity for all students, men and women, and for other related educational purposes."[25] Quickly following the American legislation, the British Sex Discrimination Act of 1975, passed by the Labor government of Harold Wilson, proclaimed "sex discrimination unlawful" in "education" as well as in "employment, training and related matters . . . , in the provision of goods, facilities and services, and in the disposal and management of premises."[26]

In the meantime, the French government of Georges Pompidou had addressed sex discrimination by passing a 1972 law calling for equal pay for equal work. Education received attention in 1974 when Françoise Giroud, Valéry Giscard d'Estaing's independent-minded appointee to the new post of secretary of state for the "condition féminine," called for eliminating differences in the education of boys and girls. At her request, the Institut national de recherche et documentation pédagogiques produced a study of feminine images in more than seventy primary school textbooks. Like Mollo, INRDP researchers found that "la femme au foyer" was more often portrayed than the working woman. An analysis of occupations depicted in three of the most widely used texts indicated that there were twice as many types of employment for males (twenty-nine) as for females (fifteen) and that feminine métiers tended to be more modest than the masculine. There was not a single male factory worker in these books, but there were six male doctors. There was not a single female doctor or female exercising any other relatively prestigious profession, but there were seven women in the traditional fields of teaching and two in nursing. The psychological profile of the typical textbook female was one of a passive, kind woman dependent upon a handsome, strong, and prosperous man for her security and subsistence. Deemed particularly offensive were scenes in *Lisons*, a *cours élémentaire* reader, where a wife cried because of her husband's displeasure with her cooking and housekeeping, and in *Avec les mots de tous les jours*, a *cours moyen* reader, where a woman proved to be incompetent as the driver of an automobile, much to the chagrin of her male passenger. Not surprisingly, the INRDP report condemned the majority of textbooks for failing to depict realistically the lives of France's many working women and also for retarding "the evolution of the feminine condition by maintaining the idea of a *société déséquilibrée* where the gap is too great between the strong [men] and the weak [women]."[27]

In detailing the evidence from textbooks that would warrant such a conclusion, the authors of the INRDP report also made the interesting observation that the principal examples of textbook women possessing an inner force which enabled them to overcome tremendous hurdles in life tended to be in extracts from nineteenth-century textbooks. By contrast, the contemporary textbook woman rarely encountered such adversity; instead, she was an "indefatigable shopper."[28] Here this study, as well as that by feminist Annie Decroux-Masson, underscored another way in which textbooks and the school system mirror the society they serve.[29] As sociologist Ida Berger observed, between the early 1950s and the 1970s France's impressive economic growth introduced more of her citizens to "embourgeoisement" and the material fruits of a "société de comsommation."[30] Textbooks' depictions of women's roles reflected that, too. During the Third Republic textbook housewives were thrifty and conserved precious resources; textbook women of the Fourth and Fifth Republics, while still depicted as bound to home, increasingly had become the managers and planners of a wide range of activities involving consumption. Whereas the instructions of 1887 for the teaching of *morale* underscored the importance of thrift, the program of 1980 called instead for lessons for the "consumer."[31] In the view of Renée Myot, a psychologist at the INRDP, women portrayed in textbooks of the 1970s spent an excessive and unrealistic amount of time shopping, watching television, and planning leisure pursuits for their families.[32]

Recent interest in textbooks' depictions of women has not, of course, been peculiar to France. American, British, and German studies, like their French counterparts, have focused on how textbooks perpetuate sexist images misrepresenting the personalities and capabilities of women and minimizing their contributions to society at large. Many would agree with the verdict of one American researcher who judged that the inadequate images of women in textbooks have contributed to a lowering of girls' self-esteem and girls' consistent demonstration of less knowledge about vocational possibilities than boys.[33] Studying British reading textbooks in 1974, G. Lobban complained that they rigidly divided human activities into male and female compartments, always portrayed parents in traditional roles, and made heroes twice as numerous as heroines.[34] A detailed content analysis of West German textbooks concluded that their female characters were distinctly lacking in "ambition, striving for self-development, striving for creature comforts, money, riches, a sense of judgment and self-confidence."[35] A comparable study of 134 American elementary-school readers—which was submitted to the Subcommittee on Equal Opportunities of the House of Representatives' Committee on Education and Labor during the hearings on the Women's Educational Equity Act—demonstrated that popular textbooks of the early 1970s contained six times as many male as female biographies, three times more adult male than female main characters, and more than twice as many boy-centered as girl-centered stories. The personality traits usually deemed necessary for success in American society—"ingenuity, creativity, bravery, perseverance, achievement, adventurousness, curiosity, sportsmanship, generativity, autonomy, self-respect"—were four times more likely to characterize textbook males than females. As for work roles, the American textbooks offered 147 possibilities for boys and only 25 for girls. There were only 3 examples in the 134 texts of working mothers, despite the fact that by the early 1970s 38 percent of all working women had children under age eighteen.[36]

The cumulative impact of such images on young girls and women could be documented in concurrent studies of the occupational aspirations of French and American boys and girls. An American investigator reported that among students from similar social backgrounds, boys tended to choose the more prestigious professions. Girls, in both fifth and tenth grades, typically opted for traditional women's careers, such as teaching, and none hoped to become lawyers, bankers, politicians, architects, or business managers.[37] Comparable vocational attitudes appeared in a 1973 French poll of 272 pupils in the last two primary grades. Teaching was the choice of 44 percent of girls but only 4 percent of boys. It should be noted, however, that since three-fifths of the children polled were the offspring of workers and farmers, the girls' interest in teaching could actually be taken to represent a much stronger desire to break with the family background than that exhibited by boys. Whereas 34 percent of the boys expected to become skilled workers and 5 percent, farmers, these occupations were the choice, respectively, of only 2 percent and 1 percent of girls. Nonetheless, boys were much more likely to aspire to the more prestigious professions of doctor, veterinarian, pharmacist, lawyer, or engineer: 34 percent of boys, as compared to 13 percent of girls, made these choices.[38]

In the French INRDP report, as in other indictments of feminine images in textbooks, recommendations for change were also forthcoming. To prepare girls for happier and more productive adult lives, Giroud's team proposed more frequent presentation of women in productive capacities, suggesting, for example, that more farm women be pictured using a tractor rather than bound to the interior of the home. They also wanted examples of civic-minded women busy with activities beneficial to communities.[39] Their recommendation that more textbook heroines be introduced and the number of weak and helpless women reduced was a suggestion which, if implemented, might some day help change the common attitude, still registered by 47 percent of women polled in 1974, that woman is "un être faible" needing special support and protection.[40] Similar changes in attitudes were desired by American feminists who called for new textbooks assigning "*all* traits we regard as human" to both sexes so that males could "show emotion" and women could "demonstrate courage and ambition."[41]

Although the government-sponsored French report and that of an independent American feminist group shared many major points, in one respect the INRDP document, which so resoundingly condemned the transmission of anachronistic images of women and male-female relationships, retained a familiar nineteenth-century French mode when it prescribed an ideal for the future. What was desired was "a more balanced society where men and women would be neither rivals, nor equals (*semblables*), neither strong, nor weak but would be able to accept each other as 'equivalent.'"[42] Thus the report restated the old idea, used a century earlier by conservatives and feminists alike, that because men and women were different it was wiser to speak of their "equivalence" than of their "equality."[43] Giroud herself would readily denounce *sexisme* but refused the label "feminist," which had more politically radical connotations in France than in the United States and also seemed to her to denote inevitable warfare between the sexes and to exclude the possibility of cooperation.[44]

Giroud's measured language undoubtedly helped persuade members of moderate or traditional women's organizations to participate in the regional groups that her office also wished to see formed to examine the depiction of women in textbooks. Although Giroud left the "feminine condition" post in 1976, her successor Monique Pel-letier continued the regional initiatives. A 1979 report issued by the "regional delegation for the feminine condition" of the Ile de France dissected textbooks' presentation of women's roles and personalities in a fashion comparable to the 1975 INRDP analysis. Among the thirty-eight women contributing to the studies on which the report was based, there were five members of the Union Féminine Civique et Sociale, a group founded in 1925 that traditionally had addressed housewives but was now seeking to modify its image, one member of the Conseil National des Femmes, a representative of the Federation of Catholic Family Associations of Paris, and two members of the Association Soutien et Promotion de la Femme au Foyer.[45] There were no members of the MDF, the more radical MLF, or the often pro-Communist Union des Femmes Françaises (UFF), a legacy of the World War II Resistance.

Both moderates and radicals who wished to eliminate sexism from French primary schools recognized that it was as essential to alter teachers' attitudes and behavior as to revise textbooks.[46] Already by 1973 teachers in the Paris area viewed women's roles differently than their counterparts of the 1950s. Only 5.5 percent of women teachers believed that women should devote themselves only to the foyer, a nearly sevenfold decrease in this view since a comparable poll of 1953. A majority of 65 percent of women teachers advocated careers for women, most of this group favoring full-time rather than part-time work. Although male teachers, a minority of only 20 percent in the teaching corps in the Paris area, were more favorable to jobs for women than those of the 1950s, they remained more traditional than female colleagues. Nearly four times as many male teachers (20 percent) as women teachers believed that woman's only place was at home, but 49 percent of the men favored women's employment. Another sign of changing values, which many textbooks had yet to mirror, was the teachers' conviction that for many women earning money for one's family might be a less important reason for working than that of fulfilling individual potential.[47]

Parisian teachers of 1973 were far less traditional in their attitudes toward women's work than the general population, for in 1970 60 percent of men and 60 percent of women disapproved of work for married women if husbands earned an income adequate for running the household.[48] Students also retained some doubts about the ac-ceptability of work for married women. In a debate in a class of fourteen-year-old boys and girls in the Nord in February 1972, a majority of students opposed a married woman's working if her husband's income was adequate or if children were small.[49]

The contrast between Parisian teachers' attitudes toward women's work, on the one hand, and the hostility of a significant part of the general population to it, on the other, further dramatized the need to remedy the disparity between idealized feminine images in textbooks and the real world of women at work. During the late 1960s and 1970s the post-World War II decline in female participation in the work force was reversed. Having fallen from 38 percent of the active population in 1946 to 33 percent in 1962, women's participation increased to 34 percent in 1968, 38 percent in 1975, and over 40 percent by 1980. Admittedly, there were regional variations in this pattern, for in 1975 women's employment ranged from a high of 46 percent of the active population in the Paris area to a low of 23 percent in the southern region of Languedoc. French women workers were also not as numerous as their American counterparts, who constituted 42.5 percent of the work force in 1980. Nonetheless, between 1968 and 1975 approximately three-fourths of the increase in the size of the French work force was due to the entry of women, many of them married and mothers.[50] Easing the burden on working mothers with small children were the *écoles maternelles*, whose soaring enrollments during the 1970s meant that by 1981 90 percent of all three-year-olds and 35 percent of all two-year-olds were in attendance.[51]

As the female work force grew and women's issues were addressed in a wide range of publications and forums, attitudes toward women's work also evolved. Fully 84 percent of the working women interviewed for a 1974 poll expressed satisfaction that they were in the work force.[52] As of 1982, a majority of working women evidently remained more likely to view their employment primarily as a way to earn a living or obtain extras for their families, rather than as a career or opportunity for self-fulfillment, but fully 68 percent of those responding to one survey also considered their role in the work force to be an important personal gain.[53]

Within the female work force certain trends from the first half of the century remained constant, while others reflected basic structural changes in the economy and the entry of more well-educated women workers. There was only a tiny decline in the feminine component of the industrial work force between 1936 and 1975 (23.2 percent, 1936; 22.9 percent, 1975), but the percentage of working women engaged in the agricultural sector dropped dramatically from 40 percent in 1936 to 9 percent in 1975. In the enlarged tertiary or service sector of the economy, the number of women professionals continued to increase. In 1968 women constituted 41 percent of the *cadres moyens* and 19 percent of the higher-earning *cadres supérieurs*; in the census seven years later they represented 45 percent of the former and 23 percent of the latter. *Institutrices, lycée* professors, and civil servants were especially numerous in the growing ranks of women professionals because the public sector of the economy remained more hospitable to female careers at the level of the *cadres moyens* and *supérieurs* than the private sector.[54]

Women in professional positions were testimony to women's enjoyment of educational opportunities considerably more advanced than those offered by the humble primary school of the Third Republic. Although a 1970 study indicated that 82 percent of young women were not yet surpassing their fathers' educational level, the corollary was that 18 percent were and this was not an insignificant advance within the space of a generation, particularly since compulsory school attendance until age sixteen took effect only in 1967.[55] Beginning in 1968, women earned the *baccalauréat* more often than men and, although *bachelières* were somewhat less likely than their male counterparts to undertake additional study, they had become as numerous as men in the ranks of university students during the 1970s.[56] What now gave cause for concern was that women's continuing preference for liberal arts programs at both the secondary and university levels did not prepare them for the higher-paying positions open to graduates of science faculties, more often attended by men, and that women were underrepresented in the prestigious *grandes écoles* that train the nation's elites.[57] In 1978, for example, the majority of recent women graduates in literature of the University of Provence had taken jobs as *employées,* a French census category with less status than the *cadre moyen,* but only 10 percent of women science graduates (and 25 percent of male degree-holders in literature) had needed to settle for such employment.[58] A disparity between the wages of male and female professionals also remained, despite the 1972 law mandating equal pay for equal work. As of early 1982, the salaries of women in the *cadres supérieurs* were, on the average, 37 percent less than those for men. Furthermore, women graduating from a university or *grande école* were less likely than men to achieve the highest professional ranks: their chances were one in four, as compared to two out of five for men.[59]

The gap between male and female earnings was also familiar to working class women, whose salaries were at least 33 percent less than those of men.[60] In 1981 fully 37 percent of all high school students opted for or were channeled into vocational or technical education, and another 14 percent entered apprenticeships.[61] Within this large group the choices of adolescent girls differed significantly from those of boys and so contributed to their lower earning potential. A study published in 1971 had demonstrated that girls attending technical high schools had noticeably lower ambitions than boys: 46

percent of girls expected to remain *ouvrières* or *employées* during their working lives, a figure three times higher than that for boys.[62] A decade later there was still evidence that women of the rural and urban working classes, like their ancestors of the Third Republic, were less likely to receive appropriate training for a lucrative career than any other group in French society. Although girls had received access to all technical training programs (*formations*) in 1966 and coeducation was officially mandated for technical high schools, 88 percent of boys elected to train for industrial jobs while 84 percent of girls chose training for sales or office work. Unfortunately, at a time of mounting unemployment, the rate of decline in the number of new jobs in the tertiary sector was twice that for skilled workers. Furthermore, young women graduating from technical high schools (*lycées d'enseignement professionnel*) found themselves at a disadvantage in competition with graduates of academic *lycées* because employers concerned about office workers' knowledge of spelling and grammar tended to prefer the latter. Thus it was not surprising that five years after completing studies in technical high schools, less than 7 percent of young men but fully 23 percent of young women were not at work.[63] Their lot was, in fact, comparable to that of young women of the mid-1950s whose schooling had stopped with the completion of primary school.

Regardless of whether they had a distinctly feminist bent, educational reformers of the early 1980s hoped that by adjusting feminine images in primary school textbooks to portray realistically woman's multifaceted role in modern society, they could better motivate girls to seek more adequate professional training—a key to self-sufficiency and the development of special talents. In July 1980 Giscard d'Estaing's Ministry of Education instructed teachers to be on guard against textbooks perpetuating outdated stereotypes, particularly those concerning "the respective roles of man and woman in social, professional, and family life."[64]

That mandate and parallel efforts of the recently founded Association pour une école non sexiste helped prompt two important publishing houses specializing in textbooks, Nathan and Magnard, to send instructions on the depiction of women *and* men to authors and illustrators of textbooks. By then one of Nathan's best-selling readers, *Daniel et Valérie* (1970), had been much maligned, as had Magnard's *Aline et René* (1973).[65] Both Nathan and Magnard based their instructions on recommendations drawn up in 1974 by the American publisher McGraw Hill for the purpose of eliminating "sexist allusions" from its future textbooks. The Association pour une école non sexiste, started in 1979 by Catherine Valabrègue, a longtime supporter of the Mouvement pour le planning familial, had supplied some twenty publishers with a translation of the McGraw Hill instructions, but by 1982 only two, Nathan and Magnard, had disseminated them.[66]

Nathan's directive, signed by Jules Soletchnik, its director of pedagogy, appeared in the widely read *Le Monde de l'éducation* in September 1980. Discussing textbooks' presentation of "socio-professional activities," Soletchnik complained that grammar and vocabulary exercises too often linked a masculine subject with the verbs "invent, work, manufacture, construct, repair, direct, organize" and a feminine subject with "gossip, wash, cook." As for family life, "the division of the roles and tasks of man and woman in modern life is . . . in evolution, and it is necessary to take that into account." Even if a child was already aware that in real life men did more often have decision-making posts and women were more likely to cook after a day at work, "that reality does not justify a 'banalisation' of the phenomenon." Instead, textbook authors should promote reflection about "the origins and causes of this situation, and contribute to creating new attitudes, new mentalities." For the sake of realism, authors and illustrators should also recognize that alongside traditional family groups there was a growing minority of women who raised their children alone. Finally, in regard to the "physical, psychological, and moral portraits of real or fictitious characters presented" in books, Soletchnik called for avoiding the pitfalls of sexism that limit girls and women to being "coquettish, frivolous, extravagant, dependent on boys/men/husbands, less enterprising" and also forbid to boys "fatigue, [and] lack of genius or virile heroism." The remedy for such sexist stereotypes? "It is necessary to portray *individuals*, not members of one sex or the other."[67]

There were also signs that pedagogical practice had begun to move in the nonsexist directions increasingly favored by the public and recommended by Giscard d'Estaing's last education minister. Already by 1975, 46 percent of women queried in one poll favored sewing and cooking lessons for boys as well as girls, and 75 percent thought that fathers could care for babies as well as mothers. In turn, newer lessons in "manual and technical education" at the junior high school level were no longer so gender-specific, at least in a formal sense. By the fall of 1980 boys in *collèges* were learning to cook and sew, and girls were having lessons at the workbenches to develop mechanical abilities.[68]

Yet it seems clear that ministerial directives and the concerns of publishers like Nathan and Magnard could not produce a recognition of *sexisme* in those who would deny that such an attitude was a problem. Nor could substantial revision of textbooks be quickly accomplished. That much remained to be done to improve the depiction of women in schoolbooks was one of the verdicts rendered in *Les Femmes en France dans une société d'inégalités* [Women in France in a Society of Inequalities], a report submitted in the spring of 1982 to Minister Yvette Roudy.

The Socialist President François Mitterrand, elected in May 1981 and backed by a legislature with a Socialist majority elected in June 1981, had appointed Roudy to head his Ministry for Women's Rights (Droits de la femme), an upgrading of the position that Giscard d'Estaing had created but kept limited to the status of a secretariat titled "the feminine condition." Given the charge of promoting measures to enhance respect for women's rights and to eliminate "all discrimination . . . and to increase the guarantees of equality, in the political, economic, social, and cultural domains," Roudy brought to her post the credentials of a respected feminist journalist, one of whose past accomplishments was the translation in 1964 of Friedan's *Feminine Mystique.*[69] Among Roudy's first initiatives as minister was a publicity campaign to disseminate information about contraception, a sign that much had indeed changed since the 1920 law prohibiting precisely such publicity had been replaced in 1967. Because France remained the only country in the European Economic Community whose labor code did not include the principle of "professional equality between the sexes," a law to guarantee equal treatment for men and women workers, beginning with the hiring process, was scheduled for presentation to the legislature in the spring of 1983.[70]

The great importance attached by Roudy and her associates to the subject of textbooks was indicated by the fact that six pages of the 188-page *Femmes en France dans une société d'inégalités* dealt with "images of women in schoolbooks." Citing some of the studies of the 1970s discussed above (Mollo, the INRDP report to Giroud, Decroux-Masson), the feminist writer, Benoîte Groult, complained that in textbooks "femininity is presented to children as a situation of weakness or dependency," regardless of the age of the woman depicted. "Despite the action of feminists and the consciousness which has resulted from it, despite the evolution of science which has deprived of all credibility theories affirming the congenital inferiority of the feminine sex, textbooks continue to present the same image [that is] not only devaluating but totally anachronistic of women and of home life." Although around 40 percent of women worked, textbooks still reproduced "a social structure dating from the nineteenth century" and depicted about 90 percent of all women as mothers staying home. As a result, even though children did not actually read that "Mama is an underdeveloped being and papa a superman," they could draw such a conclusion. Like the earlier report to Giroud, the submission to Roudy recommended revising textbooks and changing teachers' attitudes. At the same time, Groult recognized that there were obstacles to such change. She alleged that because a "striking majority" of authors and publishers of textbooks were men, they "literally do not see what can shock a feminine public." Here, however, she somewhat exaggerated the male role in authorship, for out of a group of eighteen popular readers evaluated by *Le Monde de l'éducation* in 1979, eight had women co-authors, two had women as the primary authors with male co-authors, and two were written solely by women. Nonetheless, Groult was realistic in concluding that "without a clearly expressed political will, all our pious wishes and all the recommendations of women's associations, including those of the minister for the rights of women, will remain courteously ignored."[71]

Among those praised in the Roudy report for translating convictions into actions were the members of the Association pour une école non sexiste. At a time when even the most fervent devotees of books could not deny that many people are more influenced by nonprint media than reading material, this association, with the cooperation of the Centre national de recherche scientifique (CNRS) produced such films as *Femme de ménage et homme d'affaires* and *Pour une école non sexiste* to create an awareness of sexism and the need to combat it among students, teachers, publishers, and parents.[72] With the aid of a subvention from the Ministry for Women's Rights in 1982, the association also launched such projects as an exhibition on "Sexism in Schoolbooks," which would be shown in a number of cities during the 1982–1983 school year, and sent speakers to conferences at schools and normal schools. Although no textbook was yet "exemplary" for its nonsexist presentation, the association was heartened by small changes. Whereas the 1981 edition of Hachette's "junior" dictionary had offered only *femme de ménage* and *femme de chambre* to exemplify the word *femme*, the 1982 edition added *femme d'affaires*, evidently in response to Valabrègue's pressure. Valabrègue's ultimate goal was "not to transform women into men" but to "help them to be themselves, according to their aptitudes and aspirations. All women possess a style, a *savoir-faire*, which is their own; the complement of masculine style and *savoir-faire*, this is neither its contrary, nor its double."[73] Like late nineteenth-century feminists, late twentieth-century feminists coupled egalitarian ideals with notions of male-female complementarity rather than identity.

In the meantime, other ministers and officials of the Socialist Party were voicing support for the aims of Roudy's ministry, including reforms within the schools. At a meeting of socialist women on 7 March 1982, the day before International Women's Day, Lionel Jospin, first secretary of the party, veered away from the older socialist dogma that the solution to all of women's problems lay in realizing the general egalitarian aims of the workers' movement. Instead, he recognized that emphasis on "the class struggle can be a pretext for ignoring the specific problems of women."[74]

During 1982 the education ministry of Alain Savary also drew attention to the problem of sexism. A circular of 29 April 1982 from the *directeur* of *collèges* discussed problems encountered in giving vocational advice to girls and called for a better distribution of information to both students and parents so that young women would prepare themselves for a wider variety of jobs.[75] The directive was well timed, for a recent study had indicated that 91 percent of high school girls wanted an occupation, if not a career, and that they were well aware that one out of four of the unemployed was a woman under age twenty-five.[76] As the 1982–1983 school year opened, educators received Savary's *arrêté* of 12 July 1982 which instructed them to be critical of pedagogical materials displaying "sexist stereotypes that perpetuate a nonegalitarian image of woman." Furthermore, teachers themselves should not "convey sexist stereotypes."[77] During the fall of 1982 some concerned pedagogues began acting on Savary's instructions. Because of his decree an *inspectrice* of primary education at Nantes was able to organize a two-week workshop on sexism at the departmental normal school.[78]

Noting Minister Savary's mandates, *Le Monde de l'éducation* asked in September 1982, "Will the school be able to struggle effectively against the surrounding language of a society."[79] Whatever the final answer, official educational policy at the end of a year of numerous commemorations of the centennial of the Ferry Laws was clearly directed against perpetuating only the domestic images of women predominant in the newly secularized textbooks for Ferry's schools of the 1880s.

Notes

ADP   Archives départementales de Paris (formerly Archives départementales de la Seine)
AN   Archives nationales
MDE   *Le Monde de l'éducation*
ME   Ministry of Education (Ministère de l'instruction publique until 1932; thereafter, Ministère de l'éducation nationale)
RP   *Revue pédagogique* (retitled *Enseignement public, Revue pédagogique* in 1926)

INTRODUCTION

1. For the argument that the school's influence on children has been less important than that of other institutions, see Maurice Crubellier, *L'Enfance et la jeunesse dans la société française, 1800–1950* (Paris: Armand Colin, 1979).

2. Institut national pour la recherche et documentation pédagogiques, "Images de la femme dans les manuels scolaires," *Bibliographie de France* 19, part 2 (May 7, 1975): 766–787. The INRDP is now the INRP (Institut national de recherche pédagogique).

3. Annie Decroux-Masson, *Papa lit, Maman coud, les manuels scolaires en bleu et rose* (Paris: Denoël, Gonthier, 1979).

4. Gabriel Compayré, *L'Education intellectuelle et morale* (Paris: Delaplane, n.d.), p.14.

5. James Marangé, *De Jules Ferry à Ivan Illich* (Paris: Stock, 1976), p. 197; Ida Berger and Roger Benjamin, *L'Univers des instituteurs* (Paris: Editions de Minuit, 1964), p. 141.

6. Jean Tronchère, *Une année au cours moyen,* 3d ed. (Paris: Armand Colin, 1973), p. 35.

7. Maurice Agulhon, *Marianne au combat, l'imagerie et la symbolique républicaines de 1789 à 1880* (Paris: Flammarion, 1979).

NOTES TO CHAPTER ONE: GIRLS' PRIMARY EDUCATION IN THE NINETEENTH CENTURY

1. Antoine Prost, *Histoire de l'enseignement en France, 1800–1967* (Paris: Armand Colin, 1968); R. D. Anderson, *Education in France, 1848–1870* (Oxford: Oxford University Press, 1975); François Furet and Jacques Ozouf, *Lire et écrire*, 2 vols. (Paris: Editions de minuit, 1977).

2. Abbé Hébert-Duperron, *Conseils aux institutrices* (Paris: Paul Dupont, 1865), p. 2; Ferdinand Buisson, ed., *Dictionnaire de pédagogie et d'instruction primaire*, 2 vols. (Paris: Hachette, 1882), pt. 1, 1: 1001.

3. Jean Perrel, "L'Enseignement féminin sous l'ancien régime: les écoles populaires en Auvergne, Bourbonnais et Velay," *Cahiers d'histoire* 23 (1978): 194.

4. "Voulons que l'on établisse autant qu'il sera possible des maîtres et des maîtresses dans toutes les paroisses où il n'y en a point, pour instruire tous les enfants, et nommément ceux dont les pères et les mères ont fait profession de la religion prétendue réformée, du catéchisme et des prières qui sont nécessaires . . . ; comme aussi pour apprendre à lire et même à écrire à ceux qui pourront en avoir besoin" (François Isambert, Jourdan, Decrusy, *Recueil général des anciennes lois françaises*, 29 vols. [Paris: Belin-Le Prieur, n.d.], 20: 317).

5. Furet and Ozouf, *Lire*, 1: 72–73, 199–228.

6. Anderson, *Education*, p. 158.

7. Furet and Ozouf, *Lire*, 1: 38, 2: 82–84, 243; Maurice Gontard, *L'Enseignement primaire en France de la Révolution à la loi Guizot* (Paris: Belles Lettres, n.d.), p. 22.

8. Marie-Laurence Netter, "La Demande populaire en matière d'instruction élémentaire en milieu rural: ses liens avec la politique scolaire (XVIIIe-début XIXe siécles)," paper presented to D.C. Area French Historians, January 7, 1983, pp. 6–10. In the Yonne female signatures on marriage registers rose from 20 percent in 1690 to 30 percent in 1820; in the Haute-Garonne from 6 percent to 20 percent. In both areas, however, men signed approximately twice as often as women.

9. R. Chartier, M. M. Compère, D. Julia, *L'Education en France du XVIe au XVIIIe siècle* (Paris: Société d'édition d'enseignement supérieur, 1976), pp. 231–247.

10. Gontard, *Enseignement*, pp. 24, 37–38.

11. Perrel, "Les Ecoles de filles dans la France d'ancien régime," in *The Making of Frenchmen: Current Directions in the History of Education in France, 1679–1979*, ed. Donald N. Baker and Patrick J. Harrigan (Waterloo, Ontario: Historical Reflections Press, 1980), pp. 75–83.

12. Buisson, *Dictionnaire*, 1, 1: 1012; Gontard, *Enseignement*, pp. 87, 151, 163; H. C. Barnard, *Education and the French Revolution* (Cambridge: Cambridge University Press, 1969), pp. 93–94.

13. Emmet Kennedy and Marie-Laurence Netter, "Ecoles primaires sous le Directoire," *Annales historiques de la révolution française* 53 (1981): 3–38.

14. Jean Morange and Jean-François Chassaing, *Le Mouvement de réforme de l'enseignement en France, 1760–1798* (Paris: Presses universitaires de France, 1974), p. 179.

15. Buisson, *Dictionnaire*, 1,1: 1022, Gontard, *Enseignement*, p. 237.

16. Gontard, *Enseignement*, p. 424.

17. Joseph N. Moody, *French Education Since Napoleon* (Syracuse, N.Y.: Syracuse University Press, 1978), p. 42. See Furet and Ozouf, *Lire*, for the argument that economic conditions and local traditions were more important determinants of school attendance and literacy than nineteenth-century education laws.

18. Anderson, *Education*, p. 31.

19. Michel Chausse, "La Scolarisation dans le département de la Manche (1833–1969)," *Cahiers d'histoire de l'enseignement* 5 (1977): 78.

20. Gontard, *Les Ecoles primaires de la France bourgeoise (1833–1875)* (Toulouse: CRDP, n.d.), p. 26.

21. Pierre Zind, *L'Enseignement religieux dans l'instruction primaire publique en France de 1850 à 1873* (Lyon: Centre d'histoire du catholicisme, 1973), p. 15; Françoise Mayeur, *L'Education des filles en France au XIXe siècle* (Paris: Hachette, 1979), pp. 57–83.

22. Lucille Sauvan, *Cours normal des institutrices primaires, ou Directions relatives à l'éducation physique, morale et intellectuelle, dans les écoles primaires*, 2d ed. (Paris: Pitois-Levrault, 1840), p. 26. On Sauvan, see Buisson, *Dictionnaire*, 1, 2: 2695.

23. Carolyn C. Lougee, *Le Paradis des femmes: Women, Salons, and Social Stratification in Seventeenth Century France* (Princeton, N.J.: Princeton University Press, 1976), pp. 173–187. On Fénelon, see below.

24. Sauvan, *Cours*, pp. 20–30, 81, 142.

25. Jacques Donzelot, *The Policing of Families*, trans. Robert Hurley (New York: Random House, 1979), pp. 48–95; Pierre Bourdieu and Jean-Claude Passeron, *Reproduction in Education, Society, and Culture*, trans. Richard Nice (London and Beverly Hills: Sage, 1977).

26. Anderson, *Education*, pp. 158, 240; Prost, *Enseignement*, p. 218.

27. Zind, *Enseignement*, p. 48; Prost, *Enseignement*, pp. 94–95.

28. Prost, *Enseignement*, p. 174; Moody, *French Education*, pp. 54–55. The Falloux Law modified provisions of the Guizot Law regarding qualifications of male teachers by permitting as substitutes for the *brevet de capacité* a *baccalauréat*, the title of minister in a religion officially recognized by the state, or a certificate of apprenticeship as a teacher, the latter being an especially easy way to get around the requirement of a *brevet*.

29. Jules Simon, *L'Ecole*, 12th ed. (Paris: Hachette, 1894), pp. 168–179; 1st ed., 1864.

30. Anderson, *Education*, pp. 111–112; Prost, *Enseignement*, p. 218.

31. Gontard, *Ecoles*, pp. 142–148; Zind, *Enseignement*, pp. 196–212.

32. Zind, *Enseignement*, p. 52.

33. Pierre Chevallier and B. Grosperrin, *L'Enseignement français de la Révolution à nos jours* (Paris and The Hague: Mouton, 1971), p. 267.

34. Sandra A. Horvath, "Victor Duruy and the Controversy over Secondary Education for Girls," *French Historical Studies* 9 (1975): 83–104.

35. Prost, *Enseignement*, pp. 96, 268–269. Ferry was Minister of Public Instruction from February 1879 to November 1881 and from January to August 1882; his premierships lasted from September 1880 to November 1881 and from February 1883 to March 1885.

36. Gontard, *L'Oeuvre scolaire de la troisième république, l'enseignement en France de 1876 à 1914* (Toulouse: CRDP, 1967), p. 88.

37. ME, *Statistique de l'enseignement primaire* 2 (1880): xc–xci; 3 (1884): lii; 4 (1889): liii.

38. E. Duplan, *L'Enseignement primaire public à Paris, 1877–1888*, 2 vols. (Paris: Chaix, 1889), 1: 102; Prost, *Enseignement*, p. 218.

39. Ida Berger, ed., *Lettres d'institutrices rurales d'autrefois* (Paris: Association des amis du Musée pédagogique, 1961), p. xvii; Action populaire, *Institutrices de France* (Reims: Action populaire, 1912), p. 224.

40. J. Commets, "La Formation des institutrices de Lozère de 1839 à 1899," *Bulletin du centre d'études et de recherches littéraires et scientifiques de Mende*, no. 3 (1975), pp. 25–31; Julien Clavel, *Histoire de l'école normale d'institutrices de Grenoble* (Grenoble: n.p., 1969), p. 120.

41. AN F[17] 14310 (Affaire Beaulaton); Mona Ozouf, *La Classe ininterrompue, Cahiers de la famille Sandre, enseignants, 1780–1960* (Paris: Hachette, 1979), p. 429.

42. Ozouf, *Classe*, p. 410.

43. Pierre Chevallier, ed., *La Scolarisation en France depuis un siècle* (Paris and The Hague: Mouton, 1974), p. 42. The ratio of girls to boys in private schools was 1.9 in 1911, and 1.3 in 1963.

44. A law of 2 August 1881 renamed the old *salles d'asile*, originally created for children of poor urban workers, *écoles maternelles*.

45. Action populaire, *Institutrices*, pp. 15–16; Marcel de Grandpré, *La Coéducation dans les écoles de 45 pays* (Sherbrooke: Editions Paulines, 1973), p. 285.

46. Charles Drouard, *Les Ecoles de filles, féminisme et éducation*, 2d ed. (Paris: Belin, 1907), pp. vii, 226.

47. ME, *Règlements organiques de l'enseignement primaire* (Paris, 1887), p. 344.

48. Prost, *Enseignement*, p. 261. Although the republican founders of *lycées* for girls did not intend them to prepare young women for professions or even university entrance, *lycéennes* developed precisely these ambitions and resorted to private tutoring to learn Latin and obtain the *bac*. In 1924 the *lycée* curriculum for girls and boys became identical. For this evolution see Françoise Mayeur, *L'Enseignement secondaire des jeunes filles sous la troisième république* (Paris: Presses de la foundation nationale des sciences politiques, 1977).

49. ME, *Règlements*, pp. 345–365; ME, *Statistique* 8 (1909): 70–71; *Annuaire statistique de la France* (1910), p. 33.

50. ME, *Règlements*, p. 344; Louise Murique, *Gymnastique des jeunes filles, exercices calisthéniques rédigés conformément au programme du 4 août 1905* (Paris: Hachette, 1906), p. vi.

51. Buisson, *Nouveau dictionnaire de pédagogie et d'instruction primaire* (Paris: Hachette, 1911), p. 628.

52. Jeannette Roussel, *Etre institutrice* (Paris: Editions du Cerf, 1973), p. 7; Clavel, *Histoire*, pp. 119–120.

53. Félix Pécaut, *L'Education publique et la vie nationale* (Paris: Hachette, 1897), pp. 271, 284–287.

54. Cited in Antoine Prost, "Quand l'école de Jules Ferry est-elle morte?" *Histoire de l'éducation*, no. 14 (1982): pp. 37–38.

55. Léon Deries, ed., *Journal d'une institutrice* (Paris: A. Colin, 1902), p. 59; Louise Sagnier, *L'Institutrice* (Paris: A. Colin, 1895), pp. 83–90.

56. R. P. Catillon, *Manuel pédagogique de la religieuse enseignante* (Metz: Maison de Sainte-Chrétienne, 1886); Mlle Deslys, *Aux institutrices chrétiennes*, 2d ed. (Paris: G. Beauchesne, 1905); Chanoine Beaupin, *L'Institutrice catholique dans l'enseignement libre, entretien de retraite* (Rouen: Vicomté, 1914).

57. Pierre Dauthuile, *L'Ecole primaire dans les Deux-Sèvres depuis ses origines jusqu'à nos jours* (Niort: Th. Martin, 1904), pp. 277–280.

58. ADP D¹T¹ 29, 160; Action populaire, *Institutrices*, p. 23.

59. François de Salignac de la Mothe Fénelon, *The Education of Girls*, trans. Kate Lupton (Boston: Ginn and Co., 1891), pp. 12–13.

60. Bibliothèque Nationale, *Catalogue*.

61. Fénelon, *De l'éducation des filles*, ed. Charles Defodon (Paris: Hachette, 1881), pp. xiii–xiv; Félix Hémon, "Les Lettres de Pécaut à Gréard," *RP* 55 (November 1909): 416–417; "Discours de M. Spuller à l'inauguration du lycée des jeunes filles de Versailles," *RP* 24 (May 1894): 470–472.

62. AN F¹⁷ 22316 (dossier personnel of Mme Dejean de la Bâtie); A. Eidenschenk-Patin, *Variétés morales et pédagogiques, petits et grands secrets de bonheur* (Paris: Delagrave, 1907), p. 130.

63. Jules Payot, *Avant d'entrer dans la vie, aux instituteurs et aux institutrices, conseils et directions pratiques* (Paris: A. Colin, 1897), pp. 146–149.

64. Buisson, *Nouveau dictionnaire*, p. 1061; Zind, *Enseignement*, pp. 116–117.

65. Buisson, *Nouveau dictionnaire*, p. 1063; ME, *Règlements;* P. H. Gay and O. Mortreux, eds., *French Elementary Schools, Official Courses of Study*, trans. I. L. Kandel (New York: Teachers College, Columbia University, 1926), p. 16.

66. On the division of labor within peasant families, see Martine Segalen, *Mari et femme dans la société paysanne* (Paris: Flammarion, 1980).

67. Josephine Sirey, *Petit manuel d'éducation, ou lectures à l'usage des jeunes filles de 8 à 12 ans*, 2d ed. (Paris: Belin, 1841). Sirey edited the *Journal des femmes* (1832–1836) and *La Mère de famille* (1833–1841). On the "mère-éducatrice," see Barbara Corrado Pope, "Maternal Education in France, 1815–1848," *Proceedings of the Western Society for French History* 3 (1976): 368–377.

68. AN F¹⁷ 2791. Sales figures from archives of Hachette. For more on the importance of Carraud's texts and for translations of selected portions of *Petite Jeanne* and the companion *Maurice*, see Laura Strumingher, *What Were Little Girls and Boys Made Of? Primary Education in Rural France, 1830–1880* (Albany, N.Y.: State University of New York Press, 1983).

69. ME, *Livres scolaires en usage dans les écoles primaires publiques* (Paris, 1889), p. 8. Of the half million copies printed, only 53,830 appeared after 1883 and less than 16,000 of these after 1889.

70. George Sussman, "The Wet-Nursing Business in Nineteenth-Century France," *French Historical Studies* 9 (1975): 304–323.

71. AN F[17] 11652; Lilla Pichard, *Madame Adeline, ou récits d'une institutrice à ses élèves sur l'intelligence des animaux*, 3d ed. (Paris: Belin, 1874), pp. 16, 19.

72. AN F[17] 2791; Mme Paul Caillard, *Entretiens familiers d'une institutrice avec ses élèves* (Paris: Delagrave, 1874), pp. 5–9, 26.

73. A third edition of Sauvan's manual appeared in 1853 and a fourth in 1865.

74. The abbreviated version, *Résumé d'éducation pratique par demandes et par réponses, extrait des Entretiens familiers*, appeared in three editions between 1863 and 1868 and in four more between 1870 and 1880.

75. Ernestine Wirth, *Le Livre de lecture courante des jeunes filles chrétiennes, Lectures de la division élémentaire*, 21st ed. (Paris: Hachette, 1910), pp. v–vi; *Le Livre de lecture courante des jeunes filles chrétiennes, Lectures de la division supérieure*, 14th ed. (Paris: Hachette, 1907).

76. Wirth, *Livre, élémentaire*, pp. vii–viii, 29, 55.

77. Sales figures from archives of Hachette. ME, *Livres*, p. 22.

78. Jules Michelet, *Le Prêtre, la femme et la famille* (Paris: Calmann Lévy, n.d.), p. 255.

NOTES TO CHAPTER TWO: PRESCRIBING VALUES AND BEHAVIOR: FEMININE IMAGES IN TEXTBOOKS, 1880–1914

1. Quoted in A. Viales, *La première année d'éducation et d'enseignement post-scolaire des jeunes filles en 32 réunions* (Millau: Bernat and Vent, 1911), p. 128.

2. H. Durand, "Mémoires et documents scolaires publiés par le Musée pédagogique," *RP* 16 (May 1890): 415; Pierre Caspard and Jean-Noël Luc, "Questions sur l'enseignement primaire au XIXe siècle," *Histoire de l'éducation*, no. 6 (1980), p. 52.

3. P. H. Gay and O. Mortreux, eds., *French Elementary Schools, Official Courses of Study*, trans. I. L. Kandel (New York: Teachers College, Columbia University, 1926), p. 16.

4. Antoine Prost, *Histoire de l'enseignement en France, 1800–1967* (Paris: Armand Colin, 1968), p. 294.

5. F. B., "Les nouveaux livrets de morale," *RP* 28 (April 1896): 304.

6. ME, *Livres scolaires en usage dans les écoles primaires publiques* (Paris, 1889). Of the thirty-five girls' titles on the 1889 list, twenty-three have been utilized for this study. See Bibliography II A, title nos. 2, 6, 9, 17, 21–23, 28–32, 40, 44, 45, 52, 55, 58–61, 70. Fénelon's *Education des filles* figured on one departmental list. Of the twelve titles in this group which were not consulted, eight were sewing or home economics manuals; the other four were not widely used or not available.

7. AN F[17] 11656, indicating the choices of twenty-three departments (Ain-Creuse) as of 1909. Fifty-two of these girls' titles are utilized, including eighteen already on the 1889 list. See Bibliography IIA, title nos. 1, 2, 3,

6–9, 11–17, 21–27, 29–44, 46–56, 58, 61. P. Joigneaux, *Conseils à la jeune fermière* (1st ed., 1859) was not on the 1889 list; Arsène Perier, *Leçons de droit à ma fille* (Paris: Belin, 1885) was on one departmental list but was really for secondary schools or higher primary schools.

    8. See Bibliography II. Public school texts were selected from lists collected by the education ministry (notes 6, 7). Catholic titles were chosen from those identified in Emile Boutroux, "Les récents manuels de morale et d'instruction civique," *RP* 2 (April 1883): 304–306; and from recommendations in Abbés Labelle, Porteboeuf, Quilici et un professeur d'histoire, *Le Livre scolaire catholique français* (Paris: Bloud and Gay, 1924) and the *Annuaire officiel de l'enseignement libre catholique* (Bordeaux: Delmas-Chapon-Gounouilhou, 1935).

    9. Aimé Dupuy, "Les Livres de lecture de G. Bruno," *Revue d'histoire économique et sociale* 31 (1953): 128–151. On Bruno, see below.

    10. ME, *Livres*, pp. 8, 14, 22. The 1889 list does not name individual departments. The departmental lists for 1882–1884 (AN F17 11652–11654) indicate that twenty-three departments used Carraud, twenty-one used Wirth, and twelve used both. Of the twenty-three using Carraud, ten were in the North and Northeast, five in the Southeast, five in the South and Southwest, and three in the West. In 1881–1882, when 39% of public school girls were still taught by nuns, only six of the twenty-three departments were above this average. (*Annuaire statistique de la France* [1884], pp. 270–273).

    11. Archives of Hachette.

    12. ME, *Livres*, pp. 8, 11, 14. For a comparison of *Tour de la France* and *Petit Jean*, see Dominique Maingueneau, *Les Livres d'école de la république 1870–1914, discours et idéologie* (Paris: Le Sycomore, 1979).

    13. *Le Temps*, 2 June 1886, 30 April, 1 August 1887; E. Duplan *L'Enseignement primaire public à Paris, 1877–1888*, 2 vols. (Paris: Chaix, 1889), 1: 333–340.

    14. *Bulletin administratif du ministère de l'instruction publique* 78 (19 August 1905): 479–481; Théophile Valentin, *Les Fleurs de l'histoire, dialogues, biographies et récits à l'usage de la jeunesse*, 2d ser. (Toulouse: E. Privat, 1890), pp. 232–233; Société départementale d'agriculture et d'industrie d'Ille-et-Vilaine, *Leçons d'agriculture élémentaire et d'économie domestique à l'usage des jeunes filles des écoles primaires rurales* (Ploermel: Procure générale des frères de l'instruction chrétienne, 1896), p. 10. For a comparison of Catholic and public school history textbooks, see Jacqueline Freyssinet-Dominjon, *Les Manuels d'histoire de l'école libre, 1882–1959* (Paris: Armand Colin, 1968).

    15. Dropped from the twenty-three 1909 lists in AN F17 11656 were the titles in Bibliography IIA, nos. 28, 45, 59, 60, 70.

    16. ME, *Règlements organiques de l'enseignement primaire* (Paris, 1887), pp. 353, 359–366; Gay and Mortreux, *French Elementary Schools*, pp. 16, 41. As of 1923 civic instruction was reserved for the *cours supérieur*.

    17. ME, *Règlements*, pp. 362–365; Pierre Bourdieu and Jean-Claude Passeron, *Reproduction in Education, Society and Culture*, trans. Richard Nice (London and Beverly Hills: Sage, 1977).

    18. Gabriel Compayré, *L'Education intellectuelle et morale* (Paris: Delaplane, n.d.), p. 14. On the higher primary schools, see chapter 5.

19. ME, *Plan d'études et programmes des écoles primaires supérieures de filles*, 7th ed. (Paris: Vuibert, 1936), p. 20.

20. ME, *Livres*, p. 3. Gréville was still on seventeen of the twenty-three departmental lists in AN F^{17} 11656.

21. Maurice Gontard, *L'Oeuvre scolaire de la troisième république, l'enseignement en France de 1876 à 1914* (Toulouse: CRDP, 1967), pp. 104–109.

22. *Dictionnaire de biographie française*, s.v. "Durand-Gréville, Alice"; Theodore Stanton, ed., *The Woman Question in Europe* (New York: G.P. Putnam's Sons, 1884), pp. 280–281; Barnett Singer, "Minoritarian Religion and the Creation of a Secular School System in France," *Third Republic/Troisième République* (Fall 1976), pp. 228–259.

23. It has been possible to identify twenty-four of the women authors or co-authors of pre-1914 republican textbooks sampled for this study as primary, higher primary, secondary, or normal school teachers: Berger, Bidault, Bouché, Bret, Caillard, Chalamet, Chapelot, Demailly, Eidenschenk, Fredel, Friedberg, Hocdé, Juranville, Marie, Martin, Murique, Nectoux, Sagnier, Salomon, Scordia, Sévrette, Toudy, Valette, Wirth. Best characterized as "femmes de lettres" are Becour, Bentzon (Mme Blanc), Bruno (Mme Fouillée), Carraud, Delorme, Gréville (Mme Durand-Gréville), Halt (Mme Vieu), Sage, Sirey.

24. Félix Pécaut, *L'Education publique et la vie nationale* (Paris: Hachette, 1897), pp. 266–276.

25. Mlle Ginier, "L'Inspection féminine des écoles maternelles et des écoles de filles," *RP* 38 (March 1911): 224.

26. Alice Durand-Gréville [Mme Henry Gréville], *L'Instruction morale et civique des jeunes filles* (Paris: E. Weill and G. Maurice, 1882), p. 152.

27. Ibid., pp. 134–140, 186.

28. Abbé F. Méchin, *Fleurs et épines, ou vertus ou défauts*, 14th ed. (Paris: Belin, 1895).

29. Gréville, *Instruction*, pp. 161–166.

30. Phyllis Stock, *Better Than Rubies: A History of Women's Education* (New York: G.P. Putnam's Sons, 1978), pp. 21–22, 106–107.

31. Barbara Corrado Pope, "Maternal Education in France, 1815–1848," *Proceedings of the Western Society for French History* 3 (1976): 368–377; Erna Olafson Hellerstein, "French Women and the Orderly Household, 1830–1870," in ibid., pp. 378–384; Evelyne Sullerot, *Histoire et sociologie du travail féminin* (Paris: Gonthier, 1968), pp. 78–83.

32. Gréville, *Instruction*, p. 154.

33. Ibid., pp. 166–168. Cf. H.D. Lewis, "The Legal Status of Women in Nineteenth Century France," *Journal of European Studies* 10 (1980): 178–188.

34. Gréville, *Instruction*, pp. 132–133. On Deraismes, see Patrick Kay Bidelman, *Pariahs Stand Up! The Founding of the Liberal Feminist Movement in France, 1858–1889* (Westport, Connecticut: Greenwood Press, 1982), pp. 66, 75–81.

35. Gréville, *Instruction*, pp. 158–159, 175–188.

36. Henriette Massy, *Notions d'éducation civique à l'usage des jeunes filles* (Paris: Picard-Bernheim, 1884), pp. 5–8, 100–102, 197. On Kant and republican *morale*, see John A. Scott, *Republican Ideas and the Liberal Tradition in France, 1870–1914* (New York: Columbia University Press, 1951).

37. The first editions of four Juranville textbooks appeared during the Second Empire, three during the 1870s, and eleven after 1880. Pauline Berger, an *institutrice*, co-authored five of the latter group.

38. *Annuaire de l'instruction primaire* (1887, 1905); Duplan, *Enseignement*, pp. 334–335. On the Paris list were *Premier livre des petites filles*, *Deuxième livre des petites filles*, and *Savoir-faire et le savoir-vivre*.

39. Sales figures for Juranville from archives of Larousse; others from Gontard, *Oeuvre scolaire*, p. 81.

40. Clarisse Juranville, *Manuel d'éducation morale et d'instruction civique à l'usage des jeunes filles*, 6th ed. (Paris: Larousse, 1899), pp. 20–21, 134–136, 158, 254–255.

41. *Dictionnaire de biographie française*, s.v. "Chalamet, Rose-Madeleine-Clémence-Elise"; Rose Chalamet, *La première année d'économie domestique, morale, soins du ménage, hygiène, jardinage, avec travaux manuels, suivie de notions d'instruction civique et de droit usuel* (Paris: A. Colin, 1887), pp. 2, 34–36, 194–202. Sales figures from archives of Colin. Although listed with readers rather than *morale* texts on the 1889 list (ME, *Livres*), Chalamet's text was also classified as a *morale* book by 1909 and was on twenty of the twenty-three departmental lists in AN F^{17} 11656.

42. Chalamet, *Première année*, pp. 9, 50–52; Chalamet, *Livre de maître* (Paris: A. Colin, 1893), pp. 52–53. For the other fourteen titles, see Bibliography IIA, title nos. 4, 28, 30, 32, 35, 38, 39, 43, 48, 58, 59; IIB, 20, 25, and Mme Paul Caillard, *Entretiens familiers d'une institutrice avec ses élèves*, 3d ed. (Paris: C. Delagrave, 1874).

43. Françoise Mayeur, *L'Enseignement secondaire des jeunes filles sous la troisième république* (Paris: Presses de la fondation nationale des sciences politiques, 1977), p. 467. There were fewer of the special elementary classes for girls than for boys.

44. *Dictionnaire de biographie française*, s.v. "Bentzon, Marie-Thérèse de Solms, Mme Blanc"; Mrs. Fields, "Notable Women: Mme Blanc ('Th. Bentzon')," *The Century Magazine* 66 (1903): 134–139.

45. Marie-Thérèse de Solms Blanc [Mme Thérèse Bentzon] and Mlle A. Chevalier, *Causeries de morale pratique* (Paris: Hachette, 1899), pp. 45–48, 51.

46. Theresa M. McBride, *The Domestic Revolution: The Modernization of Household Service in England and France, 1820–1929* (New York: Holmes and Meier, 1976), pp. 60–66; E. Primaire, *Manuel d'éducation morale, civique et sociale* (Paris: Bibliothèque d'éducation, 1901), p. 85; L.-P. Renaud, *La Vie morale de l'enfant* (Paris: C. Lavauzelle, 1948), p. 55. The advice that households without servants were nicer and thriftier was added to later editions of Juranville, *Savoir-faire et le savoir-vivre* (28th ed., 1919, p. 85).

47. Mayeur, *Enseignement secondaire*, pp. 204–205, citing Henri Marion, *L'Education des jeunes filles* (Paris, 1902).

48. Bentzon and Chevalier, *Causeries*, pp. 249–253.

49. Ibid., pp. 70, 122, 242. Cf. Julie Sévrette, *La jeune ménagère* (Paris: Larousse, 1904), p. 98.

50. Anne-Louise Masson, *Manuel de morale et d'instruction civique*, 3d ed. (Lyon: E. Vitte, 1922), pp. 22, 47–49, 113–116.

51. Joseph Burnichon, *Les Manuels d'éducation civique et morale et la condamnation de l'index* (Marseilles: Société anonyme de l'imprimerie marseillaise, 1883), p. 18.

52. Gabriel Compayré, *Eléments d'instruction morale et civique*, 119th ed. (Paris: Delaplane, n.d.), pp. 12–13; Ernest Lavisse [Laloi], *La première année d'instruction civique* (Paris: A. Colin, 1880), pp. 86–87.

53. Compayré, *Eléments*, pp. 127–128.

54. Eugen Weber, *Peasants into Frenchmen: The Modernization of Rural France, 1870–1914* (Stanford, Calif.: Stanford University Press, 1976), pp. 286–290.

55. Juranville, *Savoir-faire* (1883), p. 198.

56. Laloi, *Instruction*, pp. 108–109; A. Mézières, *Education morale et instruction civique* (Paris: C. Delagrave, 1883), pp. 59–60, 154.

57. ME, *Règlements*, p. 174.

58. A. Eidenschenk-Patin, *Les deuxièmes lectures des petites filles* (Paris: C. Delagrave, 1912), p. v; Alcide Lemoine and Juliette Marie, *La jeune française, 200 lectures destinées pour les jeunes filles* (Paris: Larousse, 1910), p. 5; Alcide Lemoine and Aubin Aymard, *Le jeune français, lectures éducatives, morales et littéraires* (Paris: Larousse, 1914), p. 24. Eidenschenk-Patin's first and second readers each sold more than 50,000 copies; Hachette issued 34,650 copies of Cuir's text; Larousse, at least 33,000 copies of Lemoine and Marie and 11,000 of Lemoine and Aymard. Eidenschenk-Patin's third reader offered more advice on preparing for adult life.

59. Dupuy, "Livres"; Mme Alfred Fouillée [G. Bruno], *Le Tour de la France par deux enfants*, 120th ed. (Paris: Belin, 1884); *Francinet*, 66th ed. (Paris: Belin, 1887).

60. Marie Vieu [Marie Robert Halt], *Le droit chemin* (Paris: Delaplane, 1902).

61. For boys' books discouraging expectations of social mobility and advising readers to stay in the country, see Bibliography IIB, title nos. 1, 15, 27, 29, 38, 42, 44, 45.

62. Mézières, *Education*, p. 154; Laloi, *Instruction civique*; Georges Nicolas, *Tu seras chef de famille* (Paris: A. Colin, 1891), Paul Bert, *L'Instruction civique à l'école*, 6th ed. (Paris: Picard-Bernheim, 1882), p. 95.

63. For the titles, see Bibliography IIB, nos. 2, 5, 8, 11, 25, 34, 36, 41, 42.

64. Jean Aicard, *Le Livre des petits*, 7th ed. (Paris: C. Delagrave, n.d.), pp. 172–174.

65. For girls' books explicitly discouraging expectations of social mobility and advising readers to stay in the country, see Bibliography IIA, title nos. 1, 2, 6, 8, 12–14, 26, 27, 30, 31, 41, 49, 50, 56, 62, 72, 75. Halt, *Droit chemin*; Halt, *Le Ménage de Mme Sylvain* (Paris: Delaplane, 1895).

66. Compayré, *Eléments*, p. 70; Mlle Brocard and Mlle Despiques, *Lectures morales* (Lyon: E. Vitte, 1911), p. 99; Charles Drouard *Les Ecoles de filles, féminisme et éducation*, 2d ed. (Paris: Belin, 1907), p. ix.

67. Louise A. Tilly and Joan W. Scott, *Women, Work, and Family* (New York: Holt, Rinehart and Winston, 1978), parts 1, 2.

68. Of the seven *Tu seras* books, Desmaisons ranked fourth in sales, behind Emile Lavisse, *Tu seras soldat* (182,500 copies), H. Marchand, *Tu seras agriculteur* (67,500), and Joseph Chailley-Bert, *Tu seras commerçant* (43,500). Figures from archives of Colin. Desmaisons was on eight of the twenty-three departmental lists in AN F[17] 11656.

69. Jules Simon, Préface to L. C. Desmaisons, *Tu seras ouvrière* (Paris: A. Colin, 1892), pp. iii–iv; Desmaisons, *La première année de cuisine* (Paris: A. Collin, 1895), p. 2; Desmaisons, "Le Féminisme et les institutrices," *Le Volume* 10 (19 February 1898): 172 and "Notes et remarques sur le féminisme," *Le Volume* 10 (9 April 1898): 229–231.

70. Halt, *L'Enfance de Suzette*, 17th ed. (Paris: Delaplane, 1907); *Suzette* (1889); *Le Ménage de Mme Sylvain* (1895). Sales figures from *Bibliographie de France, Livres et matériel d'enseignement* (1920), p. 446; (1932), p. 318.

71. Halt, *Suzette; Ménage*, pp. 311–312; Pierre Jakez Hélias, *The Horse of Pride*, trans. June Guicharnaud (New Haven: Yale University Press, 1978), pp. 16–17.

72. Chanoine Tournier, *Situation morale de l'école, statistique des manuels scolaires, analyse des manuels de morale* (Bourg: J. Dureuil, 1909), pp. 13–14; Duplan, *Enseignement*, 1: 340; ADP D¹T¹ 174, 177, 511. *Suzette* was on twenty of the twenty-three departmental book lists of 1909 in AN F[17] 11656 and was still used in the Seine in 1923.

73. "Le XXIIᵉ congrès de la Ligue de l'enseignement," *RP* 41 (November 1902): 446. On the Ligue, see Katherine Auspitz, *The Radical Bourgeoisie: The Ligue de l'enseignement and the Origins of the Third Republic, 1866–1885* (Cambridge and New York: Cambridge University Press, 1982).

74. Halt, *Droit chemin*, pp. 125, 135–161.

75. E. de Kereven, *Le premier livre d'Elisabeth*, 2d ed. (Lyon: E. Vitte, 1910); *La petite Elisabeth*, 2d ed. (1910); *Elisabeth*, 2d ed. (1910); Marie Thiéry, *Lisette* (Paris: A. Hatier, 1910); *Lise* (1910); *Elise*, 7th ed. (1926). Publication figures from E. Vesco de Kereven and J. Martin, *La Famille Aubert* (Lyon: E. Vitte, 1920), p. ii, and *Bibliographie de France, Livres et matériel d'enseignement* (1934), p. 85. AN F[17] 13378 indicates the use of *Lisette* and *Lise* in 1940.

76. ADP D¹T¹ 29 (Barrier); 33 (Mirman).

77. Gontard, *Oeuvre scolaire*, pp. 178–184; Christian Amalvi, "Les Guerres des manuels autour de l'école primaire en France," *Revue historique*, no. 532 (October–December 1979), pp. 359–398.

78. The *André* books were also introduced in 1910, and by 1921–1922, 55,000 copies of *Le premier livre* and 44,000 copies of *Le deuxième livre* had been issued.

79. Bonnie G. Smith, *Ladies of the Leisure Class: The Bourgeoises of Northern France in the Nineteenth Century* (Princeton, N.J.: Princeton University Press, 1981).

80. Computed from P. Bairoch, T. Deldycke, H. Gelders, J.-M. Limbor, *La Population active et sa structure* (Brussels: Institut de l'Université libre de Bruxelles, 1968), p. 167.

81. Alice Dereims, *Jeanne et Madeleine* (Paris: A. Colin, 1902), was on fourteen of the twenty-three departmental book lists of 1909 in AN F[17] 11656. Sales figures from archives of Colin.

82. Juranville and Pauline Berger, *Le troisième livre de lecture à l'usage des jeunes filles*, 2d ed. (Paris: Larousse, 1892). Sales figures from archives of Larousse.

83. For Joan of Arc, Bibliography IIA, nos. 4, 16, 20, 21, 25, 28, 30, 35, 37, 38, 59, 62, 65, 68.

84. One or more women notable in French or world history appeared in twenty-two pre-1914 girls' books in the sample. See Bibliography IIA, title nos. 4, 14, 20, 21, 25, 28, 30, 32, 33, 35, 37, 38, 48, 53, 59, 60, 62, 65, 68, 69, 71, 74. See also IIB, nos. 20, 25, 26, 30, 48, 51, 53, 55.

85. Bruno, *Francinet*, pp. 331–332; Juranville and Berger, *Le troisième livre*, p. 358.

86. AN F[17] 11652–11654, 11656; Madeleine Chambriard, "Adaptation de l'enseignement à la vie rurale," *Education* 20 (1929): 225.

87. Larousse published 364,000 copies of Juranville by 1914; Colin, 193,000 copies of Chalamet between 1886 and 1923, 185,000 of these before 1914; Hachette, 140,000 copies of Wirth by 1915; Delagrave, 300,000 copies of Hannedouche by 1940 and 188,000 of Leune and Demailly by 1932; and Larousse, 72,825 copies of Sévrette.

88. Aline Valette, *La Journée de la petite ménagère* (Paris: E. Weill and G. Maurice, 1885); A. Brémant, *Sciences et enseignement ménager* (Paris: A. Hatier, 1912); Leune and Demailly, *Cours*, p. 19; Halt, *Ménage*, Chapter 5; H. Raquet, *La première année de ménage rural*, 13th ed. (Paris: A. Colin, 1908), pp. 184–185. Cf. Bruno, *Tour*, pp. 260, 311.

89. Sales figures from archives of Colin. Michel Greff, *La Fermière*, 12th ed. (Paris: C. Delagrave, 1896), pp. 8–9; J. Huot, *Manuel d'éducation ménagère à la ville et à la campagne* (Paris: J. de Gigord, 1912), p. 281.

90. Bairoch et al, *Population*, p. 96; Martine Segalen, *Mari et femme dans la société paysanne* (Paris: Flammarion, 1980), pp. 15–16, 147, 163, 205.

91. Greff, *Fermière*, p. 141 (1st ed., 1859); Louis-Eugène Bérillon, *La bonne ménagère agricole, ou simples notions d'économie rurale et d'économie domestique*, 10th ed. (Auxerre: C. Gallot, 1888), p. 162 (1st ed., 1862).

92. Weber, *Peasants*, pp. 175, 285–286; Segalen, *Mari et femme*, p. 120.

93. Maurice Rouable, *150 lectures de morale vivante* (Paris: Vuibert, 1943), p. 147.

94. Leune and Demailly, *Cours*, p. 154.

95. Religieuses de la Providence de Saint-Brieuc, *Notions d'économie domestique à l'école primaire et dans les pensionnats de jeunes filles* (Ploermel: Procure générale des frères de l'instruction chrétienne, 1900), p. 101.

96. Halt, *Droit chemin*.

97. Kereven, *La petite Elisabeth*, pp. 110–112; Marthe Boegner, *Des deux côtés de l'estrade* (Paris: Editions du scorpion, 1964), p. 27.

98. Sévrette, *Jeune ménagère*, p. 126; Marie Delorme, *Les petits cahiers de Mme Brunet* (Paris: A. Colin, 1888), p. 274; Chalamet, *Première année*, p. 34. See also Lilla Pichard, *La Choix d'un état, arts et métiers propres aux femmes* (Paris: G. Téqui, 1879), pp. 422–449.

99. Ida Berger, ed., *Lettres d'institutrices rurales d'autrefois, rédigées à la suite de l'enquête de Francisque Sarcey en 1897* (Paris: Association des amis du Musée pédagogique, 1961), p. 65.

100. Of the 76 pre-1914 girls' books in the sample, 35 explicitly mentioned one or more feminine personality traits, and in most others the notion of a special feminine personality was implicit in the behavior of a little girl or woman. Public school books were just as likely to speak of distinctive feminine traits (28 of 61 books) as were Catholic books (7 of 15). For the titles, see Bibliography IIA, Nos. 1, 2, 4, 5, 7, 8, 11, 12, 14, 17, 25–28, 30, 32, 39, 43–45, 47–50, 53, 58–60, 64, 65, 68–71, 73. For the same theme in books for boys or mixed classes, see IIB, nos. 26, 41, 44, 48, 57.

101. See Bibliography IIA, title nos. 4, 26, 30, 36, 38, 53, 71.

102. See Bibliography IIA, title nos. 4, 30, 48, 53, 69.

103. For a summary of textbook treatments of women's work and the actual role of women in the work force, see chapter 5.

104. Woman's suffrage was mentioned in six girls' books, five opposing it (Juranville, *Manuel;* Masson; Massy; Sage; Wirth, *Future ménagère*) and one (Bentzon and Chevalier) supporting it tactfully: "While waiting until she has her say in the councils of the nation, the woman will form citizens" (p. 70). Alphonse Aulard, *Eléments d'instruction civique* (Paris: Edouard Cornely, 1907) mentioned the issue but took no stance.

105. Lemoine and Marie, *La jeune française,* p. 289.

106. See Bibliography IIA, title nos. 1, 2, 5, 7, 8, 17, 30, 36, 38, 43, 47, 48, 56, 58, 71, 72. In addition, two textbooks (Halt, *Ménage;* Juranville, *Savoir-faire,* 1882) showed husband and wife doing accounts together; two (Lemoine and Marie; Juranville, *Savoir-faire,* 1919) showed men in control of family finances; and two (Massy; Kereven, *Elisabeth*) assigned household accounts to the woman but clearly not control of the family fortune.

107. In twenty-four girls' books (eighteen republican, six Catholic) the "interior" was explicitly designated as woman's domain, and in most others the story line made the message implicit. See Bibliography IIA, title nos. 2, 4, 5, 7, 8, 14, 17, 25, 26, 29, 30, 32, 34, 38, 40, 42, 53, 60, 64, 69, 71–74.

108. Anna Davin, "'Mind That You Do As You Are Told': Reading Books for Board School Girls," *Feminist Review* 3 (1979): 89–98; Carol Dyhouse, "Good Wives and Little Mothers: Social Anxieties and the Schoolgirl's Curriculum, 1890–1920," *Oxford Review of Education* 3 (1977): 21–34; Renate Schäfer, "Die gesellschaftliche Bedingtheit des Fibelinhalts: Ein Beitrag zur Geschichte des Erstlesebuchs," *Jahrbüch für Erziehungs- und Schulgeschichte* 2 (1972): 71–84; Ruth Miller Elson, *Guardians of Tradition: American Schoolbooks of the Nineteenth Century* (Lincoln: University of Nebraska Press, 1964), pp. 301–312.

109. Mary S. Hartman, *Victorian Murderesses* (New York: Schocken Books, 1977), p. 274.

110. Theodore Zeldin, *France, 1848–1945,* vol. 1: *Ambition, Love and Politics* (Oxford: Oxford University Press, 1973), p. 346.

111. Bidelman, *Pariahs,* pp. 199–201; Karen M. Offen, "Depopulation, Nationalism, and French Feminism during the Belle Epoque," paper presented

to the Society for French Historical Studies, Bloomington, Indiana, March 1981.

112. See Bibliography IIA, title nos. 2, 4, 5, 8, 12, 13, 15, 17, 24, 30, 32, 38, 39, 45, 48, 50, 53, 56, 58–60, 65, 69, 71–74. For the message in books for mixed classes, IIB, nos. 27, 44.

NOTES TO CHAPTER THREE: THE SCHOOL'S DISSEMINATION OF FEMININE IMAGES AND REACTIONS TO THEM, 1880–1914

1. ADP D^{1}T^1 28–35, 153–195, 345, 360, 379–381, 411–418, 483–484, 500–511, 540, 610, 673, 704 (dossiers personnels of teachers). For an example of an uncooperative teacher, see AN F^{17} 14310 (Affaire Beaulaton).

2. For inspections from the interwar years, see Oreste Auriac, L'Ecole exemplaire (Paris: A. Colin, 1948); for the similarity of Fifth Republic inspections to earlier ones, Josette Voluzan, L'Ecole primaire jugée (Paris: Larousse, 1975).

3. ADP D^{1}T^1 176.

4. ADP D^{1}T^1 162.

5. ADP D^{1}T^1 153, 184, 345.

6. ADP D^{1}T^1 192 (Colle), 412 (Badour).

7. ADP D^{1}T^1 484 (Assénat), 610 (Bendelé).

8. ME, Inspection de l'enseignement primaire (Paris, 1900), p. 158.

9. E. Duplan, L'Enseignement primaire public à Paris, 1877–1888, 2 vols. (Paris: Chaix, 1889), 1: 182.

10. "Leçon pratique d'économie domestique," RP 7 (September 1885): 282.

11. ADP D^{1}T^1 153 (Astaix).

12. For the use of the same question in the Seine in 1892, see AN F^{17} 11629 (excerpt from L'Instituteur pratique).

13. Philippe Maurer, ed., Les Cahiers du devoir, essai d'anthologie scolaire illustrée (1880–1906), in Cahiers d'histoire de l'enseignement, numéro spécial (1976), pp. 18, 40, 42, 44, 76.

14. Archives départmentales de Maine-et-Loire, "Choix de documents d'archives sur l'école, Ecole de la vie: cahiers d'une fillette angevine (1904–1908)."

15. Maurer, Cahiers, p. 48.

16. Musée national de l'éducation, Enseignement primaire cahiers, 1880–1889, 1910–1914 cartons.

17. G. Lefèvre, "Une enquête pédagogique dans les cours moyens des écoles primaires du Nord," RP 36 (January 1900): 9–10. This article is discussed below.

18. Musée national de l'éducation, Cahiers, 1900–1909 carton.

19. AN F^{17} 11630.

20. Ibid.

21. Ibid.

22. Pierre Déghilage, La Dépopulation des campagnes (Paris: F. Nathan, 1900), p. 21; Bulletin de la statistique générale de la France 25 (1936): 327. For girls' earning of the c.e.p., see chapter 5.

23. ME, *Règlements organiques de l'enseignement primaire* (Paris, 1887), pp. 424–427; "Chronique de l'enseignement primaire en France," *RP* 31 (August 1897): 184–185.

24. Jean Marie Coudert and A. F. Cuir, *Mémento pratique du certificat d'études primaires* (Paris: A. Colin, 1887); A. Pierre and A. Minet, *1300 sujets de rédaction pour la préparation de certificat d'études* (Paris: F. Nathan, 1892); C. Wirth, *Le Livre de composition française des jeunes filles*, 6th ed. (Paris: Hachette, 1912); ADP D^2T^1 110–134 (*régistres*).

25. AN F^{17} 14310 (Affaire Beaulaton); Wirth, *Livre*, p. 116.

26. Coudert and Cuir, *Mémento*, p. 93; *L'Ecole française* (8 March 1898); Pierre and Minet, *1300 sujets*, pp. 156–157.

27. Coudert and Cuir, *Mémento*, pp. 128, 135, 145, 201, 348, 432.

28. Ibid., p. 251.

29. Wirth, *Livre*, pp. 232–233, 282; Pierre and Minet, *1300 sujets*, p. 40.

30. ADP D^2T^1 *régistres* 113–133.

31. Musée national de l'éducation, Cahiers, 1890–1894 carton, 1890 *cahier* of Juliette Devillers.

32. Wirth, *Livre*, p. 366. Cf. Pierre and Minet, *1300 sujets*, pp. 26–27.

33. AN F^{17} 11629.

34. C. Chabot, "Une enquête pédagogique dans les écoles primaires de Lyon," *RP* 34 (April 1899): 329–332.

35. Lefèvre, "Une enquête pédagogique," p. 8.

36. Octave Gréard, *L'Enseignement primaire à Paris et dans le département de la Seine de 1867 à 1877* (Paris: Chaix, 1878), pp. 267–593.

37. Henriette Sourgen, "L'Enseignement ménager," in *Encyclopédie pratique de l'éducation en France*, ed. Institut pédagogique national (Paris, 1960), pp. 801–802; Marie Mauron, *Les Cas de conscience de l'instituteur* (Paris: Perrin, 1966), p. 57.

38. M. Bec, "Congrès international d'enseignement ménager de Gand," *RP* 64 (May 1914): 462; Eugen Weber, *Peasants into Frenchmen: The Modernization of Rural France, 1870–1914* (Stanford, Calif.: Stanford University Press, 1976), p. 329.

39. Gréard, *Enseignement*, pp. 267–593. Gréard's data is interpreted in John W. Shaffer, "Family, Class, and Young Women: Occupational Expectations in Nineteenth Century Paris," *Journal of Family History* 3 (1978): 62–77.

40. Lefèvre, "Une enquête," pp. 9–10.

41. Marguerite Bodin, *Les Surprises de l'école mixte* (Paris: Librairie universelle, 1905), p. 105. Cf. Louise Michel, *L'Ecole de campagne* (Bordeaux: Nouveaux cahiers de jeunesse, 1968), p. 67.

42. Jeanne Bouvier, *Mes mémoires, ou 59 années d'activité industrielle, sociale et intellectuelle d'une ouvrière* (Paris: Action intellectuelle, 1936), p. 22; Simone de Beauvoir, *Mémoires d'une jeune fille rangée* (Paris: Gallimard, 1958), p. 94; Germaine de Maulny, *Les Bottines à boutons* (Paris: Editions France-Empire, 1978), p. 40; Marie Gasquet, *Une Enfance provençale, suivie de Gai-savoir* (Paris: Flammarion, 1967), p. 298.

43. Sidonie Gabrielle Colette, *Claudine à Paris*, 92d ed. (Paris: P. Ollendorff, 1903), pp. 91–95; *Claudine at School*, trans. Antonia White (London: Secker and Warburg, 1956).

44. ADP D²T¹ 17; D¹T¹ 380 (Van Beck); D²T¹ 13.

45. Musée pédagogique, *Congrès international de l'enseignement primaire, analyse des memoires*, Mémoires et documents scolaires, fascicule 91 (Paris, 1889), pp. 199–230.

46. The published summaries of the position papers often excluded the statements about womanhood in the original manuscripts. The Archives Nationales (Congrès international de l'enseignement primaire) has forty-seven manuscripts by French delegates, twenty-two by women and twenty-five by men; the published summary contains three additional position papers by women. Formerly at the Institut pédagogique national, the manuscripts do not yet have a classification number at the Archives Nationales. I wish to thank Mme Paule René-Bazin for directing me to them.

47. AN, "Congrès"; Musée pédagogique, *Congrès international de l'enseignement primaire, compte rendu des séances*, Mémoires et documents scolaires, fascicule 95 (Paris, 1889), pp. 21–24, 89. Section one discussed the extent to which professional education (commercial, industrial, and agricultural) should be given in primary, higher primary, and normal schools; section three discussed the role of the *écoles annexes* of normal schools. For the role of women in school inspection before 1889, see *Recueil des monographies pédagogiques publiées à l'occasion de l'exposition universelle de 1889*, 6 vols. (Paris, 1889), 1: 483–487.

48. AN, "Congrès"; Musée pédagogique, *Compte rendu*, pp. 23, 73–75.

49. AN, "Congrès" (Bisson, Bosse, Chapalain, Gillot, Mantoz-le-Gad, Scordia, Szumlanska, Vilain-Philippe); Musée pédagogique, *Compte rendu*, pp. 20, 23 (Kergomard).

50. AN, "Congrès" (Bonnet, Bonnefous, Scordia, Venot, Verdelhan).

51. Ibid. (Defretières, Gaudel).

52. Ibid. (Bisson, Bonnet, Mantoz-le-Gad, Simboiselle, Scordia); Musée pédagogique, *Compte rendu*, pp. 68–70 (Kergomard).

53. AN F¹⁷ 23609 (Kergomard dossier). Kergomard (1838–1925) was the daughter of a Protestant school inspector from Bordeaux, the cousin of the anarchist geographer Elisée Reclus, and the wife of Jules Duplessis Kergomard (1822–1901), an aspiring author. As an *inspectrice générale* of *écoles maternelles* from 1879 to 1917, she presided over their transition from the *salles d'asile*, regarded as suitable only for the offspring of the urban poor, to institutions which combined features of a nursery, kindergarten, and preparatory class for elementary school.

54. Musée pédagogique, *Compte rendu*, p. 19, 68–69.

55. Ibid., pp. 72, 76.

56. In 1887, 71 percent of *écoles mixtes* were taught by men; in 1906, 65 percent (André Balz, "L'Expansion féminine dans l'enseignement primaire," *Manuel général de l'instruction primaire* [25 August 1906], p. 559).

57. "Les Inspections des écoles primaires," *RP* 18 (February 1891): 184–185; M. Ginier, "L'Inspection féminine des écoles maternelles et des écoles de filles," *RP* 58 (1911): 218. The Seine-et-Oise appointed a woman inspector

in 1891; the Seine, in 1895. Additional Seine inspection posts were opened to women in 1897, 1904, and 1912.

58. Jacques Ozouf, ed., *Nous les maîtres d'école* (Paris: Gallimard, 1967).

59. Ida Berger, ed., *Lettres d'institutrices rurales d'autrefois, rédigées à la suite de l'enquête de Francisque Sarcey en 1897* (Paris: Association des amis du Musée pédagogique, 1961); Danielle Delhome, Nicole Gault, Josiane Gonthier, *Les premières institutrices laïques* (Paris: Mercure de France, 1980), pp. 105–199.

60. Léon Deries, ed., *Journal d'une institutrice* (Paris: A Colin, 1902), p. 77; Louise Sagnier, *L'Institutrice* (Paris: A. Colin, 1895), pp. 90–91.

61. AN AJ¹⁶ 234; ADP D¹T¹ 51.

62. Deries, *Journal*, p. 59.

63. Mona Ozouf, ed., *La Classe ininterrompue, Cahiers de la famille Sandre, enseignants, 1780–1960* (Paris: Hachette, 1979), pp. 429–434.

64. Yves Sandre, *Marie des autres* (Paris: Editions du Seuil, 1964).

65. Bodin, *L'Institutrice* (Paris: Octave Doin, 1922), pp. 307–309; Bodin, *Surprises*, pp. 188–191.

66. "De l'éducation qui convient aux femmes, composition d'une élève de l'école de Fontenay-aux-Roses," *RP* 13 (August 1888): 152–156.

67. Barbara Greven-Aschoff, *Die bürgerliche Frauenbewegung in Deutschland, 1894–1933* (Göttingen: Vandenhoeck und Ruprecht, 1981), pp. 59–67; Sara Delamont, "The Domestic Ideal and Women's Education," in *The Nineteenth Century Woman: Her Cultural and Physical World*, ed. Delamont and Lorna Duffin (London: Croom Helm, 1978), pp. 164–187; Carol Dyhouse, *Girls Growing Up in Late Victorian and Edwardian England* (London: Routledge and Kegan Paul, 1981), pp. 79–114, 170–175.

68. Patrick Kay Bidelman, *Pariahs Stand Up! The Founding of the Liberal Feminist Movement in France, 1858–1889* (Westport, Conn.: Greenwood Press, 1982), pp. 199–201; Richard J. Evans, *The Feminists* (London: Croom Helm and New York: Barnes and Noble, 1977), p. 36.

69. Persis Charles Hunt, "Teachers and Workers: Problems of Feminist Organizing in the Early Third Republic," *Third Republic/Troisième République*, nos. 3–4 (1977), p. 171. Cf. Anne-Marie Sohn, *Féminisme et syndicalisme, les institutrices de la Fédération unitaire d'enseignement de 1919 à 1935* (Paris: Hachette, 1975), Microfiche.

70. Pauline Kergomard, *L'Education maternelle dans l'école*, 2 vols. (Paris, 1886, 1895), 1:37, as quoted in Françoise Derkenne, *Pauline Kergomard et l'éducation nouvelle enfantine (1838–1935)* (Paris: Editions du Cerf, 1938), p. 171.

71. M. Prélat, "Le Congrès de Lille," *RP* 47 (October 1905): 309–313; Francis McCollum Feeley, "A Study of French Primary School Teachers (1880–1919), The Conditions and Events which Led a Group of Them into the Revolutionary *Syndicaliste* Movement" (Ph.D. dissertation, University of Wisconsin, 1976), pp. 216–220. In 1907 the *amicales* had 85,000 supporters, or more than 70% of public school teachers. (Antoine Prost, *Histoire de l'enseignement* en *France, 1800–1967* [Paris: A. Colin, 1967], p. 391).

72. Theodore Zeldin, *France 1848–1945*, vol. 1: *Ambition, Love and Politics* (Oxford: Oxford University Press, 1973), pp. 347–350. For a more sympathetic account, see Steven C. Hause and Anne R. Kenney, "The Limits of Suffragist

Behavior: Legalism and Militancy in France, 1876–1922," *American Historical Review* 86 (October 1981): 781–806.

73. *Manuel général de l'instruction primaire* (27 March 1909): 393–395; (14 April 1909): 432; A. Eidenschenk-Patin, *Variétés morales et pédagogiques, petits et grands secrets de bonheur* (Paris: C. Delagrave, 1907), p. 117; Yvonne Oulhiou, *L'Ecole normale supérieure de Fontenay-aux-Roses à travers le temps, 1880–1980* (Fontenay-aux-Roses, Cahiers de Fontenay, 1981), p. 161. On Eidenschenk-Patin, see the previous references in chapters 1, 2, and Amicale des anciennes élèves de l'école normale d'institutrices du Nord, *Madame Eidenschenk* (Lille: n.p., 1978).

74. Eidenschenk-Patin, *Variétés*, pp. 117, 122. The author's textbook, *Troisièmes lectures des petites filles* (1913), offered impressive examples of female heroism but no complaints comparable to those in her manual for teachers.

75. Marilyn J. Boxer, "Foyer or Factory: Working Class Women in Nineteenth Century France," *Proceedings of the Western Society for French History* 2 (1975): 192–203.

76. Groupe des étudiants socialistes révolutionnaires internationalistes, *Comment l'état enseigne la morale* (Paris: Temps nouveaux, 1897), pp. 97–101; Le Congrès de Lyon, *La Française*, 6 June 1914.

77. Ginier, "Inspection," p. 217; E. Dodeman, "L'Inspection féminine dans les écoles de filles," *RP* 59 (July 1911): 66–71.

78. ADP D^1T^1 414 (Boissel).

79. ADP D^1T^1 500 (Debesson).

80. Persis Charles Hunt, "Revolutionary Syndicalism and Feminism among Teachers in France, 1900–1921" (Ph.D. dissertation, Tufts University, 1975), p. 261; Delhome et al, *Les premières institutrices*, p. 217.

81. André Retail, *Instituteur en pays de chouannerie* (Les Sables-d'Olonne: Editions le cercle d'or, 1979), p. 68.

82. Action populaire, *Institutrices de France* (Reims: Action populaire, 1912), p. 233.

83. Peter V. Meyers, "From Conflict to Cooperation: Men and Women Teachers in the Belle Epoque," in *The Making of Frenchmen: Current Directions in the History of Education in France, 1679–1979*, ed. Donald N. Baker and Patrick J. Harrigan (Waterloo, Ontario: Historical Reflections Press, 1980), p. 501.

NOTES TO CHAPTER FOUR: FROM WORLD WAR I TO WORLD WAR II: CONTINUITY AND CHANGE IN CURRICULUM AND TEXTBOOKS

1. Marguerite Bodin, *L'Institutrice* (Paris: O. Doin, 1922), p 47.

2. John E. Talbott, *The Politics of Educational Reform in France, 1918–1940* (Princeton, N.J.: Princeton University Press, 1969).

3. P. H. Gay and O. Mortreux, eds., *French Elementary Schools, Official Courses of Study*, trans. I. L. Kandel (New York: Teachers College, Columbia University, 1926), pp. 34, 55, 65, 100.

4. Ibid., pp. 92–93, 105, 117; Préfecture de Paris, Direction de l'enseignement, *Liste des ouvrages classiques qui peuvent être fournis gratuitement aux
frais de la ville de Paris dans les écoles primaires, collèges d'enseignement
général, communal et industriel* (Paris, 1971).

5. Gay and Mortreux, *French Elementary*, p. 92.

6. For background, see Joseph J. Spengler, *France Faces Depopulation* (Durham, N.C.: Duke University Press, 1938); Robert Talmy, *Histoire du mouvement familial en France (1896–1939)*, 2 vols. (Paris: Union nationale des caisses
d'allocations familiales, 1962); Karen M. Offen, "Depopulation, Nationalism,
and French Feminism during the Belle Epoque," paper presented to the
Society for French Historical Studies, Bloomington, Indiana, March 1981. I
wish to thank Karen Offen for information about the 27 May 1920 decree
establishing motherhood medals: bronze for those with at least five living
children, silver for eight, and gold for ten.

7. "Séance du 22 décembre 1912," *Eugénique* 1 (1913): 54–60; Offen,
"Depopulation."

8. *Deuxième congrès international des oeuvres et institutions féminines, Paris
1900, compte rendu des travaux* (Paris: Charles Blot, 1902), pp. 274–280;
Adolphe Pinard, *La Puériculture du premier age* (Paris: A. Colin, 1904), pp.
ix–x; Ferdinand Buisson, ed., *Nouveau dictionnaire de pédagogie et d'instruction
primaire* (Paris: Hachette, 1911), pp. 816, 1711; AN F¹⁷ 11656.

9. Diocèse de Paris, Direction de l'enseignement libre, *Organisation pédagogique et programme d'enseignement des écoles primaires libres* (Paris: L'Ecole,
1922), p. 66.

10. See Bibliography III.

11. M. Miraton and M. Farges, *L'Education morale et civique par la suggestion
artistique et littéraire*, 9th ed. (Paris: Delalain, 1923), p. 5; Henri Chatreix,
"Une morale d'Etat," in *Encyclopédie française* 15: 15'40–14.

12. Kléber Seguin, *Histoire de trois enfants* (Paris: Hachette, 1927).

13. Aimé Souché, *Le second livre de morale de la jeune française* (Paris:
Librairie d'éducation nationale, A. Picard, 1926), pp. 233–234; G. Imbert,
Leçons de morale, 3d ed. (Paris: Belin, 1935), p. 250; L. Emery, *Devant la vie*
(Paris: Société universitaire d'éditions et de librairie, 1936), p. 215; Félicien
Challaye and Marguerite Reynier, *Cours de morale à l'usage des écoles primaires
supérieures et cours complémentaires*, 8th ed. rev. (Paris: Félix Alcan, 1939),
p. 252.

14. Miraton and Farges, *Education morale*, pp. 137–139.

15. Charles Ab der Halden, *Hors du nid* (Paris: Editions Bourrelier, 1934),
p. 20; Imbert, *Leçons*, p. 323.

16. René Bazin and P. Dufrenne, *Lectures françaises, Il était quatre petits
enfants, cours élémentaire et moyen*; ibid., *cours moyen et supérieur*; Abbé E.
Bourceau and Raymond Fabry, *Lectures littéraires expliquées avec enseignement
moral et civique, cours supérieur* (Paris: Librairie de l'Ecole, 1933), p. 125;
Msgr. Marcel Hamayon and Abbé A. Bragade, *André et Jacqueline, deux
enfants de France* (Paris: Editions de l'Ecole, 1940), p. 75.

17. Ab der Halden and Marguerite Lavaut, *Pour enseigner la morale* (Paris:
F. Nathan, 1930), pp. 206–207; Charles Charrier, *Pédagogie vécue*, 15th ed.

(Paris: F. Nathan, 1936), p. 447; Edouard Bled, *Mes écoles* (Paris: R. Laffont, 1977), p. 245.

18. *Bibliographie de la France, Livres et matériel d'enseignement* (Paris: 1934, 1936).

19. Colin issued 79,000 copies of Payot's text between 1908 and 1939, 63,000 appearing before 1914.

20. Miraton and Farges, *Education morale*, pp. 5, 16–17, 20–21.

21. Ibid., pp. 56–57.

22. Souché, *Second livre*, pp. 5, 225.

23. Ibid., pp. 33–36.

24. Alice Durand-Gréville [Mme Henry Gréville], *L'Instruction morale et civique des jeunes filles* (Paris: E. Weill and G. Maurice, 1882), pp. 36–37; Stella, *Lectures pour les jeunes filles* (Tours: A. Mame, 1911), p. 99; Alcide Lemoine and Aubin Aymard, *Le jeune français* (Paris: Larousse, 1914), pp. 280–281.

25. See the titles in Bibliography IIIA, nos. 10, 13, 14, 18; IIIB 5, 6, 7, 9, 14, 24, 25, 27. The theme is implicit in the *puériculture* lessons in home economics and girls' science books.

26. Jean Cornec, *Josette et Jean Cornec, Instituteurs* (Paris: Clancier-Guénaud, 1980), pp. 24–25.

27. Souché, *Second livre*, p. 188. Only five books in the 1914–1940 sample mentioned the vote; on the other four, see below.

28. Ibid., pp. 165–166; Miraton and Farges, *Education morale*, pp. 124–135.

29. Marie-José Chombart de Lauwe, Paul-Henry Chombart de Lauwe et al., *La Femme dans la société, son image dans différents milieux sociaux* (Paris: Editions du C.N.R.S., 1963), pp. 157–158.

30. Emery, *Devant la vie*, pp. 143–158.

31. Souché, *Second livre*, pp. 68, 106; Mme Foulon-Lefranc and G. Laurent, *L'Ecole du bonheur* (Paris: Magnard, 1938), p. 14; Mlle Darcey, *Petit cours d'enseignement ménager*, 8th ed. (Lyon: E. Vitte, 1935), p. 8.

32. M. Bellenoue, *Entretiens familiers sur la morale sociale* (Paris: Spes, 1923), p. 52; Bourceau and Fabry, *Lectures, cours supérieur*, pp. 350, 369, By 1933, 70,000 copies of Bourceau and Fabry had been issued, and both books were recommended in the *Annuaire officiel de l'enseignement libre catholique* (Bordeaux: Delmas-Chapon-Gounouilhou, 1935), p. 518.

33. Steven C. Hause, "The Rejection of Women's Suffrage by the French Senate in November 1922: A Statistical Analysis," *Third Republic/Troisième République*, nos. 3–4 (1977), pp. 205–235.

34. Foulon-Lefranc, *La Femme au foyer* (Paris: L'Ecole, 1938), p. 15; and the more secular Foulon-Lefranc and Laurent, *Ecole du bonheur*, p. 15.

35. Une ancienne institutrice, *Aux jeunes filles* (Avignon: Aubanel, 1928), p. 40.

36. Bellenoue, *Entretiens*, pp. 67–68; Marie Thiéry, *Elise*, 7th ed. (Paris: A. Hatier, 1926), p. 52.

37. J. Leday, *Mon petit livre, lectures courantes pour les jeunes filles* (Paris: J. de Gigord, 1921), pp. 96, 187–194; Abbé Mathieu, *La Lecture expliquée au cours moyen*, 21st ed. (Paris: A. Hatier, 1945), p. 230; Bourceau and Fabry, *Lectures, cours supérieur*, p. 351.

38. For the titles of girls' readers available in 1932, see Bibliography IIA, nos. 18–20, 29, 31, 33, 35, 38, 54–56, 65–67, 73–76 and IIIA, 17, 19. The other three titles were Juranville, *La Civilité des petites filles* (1894); Stella, *Lectures des petites filles* (1903); and Antonin Franchet, *Livre de nos filles* (1922).

39. Bled, *Mes écoles*, p. 270; Pierre Dandurand, "Dynamique culturelle en milieu scolaire, une étude diachronique de manuels de l'école élémentaire française," *Revue française de sociologie* 13 (1972): 196.

40. Gay and Mortreux, *French Elementary*, p. 67; *RP* 120 (November 1938): 315.

41. ADP D¹T¹ 500.

42. Clément Brun, *Trois plumes de chapeau ou l'instituteur d'autrefois* (Grenoble and Paris: B. Arthaud, 1950), p. 94; Bled, *Mes écoles*, p. 55; *RP* 120 (1938): 314–315.

43. Chatreix, "Une morale d'Etat," pp. 15′40–14.

44. Dandurand, "Dynamique culturelle," pp. 193–212.

45. Octave Forsant and Pierre Dudouit, *La Vie des champs* (Paris: Larousse, 1930), pp. 5, 83–85, 115. Cf. F. Chadeyras, *Belles lectures françaises* (Paris: C. Delagrave, 1921), p. 48.

46. Laetitia Dès, *Jean et Lucie* (Paris: F. Nathan, 1920), pp. 176, 345; Bazin and Dufrenne, *Il était, cours moyen et supérieur*, pp. 91, 147. The latter was still for sale after 1945.

47. See chapter 5.

48. Ab der Halden, *Hors du nid*; a final edition appeared in 1954.

49. Hamayon and Bragade, *André et Jacqueline*. The introduction is dated March 1940. On the 1950 edition, see chapter 6.

50. Z., "Enseignement de la couture et des travaux du ménage," *RP* 25 (September 1894): 251; "Discours de M. Bayet au VIIᵉ congrès international contre l'alcoolisme," *RP* 35 (July 1899): 68.

51. Henriette Sourgen, "L'Enseignement ménager," in *Encyclopédie pratique de l'éducation en France* (Paris: Institut pédagogique national, 1960), pp. 801–802; Marie Mauron, *Les Cas de conscience de l'instituteur* (Paris: Perrin, 1966), p. 57; Alix Gautier, "L'Enseignement du travail manuel à l'école primaire," *RP* 81 (December 1922): 431.

52. "L'Enseignement du travail manuel dans les écoles primaires élémentaires de filles et dans les écoles normales d'institutrices," *RP* 33 (November 1898): 448.

53. Oreste Auriac, *L'Ecole exemplaire* (Paris: A. Colin, 1948), p. 113; Gaston Bonheur, *Qui a cassé le pot au lait* (Paris: R. Laffont, 1970), p. 49.

54. ME, *Règlements organiques de l'enseignement primaire* (Paris, 1887), p. 321.

55. "Congrès international de l'enseignement primaire," *RP* 37 (October 1900): 352–357; Maurice Souriau, "Un cours d'économie ménagère à Caen," *RP* 37 (August 1900): 199–201; C. Driessens, "L'Enseignement ménager dans l'académie de Lille," *RP* 39 (September 1901): 258.

56. ADP D²T¹ 13; C. Dolidon, "L'Education ménagère à l'école primaire," *RP* 69 (November 1916): 470–478.

57. ADP D²T¹ 13; Charrier, *Pédagogie*, p. 451; Gay and Mortreux, *French Elementary*, p. 92.

58. Sourgen, "Enseignement ménager," p. 806; "L'Education ménagère à l'école primaire," *RP* 40 (March 1902): 315–318.

59. In the girls' edition of Chanoine C. Grill and P. Le Floch, *L'Enseignement scientifique par l'observation et l'expérience* (Paris: L'Ecole, 1937), 12% of the pages dealt with home economics; in A. Roudil and Mme Bartoli, *Les Sciences physiques et naturelles* (Paris: Larousse, 1932), 14%; in A. Allard and Mlle Bergevin, *Cours méthodique de sciences physiques et naturelles et d'enseignement ménager* (Paris: Belin, 1923), 25%.

60. Roudil and Bartoli, *Sciences*, p. 235 (60,000 copies in the first two printings in 1932); Grill and Le Floch, *Enseignement scientifique*, pp. 264–265, 395.

61. Allard and Bergevin, *Cours*, p. 103; Roudil and Bartoli, *Sciences*, p. 267.

62. Miraton and Farges, *Education morale*, p. 16.

63. Roudil and Bartoli, *Sciences*, p. 269; Grill and Le Floch, *Enseignement scientifique*, p. 403.

64. Mme Georges Coulon, *Puériculture* (Paris: Hachette, 1925), pp. 24–27.

65. Pinard, *Puériculture*, p. 126 (figures from archives of Colin); Foulon-Lefranc, *Ecole du bonheur*, p. 202; *La Femme au foyer*, p. 192; George Sussman, "The Wet-nursing Business in Nineteenth-Century France," *French Historical Studies* 9 (1975): 304–328.

66. B. R. Mitchell, *European Historical Statistics, 1750–1950*, abridged ed. (New York: Columbia University Press, 1978), p. 43.

67. Solange Robert, *Septoures, chroniques villageoises* (Brioude: S. Frayssinet-Robert, 1973), p. 65.

68. Départements de la Mayenne et de la Sarthe, *Recueil des compositions données aux examens de 1935*, 2 vols. (Laval: A. Vade, 1935), 1: 5, 28, 37; 2: 63.

69. ADP D²T¹ 12. Entries on *puériculture* were interspersed with other subjects in the 1930–1931 notebooks of the Ecole de filles, rue Jules Ferry, in the Paris suburb of Clamart (Musée national de l'éducation, Enseignement primaire cahiers, 1930–1931 carton).

70. ADP D²T¹ 2 (report of Mme Pouillot); Gay and Mortreux, *French Elementary*, p. 92.

71. Bodin, *L'Institutrice*, p. 150.

72. Mlle Guennard, *Le Trésor de la ménagère* (Lyon: Vitte, 1935), p. 5; Darcey, *Petit cours d'enseignement ménager*, p. 7.

73. Foulon-Lefranc, *La Femme au foyer*, pp. 225–227.

74. Bourceau and Fabry, *Lectures, cours supérieur*, p. 369.

75. Fleury Marduel, *La Morale de la ménagère* (Paris: L'Ecole, 1938), pp. 20–21.

76. Guennard, *Trésor*, p. 543; Foulon-Lefranc, *La Femme au foyer*, p. 71, *Ecole du bonheur*, p. 81.

77. Talbott, *Politics of Educational Reform*.

78. Ibid., pp. 79, 226–227, 235–244.

79. Between 1930 and 1937 enrollment in all kinds of secondary establishments increased by 63%; it jumped 73% in *lycées* (ibid., p. 230).

80. P. Barrier, "La Réforme du certificat d'études et les nouveaux programmes et horaires de l'enseignement primaire élémentaire," *RP* 119 (June 1938): 487.

81. "Arrêté du 23 mars 1938 fixant les programmes du cours de fin d'études primaires," *RP* 119 (June 1938): 562; "Instructions relatives à l'application des arrêtés du 23 mars 1938 et du 11 juillet 1938," *RP* 120 (September 1938): 295.

82. "Arrêté du 23 mars 1938," pp. 548–549; Barrier, "Réforme," p. 487.

83. "Instructions," p. 280.

84. Jeannette Roussel, *Etre institutrice* (Paris: Editions du Cerf, 1973), p. 13.

85. Jean Zay, "Travail manuel féminin et enseignement ménager," *RP* 123 (February 1940): 126–127.

86. Mme Ellichabe, "L'Enseignement secondaire féminin," *Education* 23 (April 1932): 389–390.

87. Pierre Chevallier, ed., *La Scolarisation en France depuis un siècle* (Paris and The Hague: Mouton, 1974), p. 42.

88. Harry W. Paul, *The Second Ralliement: The Rapprochement between Church and State in France in the Twentieth Century* (Washington, D.C.: Catholic University Press, 1967).

89. Andrée Michel and Geneviève Texier, *La Condition de la française d'aujourd'hui, mythes et réalités*, 2 vols. (Paris: Gonthier, 1964), 1: 177; Hause, "The Rejection of Woman's Suffrage."

90. D. Billotey, "L'Enseignement primaire féminin," *Education* 23 (April 1932): 402.

91. AN F¹⁷ 14300.

Notes to Chapter Five: The Feminine Image and Social and Economic Realities, 1880–1940

1. ADP D²T¹ 15 (Mme Pouillot-Lombard).

2. E.g., Alice Durand-Gréville [Mme Henry Gréville], *L'Instruction morale et civique des jeunes filles* (Paris: E. Weill and G. Maurice, 1882), pp. 163–164; Stella, *Lectures pour les jeunes filles* (Tours: A. Mame, 1911), pp. 31–32. This message was explicit in 21 of 76 pre-1914 girls' textbooks in the sample; it was implicit in the depiction of women earning money in 12 others. Of 49 1914–1940 textbooks, 16 advised girls to prepare for work or depicted women at work. See Bibliography IIA, title nos. 2, 6, 8, 11–15, 17, 24, 29, 30, 35, 38, 40, 43, 48–50, 53–56, 58, 65–67, 69, 71, 73–76; IIA, nos. 32 (1919), 69 (1922); IIIA, 5, 9, 10, 11, 13; IIIB 1, 3, 6, 15–17, 19, 24, 28.

3. Jules Payot, *La Morale à l'école*, 3d ed. (Paris: A. Colin, 1908), p. 191; Aimé Souché, *Le second livre de morale de la jeune française* (Paris: A. Picard, 1926), pp. 5–6; Marie Thiéry, *Lisette* (Paris: A. Hatier, 1910), p. 32; Mlle Darcey, *Petit cours d'enseignement ménager*, 8th ed. (Lyon: E. Vitte, 1935), pp. 7–8. See also Bibliography IIB, title nos. 16, 18, 44; IIIA, 13, 14, 16, 18;

IIIB, 6; and the discussion of higher primary school textbooks at the end of this chapter.

4. Mme Foulon-Lefranc and G. Laurent, *L'Ecole du bonheur* (Paris: Magnard, 1938), p. 9.

5. Ernest Lavisse [Laloi], *La première année d'instruction civique* (Paris: A. Colin, 1880), p. 89; Anne-Louise Masson, *Manuel de morale et d'instruction civique à l'usage de l'enseignement primaire*, 3d ed. (Lyon: E. Vitte, 1922), p. 115. See also Bibliography IIA, title nos. 9, 13, 17; IIB, 36; IIIA, 9, 10, 16; IIIB, 1.

6. Henri Nolleau, "Les Femmes dans la population active de 1856 à 1954," *Economie et Politique* (October 1960): 11; Louise A. Tilly and Joan W. Scott, *Women, Work, and Family* (New York: Holt, Rinehart and Winston, 1978), pp. 104–145.

7. Emile Devinat, *Livre de lecture et de morale*, 17th ed. (Paris: C. Delagrave, n.d.), p. 50; Charles Ab der Halden, *Hors du nid* (Paris: Editions Bourrelier, 1934), p. 60.

8. Souché, *Second livre*, pp. 13, 103–106. See also Bibliography IIA, title nos. 16, 24, 38, 50; IIIA, 5, 14; IIIB, 1, 7, 15, 17; and for the higher primary schools, Félicien Challaye and Marguerite Reynier, *Cours de morale à l'usage des écoles primaires supérieures et cours complémentaires*, 8th ed. rev. (Paris: Félix Alcan, 1939), and Mathilde Salomon, *A nos jeunes filles, lectures et leçons de morale* (Paris: L. Cerf, 1893).

9. Nolleau, "Les Femmes," pp. 2–21, Souché, *Second livre*, pp. 13, 103–106; Foulon-Lefranc and Laurent, *Ecole*, p. 10.

10. Even in a reader by the feminist Marguerite Bodin, the girl sewed and helped her mother in the kitchen while the brother tidied up the father's workshop (*Jacques et Zette* [Paris: A. Colin, 1928], pp. 49–50). For rare examples of boys doing housework, see Bibliography IIA, 24; IIIA, 3; IIIB, 20.

11. Computed from figures in P. Bairoch, T. Deldycke, H. Gelders, J.-M. Limbor, *La Population active et sa structure* (Brussels: Institut de l'université libre, 1968), p. 167. Women were 31.2% of the work force in 1876, 33.6% in 1886, 33.6% in 1896, 37.2% in 1906, 36.6% in 1926, and 36.1% in 1936. In 1906 census takers began a deliberate effort to count farm wives in the work force.

12. Jean Daric, *L'Activité professionnelle des femmes en France* (Paris: Presses universitaires de France, 1947), p. 80; W. S. Woytinsky and E. S. Woytinsky, *World Population and Production: Trends and Outlook* (New York: The Twentieth Century Fund, 1953), p. 389; Bairoch, *La Population active*, p. 169.

13. See Bibliography IIA, title nos. 2, 3, 6, 8, 12, 13, 14, 16, 30, 49, 50, 56, 65, 71, 73; IIB, 13, 16, 27, 44, 57; IIIB, 1, 6, 15, 28.

14. See Bibliography IIA, title nos. 8, 14, 30, 40, 49, 50, 55, 56, 65, 73; IIB, 9, 16, 27, 57; IIIB, 1.

15. A. Mézières, *Education morale et instruction civique* (Paris: C. Delagrave, 1883), pp. 60, 154; Armand Ligny, *En route pour la vie*, 7th ed. (Paris: A. Colin, 1919), p. 162; Chanoine C. Grill and P. Le Floch, *L'Enseignement scientifique par l'observation et l'expérience (Garçons)* (Paris: L'Ecole, 1937), p. 393. See the discussion of this theme in Chapters 2, 4.

16. For enrollments in post-primary schools, see Antoine Prost, *Histoire de l'enseignement en France, 1880–1967* (Paris: A. Colin, 1968), p. 346, and Table 17, p. 149.

17. Stanley Hoffmann, "Paradoxes of the French Political Community," in *In Search of France*, ed. Hoffmann et al (Cambridge, Mass.: Harvard University Press, 1965), p. 3; Georges Dupeux, *French Society 1789–1970*, trans. Peter Wait (New York: Barnes and Noble, 1976), Chapters 4, 5.

18. Patrick J. Harrigan, *Mobility, Elites and Education in French Society of the Second Empire* (Waterloo, Ontario: Wilfrid Laurier University Press, 1980), pp. 151–160; Robert Gildea, "Education and the *Classes Moyennes* in the Nineteenth Century," in *The Making of Frenchmen: Current Directions in the History of Education in France, 1670–1979*, ed. Donald N. Baker and Patrick J. Harrigan (Waterloo, Ontario: Historical Reflections Press, 1980), pp. 275–299.

19. Gildea, "Education and the *Classes Moyennes*," p. 299.

20. Francine Muel, "Les Instituteurs, les paysans et l'ordre républicain," *Actes de recherche en sciences sociales*, nos. 17–18 (November 1977), pp. 40–42.

21. J. E. S. Hayward, "The Official Philosophy of the French Third Republic: Léon Bourgeois and Solidarism," *International Review of Social History* 6 (1961): 19–48.

22. Prost, *Enseignement*, pp. 390–393; Ida Berger and Roger Benjamin, *L'Univers des instituteurs, étude sociologique sur les instituteurs et institutrices du département de la Seine* (Paris: Editions de Minuit, 1964), pp. 141–157.

23. Anne-Marie Sohn, "Exemplarité et limites de la participation féminine à la vie syndicale: Les institutrices de la C.G.T.U.," *Revue d'histoire moderne et contemporaine* 24 (1977): 413; Danielle Delhome, Nicole Gault, Josiane Gonthier, *Les premières institutrices laïques* (Paris: Mercure de France, 1980), p. 214.

24. Anne-Marie Sohn, *Féminisme et syndicalisme, les institutrices de la Fédération unitaire d'enseignement de 1919 à 1935* (Paris: Hachette, 1975; microfiche), p. 67.

25. Ibid., pp. 42, 126, 143.

26. B. R. Mitchell, *European Historical Statistics, 1750–1970*, abridged ed. (New York: Columbia University Press, 1978), pp. 20–31; Joseph J. Spengler, *France Faces Depopulation* (Durham: Duke University Press, 1938).

27. Mitchell, *Statistics*, p. 27.

28. L. Leterrier, "Comment ils nous jugent," *RP* 87 (July 1925): 22; John W. Shaffer, "Family, Class, and Young Women: Occupational Expectations in Nineteenth Century Paris," *Journal of Family History* 3 (1978): 62–77.

29. Gaston Lecordier, *La Morale du travail pour les jeunes filles des milieux urbains, industriels et commerciaux* (Paris: Spes, 1947), p. 52.

30. Prost, *Enseignement*, pp. 10–12, 330.

31. E. Leroy, *La Composition française au c.e.p. et au concours de bourses nationales* (Paris: F. Nathan, 1934), p. 62.

32. Ida Berger, *Les Instituteurs d'une génération à l'autre* (Paris: Presses universitaires de France, 1979), p. 175.

33. Edouard Bled, *Mes écoles* (Paris: Robert Laffont, 1977), pp. 285–286.

34. Jacques Caroux-Destray, *Un couple ouvrier traditionnel, la vieille garde autogestionnaire* (Paris: Editions Anthropos, 1974), pp. 104–105; Marthe Boegner, *Des deux côtés de l'estrade* (Paris: Editions du Scorpion, 1964), p. 187.

35. Jane Marceau, *Class and Status in France: Economic Change and Social Immobility, 1945–1975* (Oxford: Oxford University Press, 1977), pp. 100–128; James Marangé, *De Jules Ferry à Ivan Illich* (Paris: Stock, 1976), p. 25; Marie Mauron, *Les Cas de conscience de l'instituteur* (Paris: Perrin, 1906), p. 117.

36. Computed from statistics in ME, *Statistique de l'enseignement primaire* 3 (1884): 248–249; 8 (1909): 266–269; *Bulletin de la Statistique générale de la France* 25 (1936): 327.

37. *Bulletin de la Statistique générale* 25 (1936): 327; *Annuaire statistique de la France* (1956), pp. xxii–xxiii. No educational data are given in the 1954 census for 3.3% of women and 2.6% of men.

38. ADP D²T¹ 2. Lacking statistics on the exact number of 12-year-olds in primary schools, I have computed the number of students potentially eligible to take the exam by dividing the total primary school enrollment (either public or private) by six. The results obtained for public school pupils are comparable to an official 1936 estimate (cited in note 37) that 50% of these pupils tried the exam and about 40% passed.

39. ADP D²T¹ 17.

40. ME, *Statistique* 8 (1909): 266–269.

41. Eugen Weber, *Peasants into Frenchmen: The Modernization of Rural France, 1870–1914* (Stanford, Calif.: Stanford University Press, 1976), p. 68.

42. ME, *Statistique* 8 (1909): clxix.

43. *Annuaire statistique de la France* (1909), pp. 30–31.

44. André Retail, *Instituteur en pays de Chouannerie* (Les Sables-d'Olonne: Editions le Cercle d'Or, 1979), p. 89; Pierre-Jakez Hélias, *The Horse of Pride: Life in a Breton Village*, trans. June Guicharnaud (New Haven, Conn.: Yale University Press, 1978), p. 137; Michel Ostenc, "L'Enseignement catholique pour les jeunes filles en Ardèche au début du XXᵉ siècle," in *Education et images de la femme chrétienne en France au début du XXᵉ siècle*, ed. Françoise Mayeur and Jacques Gadille (Lyon: Hermès, 1980), p. 138.

45. Statistique générale, *Résultats du recensement de 1901*, 3: 135, 169, 187, 257, 427, 623, 759, 867; 4: 251, 510–513, 866–869.

46. *Annuaire statistique* (1956), pp. xxii–xxiii.

47. Michel Vovelle, "Y-a-t-il une révolution culturelle au XVIIIe siècle: A propos de l'éducation populaire en Provence," *Revue d'histoire moderne et contemporaine* 22 (1975): 92–93, 127–131.

48. ME, *Statistique* 3 (1884): 248–249; 8 (1909): clxix, 266–269; *Annuaire statistique* (1909), pp. 30–31.

49. Peter V. Meyers, "From Conflict to Cooperation: Men and Women Teachers in the Belle Epoque," in *Making of Frenchmen*, ed. Baker and Harrigan, p. 494; *Annuaire statistique* (1909), pp. 36–37. There were more girls than boys in primary schools in the Alpes-Maritimes, Vaucluse, and Rhône in 1907.

50. L. M. Goreux, "Les Migrations agricoles en France depuis un siècle et leur rélations avec certains facteurs économiques," *Etudes et conjonctures* 11 (1956): 356–357.

51. *Résultats du recensement de 1901*, 4: 866–869.

52. Weber, *Peasants*, p. 182.

53. *Annuaire statistique* (1956), pp. xxii–xxiii.

54. Ibid., p. xix.

55. Theodore Zeldin, *France 1848–1945*, vol. 1: *Ambition, Love and Politics* (Oxford: Oxford University Press, 1973), p. 173. See also Pierre Déghilage, *La Dépopulation des campagnes* (Paris: F. Nathan, 1900); Catherine Bodard Silver, "France," in *Women, Roles and Status in Eight Countries*, ed. Janet Zollinger Giele and Audrey Chapman Smock (New York: John Wiley, 1977), p. 272.

56. Prost, *Enseignement*, p. 346.

57. Ibid.; *Annuaire statistique* (1966), pp. 139, 141.

58. ME, *Règlements organiques de l'enseignement primaire* (Paris, 1887), pp. 366–383; ME, *Plan d'études et programmes des écoles primaires supérieures de filles*, 7th ed. (Paris: Vuibert, 1937), pp. 90–95.

59. ME, *Plan . . . filles*, p. 75.

60. Emilien Constant, "Les Débuts de l'enseignement secondaire (et primaire supérieur) des jeunes filles dans le Var, 1867–1925," in *Making*, ed. Baker and Harrigan, p. 309.

61. Suzanne Mathiot, "Une année dans un cours complémentaire en 1939–1940," *Cahiers d'histoire de l'enseignement* 3 (1975): 131–139.

62. Gildea, "Education and the *Classes Moyennes*, pp. 275–279.

63. ME, *Plan . . . filles*; *Plan d'études et programmes des écoles primaires supérieures de garçons*, 7th ed. (Paris: Vuibert, 1937).

64. Ibid. (*filles*), p. 33.

65. Germaine Bourgade, *Contribution à l'étude d'une histoire de l'éducation féminine à Toulouse de 1830 à 1914* (Toulouse: Publications de l'Université de Toulouse-Le Mirail, 1980), p. 255.

66. Mathiot, "Une année," p. 137.

67. D. Levesque, "La Formation professionnelle dans les écoles primaires supérieures," *RP* 77 (October 1920): 266; Françoise Mayeur, *L'Enseignement secondaire des jeunes filles sous la troisième république* (Paris: Presses de la fondation nationale des sciences politiques, 1977), pp. 388–398, 400–428.

68. Amélie Gayraud, *Les jeunes filles d'aujourd'hui* (Paris: G. Oudin, 1914), pp. 116, 222; Louise Weiss, *Mémoires d'une européenne*, vol. 1: *1893–1919* (Paris: Payot, 1968), pp. 56, 74–85, 134; Ménie Grégoire, *Telle que je suis* (Paris: R. Laffont, 1976), pp. 121–129.

69. ME, *Plan . . . garçons*, pp. 12–33.

70. E. Segond, *Mes premières lectures, à l'usage des écoles et maisons d'éducation de jeunes filles* (Paris: A. Hatier, 1927), pp. 103–104.

71. Salomon, *A nos jeunes filles*, pp. 21–25, 34–38, 126–127. On Salomon, see Mayeur, *Enseignement*, pp. 88–90, 228.

72. Albert Pierre and A. Martin, *Cours de morale théorique et pratique (filles et garçons)*, 9th ed. (Paris: F. Nathan, 1911), pp. 133, 137.

73. Bairoch, *La Population active*, p. 179.

74. ME, *Statistique* 8 (1909): ci–civ. Data on the occupations of parents of some girls in *écoles primaires supérieures* are in AN F[17] 9819.

75. Gildea, "Education and the *Classes Moyennes*." Gildea uses the "Statistique des cours complémentaires des écoles primaires" in AN F^{17} 11681–11690.

76. AN F^{17} 11688–11690.

77. AN F^{17} 11688–11689.

78. Emilie Carles, *Une soupe aux herbes sauvages* (Paris: Editions Jean-Claude Simoën, 1977), pp. 59–77.

79. "La Guerre et l'apprentissage," *RP* 71 (September 1917): 268.

80. Frances I. Clark, *The Position of Women in Contemporary France* (London: P. S. King, 1937), p. 39.

81. Daric, *Activité*, p. 31; Bairoch, *La Population active*, pp. 167, 172–173.

82. Nolleau, "Les Femmes," p. 11; Daric, "Aperçu général de l'évolution du travail féminin en France," *Avenirs*, nos. 53–54 (March-April 1953), p. 11.

83. Bairoch, *La Population active*, pp. 172–173.

84. Clark, *Position of Women*, p. 75; *Annuaire statistique* (1936), p. 315.

85. Bairoch, *La Population active*, pp. 96, 172–173.

86. Challaye and Reynier, *Cours de morale*, pp. 140–145.

87. Ibid., p. 169; Louis-Eugène Rogie, M. Bornecque, and Mme Levesque, *Nouvelles lectures professionnelles* (Paris: Gedalge, 1928), pp. 157–184.

88. ADP D^{2}T^1 15 (Mme Pouillot-Lombard, cited in note 1); Marguerite Charles, *L'Enseignement du travail à l'école primaire, garçons et filles* (Paris: Gedalge, 1927), p. 63.

89. Denise Billotey, "Travail féminin," *RP* 110 (October 1933): 128.

NOTES TO CHAPTER SIX: FROM VICHY THROUGH THE FOURTH REPUBLIC

1. Gaston Lecordier, *Morale civique et sociale, deuxième année* (Paris: Bloud and Gay, 1959), p. 81.

2. Félicien Challaye and Marguerite Reynier, *Cours de morale et instruction civique, deuxième année* (Paris: Presses universitaires de France, 1941), p. 6. On the support for Vichy of secondary professor Challaye and inspector and textbook author Léon Emery, see Paul Delanoue, *Les Enseignants, la lutte syndicale du front populaire à la libération* (Paris: Editions sociales, 1973), pp. 46, 131, 193, 200, 214.

3. James Marangé, *De Jules Ferry à Ivan Illich* (Paris: Stock, 1976), p. 49. See also W. D. Halls, *The Youth of Vichy France* (Oxford: Oxford University Press, 1981), pp. 103–131; Jean Vial, *Les Instituteurs* (Paris: J.-P. Delarge, 1980), pp. 219–222.

4. Philippe Pétain, "L'Education nationale," *RP* 124 (May-June 1941): 88.

5. "Organisation de l'enseignement primaire élémentaire," *RP* 124 (May-June 1941): 193; Robert O. Paxton, *Vichy France: Old Guard and New Order, 1940–1944* (New York: Alfred A. Knopf, 1972), p. 151. Carcopino, education minister from February 1941 to April 1942, simply allowed free time for "voluntary religious instruction off school premises."

6. Pétain, "Education," p. 88.

7. "Organisation," pp. 178–180.

8. Paxton, *Vichy France*, p. 160.

9. AN F¹⁷ 13378.

10. See Bibliography IV.

11. L. P. Renaud, *Notre morale "servir"* (Paris: C. Lavauzelle, 1944), pp. 26–27.

12. Maurice Rouable, *150 lectures de morale vivante* (Paris: Vuibert, 1943), p. 2; Rose Guillaume, *Sciences appliquées et travaux pratiques, enseignement ménager, puériculture, hygiène* (Paris: Bourrelier, 1943), p. 244.

13. Evelyne Sullerot, "La Démographie en France," in *Société et culture de la France contemporaine*, ed. George Santoni (Albany, N.Y.: State University of New York Press, 1981), p. 73.

14. Henriette Sourgen, "L'Enseignement ménager," in *Encyclopédie pratique de l'éducation en France* (Paris: Institut pédagogique national, 1960), p. 802; Halls, *Youth*, p. 99.

15. Mme Foulon-Lefranc, *L'Ecole du bonheur*, 6th ed. (Paris: Magnard, 1943), p. 359; *La Femme au foyer*, 11th ed. (Paris: L'Ecole, 1953), pp. 355–357.

16. Challaye and Reynier, *Cours*, p. 6; Rouable, *150 lectures*, p. 292.

17. Renaud, *Notre morale "servir"*, pp. iv, 67, and *La Vie morale de l'enfant* (Paris: C. Lavauzelle, 1949), p. 67; Challaye and Reynier, *Cours*, p. 4; Groupe de travail de la maison d'école à Montceau-les-Mines, *Cent ans d'école* (Seyssel: Editions du Champ Vallon, 1981), p. 173.

18. Mattei Dogan and Jacques Narbonne, *Les Françaises face à la politique, comportement politique et condition sociale* (Paris: A. Colin, 1955), p. 181; A. Godier and G. Salesse, *Préparons-nous à la vie sociale* (Paris: Bourrelier, 1954), p. 98.

19. Andrée Michel and Geneviève Texier, *La Condition de la française d'aujourd-hui*, 2 vols. (Paris: Gonthier, 1964), 1: 181; Catherine Bodard Silver, "France," in *Women, Roles and Status in Eight Countries*, ed. Janet Zollinger Giele and Audrey Chapman Smock (New York: John Wiley, 1977), p. 290; *Le Monde*, 23 June 1981.

20. Alain Girard, "Les Femmes sont-elles féministes? Travail féminin et participation sociale," *L'Esprit* 29 (May 1961): 922; Charles Roig and Françoise Billon-Grand, *La Socialisation politique des enfants* (Paris: A. Colin, 1968), pp. 71, 87, 115; Betty Friedan, *The Feminine Mystique* (New York: Norton, 1963).

21. Groupe de travail, *Cent ans*, p. 176.

22. Lecordier, *Morale, deuxième année*, p. 140.

23. Lecordier, *Morale du travail pour des jeunes filles des milieux urbains, industriels et commerciaux* (Paris: Spes, 1947), p. 38.

24. H. Michard and A. Glossinde, *Condition et mission de l'instituteur* (Paris: Aubier, 1945), pp. 128–129.

25. See Bibliography V B, title nos. 6, 8, 14, 16.

26. Raymond Bauduin, "Sciences d'observation," in *Encyclopédie pratique de l'éducation*, p. 723.

27. "Evolution de l'emploi féminin dans la société française," *Avenirs*, nos. 268–269 (November-December 1975), p. 11.

28. Robert Colin, "Prémices et développement de la législation familiale française," in *Renouveau des idées sur la famille*, ed. Robert Prigent (Paris:

Presses universitaires de France, 1954), pp. 171–174; G. Mauco and M. Grandazzi, *La Démographie à l'école, manuel à l'usage des maîtres* (Paris: Alliance nationale contre la dépopulation, 1948), pp. 60–63.

29. See Bibliography V A, title nos. 6, 9, 12; V B, 14.

30. Marie Ravaudet, *Courage* (Villefranche: Editions du C.e.p. beaujolais, 1953), p. 45; M. Ballot and R. Aveillé, *Education morale et civique* (Paris: C. Lavauzelle, 1952), p. 86; Lecordier, *Morale du travail*.

31. Aimé Souché, *Les nouvelles leçons de morale au cours moyen* (Paris: F. Nathan, 1947), pp. 41, 163, 219–220.

32. André Godier, "Les nouveaux programmes de sciences appliquées," *Education nationale; Ecole publique* (19 November 1953): 5.

33. Ballot and Aveillé, *Education*, p. 260; Godier and Salesse, *Préparons*, p. 154. See also Bibliography V B, title nos. 7, 14, 15.

34. Jean Anscombre, *Mon mémento de sciences (Filles, écoles rurales et urbaines)* (Saint-Germain-en-Laye: Maison des instituteurs, 1956), p. 18.

35. Godier and Salesse, *Préparons*, p. 120.

36. Michel and Texier, *Condition*, 1: 41; B. R. Mitchell, *European Historical Statistics, 1750–1970*, abr. ed. (New York: Columbia University Press, 1978), p. 27; Francis Ronsin, *La Grève des ventres, propagande néo-malthusien et baisse de la natalité française* (Paris: Aubier, 1980), p. 14. By 1978 the birthrate hit an alltime low of 138 per 10,000.

37. Lecordier, *Morale du travail*, pp. 21–57.

38. Pierre Dandurand, "Dynamique culturelle en milieu scolaire, une étude diachronique de manuels de l'école élémentaire française," *Revue française de sociologie* 13 (1972): 196, 201, 207.

39. In 1939 girls were 33% of the public secondary school population; in 1952, nearly 50% (*Annuaire statistique de la France*, 1966, pp. 139–140).

40. Mgr Marcel Hamayon and Abbé A. Bragade, *André et Jacqueline, deux enfants de France*, 7th ed. (Paris: Editions de l'Ecole, 1951), pp. 59, 242–245, 325–327.

41. Jeanne Séguin and Pauline Millett, *Pour nos filles* (Paris: Larousse, 1957), pp. 88, 238–239.

42. Letter from Jeanne Séguin, June 1981. Sales figures from archives of Larousse. No other girls' reader is advertised in the 1957 textbook supplement of the *Bibliographie de France*.

43. Hélène Sourgen, *L'Education civique des femmes, quelques suggestions pratiques* (Paris: UNESCO, 1954), pp. 17–18, 46, 55, 103.

44. Roig and Billon-Grand, *Socialisation*, pp. 71, 87, 115.

45. Sourgen, "Enseignement ménager," pp. 801–802; Marthe Broussin, "Sciences, techniques et arts, section féminines," in *Encyclopédie*, pp. 789, 798.

46. Ballot and Aveillé, *Education*, p. 86.

47. Ida Berger and Roger Benjamin, *L'Univers des instituteurs, étude sociologique sur les instituteurs du département de la Seine* (Paris: Editions de minuit, 1964), p. 105; Marie-José Chombart de Lauwe, Paul-Henry Chombart de Lauwe et al., *La Femme dans la société, son image dans différents milieux sociaux* (Paris: Centre national de la recherche scientifique, 1963), pp. 212–213.

48. Jeanne Burniaux, *L'Education des filles* (Paris: Editions universitaires, 1965), pp. 34–36.

49. G. Villard, *La Morale en action* (Paris: F. Nathan, 1960), p. 193; Jeannette Roussel, *Etre institutrice* (Paris: Editions du Cerf, 1973), p. 14.

50. P. Bairoch, T. Deldycke, H. Gelders, J.-M. Limbor, *La Population active et sa structure* (Brussels: Institut de l'université libre, 1968), pp. 170–171.

51. *Sondages* (16 January 1947), p. 18.

52. Berger and Benjamin, *Univers*, p. 105.

53. Chombart de Lauwe, *La Femme*, pp. 198–215.

54. Ibid., p. 359.

55. Madeleine Chapsal, *Vérités sur les jeunes filles* (Paris: Grasset, 1960), p. 186.

56. Bianka Zazzo, "Etude différentielle de l'image du soi," *L'Enfance* 11 (1958): 363–367, 372. Zazzo studied 133 apprentices and 42 secondary students.

57. Zazzo, "La Représentation de la réussite chez les adolescents," *L'Enfance* 15 (1962): 275–289.

58. *Sondages* (Summer 1950), p. 19.

59. *Annuaire statistique de la France* (1952), p. 54.

60. Laurence Wylie, *Village in the Vaucluse*, 3d ed. (Cambridge, Mass.: Harvard University Press, 1974), pp. 91–94; Edouard Bled, *Mes écoles* (Paris: R. Laffont, 1977), p. 355; Roussel, *Etre institutrice*, p. 16.

61. Jean Auvinet, *L'Ecole et la réussite scolaire* (Paris: J. Vrin, 1968), p. 295.

62. Claude Vimont and Geneviève Gontier, "Une enquête sur les femmes fonctionnaires," *Population* 20 (1965): 32.

63. A. Girard, "Enquête nationale sur l'orientation et la sélection des enfants d'age scolaire," *Population* 9 (1954): 615; Viviane Isambert-Jamati, "Le Choix du métier," *L'Esprit* 29 (1961): 892–903.

64. Girard, "Enquête," p. 616.

65. Michel and Texier, *Condition*, 1: 166.

66. Madeleine Guilbert and Viviane Isambert-Jamati, "Une étude de biographies professionnelles," *Population* 13 (1958): 647–662.

67. René Kaes, *Quelques attitudes ouvrières à l'égard de l'école et de l'enseignement, enquête dans deux entreprises françaises, 1961* (Strasburg: University of Strasburg, 1964); "La Formation initiale," *Avenirs* (1975), p. 297; Isambert-Jamati, "Choix."

68. Girard, "Enquête," pp. 621, 623.

69. Isambert-Jamati, "Choix," pp. 893–895.

70. Alain Girard and Henri Bastide, "Orientation et sélection scolaires, une enquête sur les enfants à la sortie de l'école primaire," *Population* 10 (1955): 606, 614.

71. Berger and Benjamin, *Univers*, pp. 58–59.

72. Fritz K. Ringer, *Education and Society in Modern Europe* (Bloomington, Ind.: Indiana University Press, 1979), p. 147; Françoise Lantier, *Le Travail et la formation des femmes en Europe* (Paris: Documentation française, 1972), p. 26.

NOTES TO CHAPTER SEVEN: THE FIFTH REPUBLIC: EDUCATIONAL
REFORMS AND REEVALUATIONS OF GIRLS' SCHOOLING

1. Danièle Granet, "La Gare de triage de la troisième," *L'Express* (13 June 1977), p. 104.

2. W. Fraser, *Reforms and Restraints in Modern French Education* (London: Routledge and Kegan Paul, 1971), p. 130.

3. Antoine Prost, *Histoire de l'enseignement en France, 1800–1967* (Paris: A. Colin, 1968), pp. 413, 423.

4. Ibid., pp. 477–482.

5. Antoine Prost, "Quand l'école de Jules Ferry est-elle morte?" *Histoire de l'éducation,* no. 14 (1982), p. 36.

6. ME, *L'Enseignement en France, textes fondamentaux* (Paris, 1961), pp. 239–240; Jean Tronchère, *Une année au cours moyen,* 3d ed. (Paris: A. Colin, 1978), p. 43; P. H. Gay and O. Mortreux, eds., *French Elementary Schools: Official Courses of Study,* trans. I. L. Kandel (New York: Teachers' College, Columbia University, 1926), p. 34. As of 1978 "activités d'éveil" received one more hour and physical education one less (L. Leterrier, *Programmes, instructions,* ed. M. Pierre and N. Babin [Paris: Hachette, 1981], p. 360).

7. Pierre Dandurand, "Dynamique culturelle en milieu scolaire, une étude diachronique de manuels de l'école élémentaire française," *Revue française de sociologie* 13 (1972): 200, 208.

8. Christian Baudelot and Roger Establet, *L'Ecole primaire divise* (Paris: F. Maspéro, 1975), pp. 19, 29, 73–75.

9. Michèle Saltiel, "L'Echec à l'école primaire," *Le Monde de l'éducation,* no. 67 (December 1980), p. 9.

10. *Sondages,* nos. 3–4 (1974), p. 51.

11. Saltiel, "L'Echec," pp. 10–14.

12. Marie-Claude Betbeder, "Maternelle: les inquiétudes d'une école heureuse," *MDE,* no. 88 (November 1982), p. 22.

13. "La Formation initiale," *Avenirs,* nos. 268–269 (1975), p. 297.

14. ME, *Informations statistiques,* No. 101 (March 1968), p. 171. By 1972–1973 the education ministry's statistics no longer classified public primary schools by sex but continued to do so for private schools.

15. ME, *Informations statistiques,* No. 101, p. 210; *Statistique des enseignements,* No. 1 (1975), p. 17.

16. Interview with the *directeur* of the *école primaire,* rue Victor Cousin, June 1979.

17. Jeanine de Caumont, "L'Ecole primaire, pourquoi l'enseignement n'est-il pas mixte," *Education* (February 1969), pp. 5–7; B. Zazzo, "La Coéducation," *Ecole des parents* (April 1964), pp. 2–11.

18. Edouard Breuse, *La Coéducation dans les écoles mixtes* (Paris: Presses universitaires de France, 1970), pp. 17–18.

19. Philippe Baillat et al., *A la Communale* (Paris: Hachette, 1976), pp. 184–185.

20. Marie-José Chombart de Lauwe, "Quelle image la petite fille d'aujourd'hui a-t-elle de la femme," in *Dans la société d'aujourd'hui devenir une*

femme, propos sur l'éducation des filles, ed. Bernadette Aumont (Paris: Editions Fleurus, 1970), p. 20.

21. Louise Michel, *L'Ecole de campagne* (Bordeaux: Nouveaux cahiers de jeunesse, 1968), p. 67.

22. Margaret Collins Weitz, "The Status of Women in France Today," *Contemporary French Civilization* 3 (1978): 40–42.

23. Suzanne Mollo, *L'Ecole et la société, psychosociologie des modèles éducatifs* (Paris: Dunod, 1970), pp. 87–92, 122, 158.

24. *Daniel et Valérie* was published by F. Nathan. Ligue du droit des femmes, Groupe manuels scolaires, "Le Sexisme dans les manuels scolaires," *Les Temps modernes* 30, no. 340 (November 1974): 450–462. See also the special issue, "Petites filles en éducation," *Les Temps modernes* 31, no. 358 (May 1976).

25. Mary Ellen Verheyden-Hilliard, *A Handbook for Workshops on Sex Equality in Education* (Washington, D.C.: American Personnel and Guidance Association, n.d.), p. 18; U.S., Congress, House, Committee on Education and Labor, *The Women's Educational Equity Act,* Hearings before the Subcommittee on Equal Opportunities of the House Committee on Education and Labor on H.R. 208, 93d Cong., 1st sess., 1973, p. 1.

26. Rosemary Deem, *Women and Schooling* (London: Routledge and Kegan Paul, 1978), p. 79.

27. Institut national de la recherche et de la documentation pédagogiques, "Images de la femme dans les manuels scolaires," *Bibliographie de France* 19, part 2 (May 7, 1975): 766–787. *Lisons* was published by F. Nathan; *Avec les mots de tous les jours,* by Hachette. The INRDP is now the INRP (Institut national de recherche pédagogique.

28. Ibid., pp. 772, 779.

29. Annie Decroux-Masson, *Papa lit, maman coud, les manuels scolaires en bleu et rose* (Paris: Denoël and Gonthier, 1979).

30. Ida Berger, *Les Instituteurs d'une génération à l'autre* (Paris: Presses universitaires de France, 1979), p. 171.

31. Leterrier, *Programmes,* p. 459.

32. Renée Myot, "Image de la femme dans les manuels scolaires," *Pédagogie,* no. 7 (September 1975), p. 63. This article reproduces INRDP, "Images," pp. 775–780.

33. Janice Pottker, "Psychological and Occupational Sex Stereotypes in Elementary-School Readers," in *Sex Bias in the Schools,* ed. Pottker and Andrew Fishel (Cranbury, N.J.: Associated University Presses, 1977), pp. 101–110.

34. G. Lobban, "Presentation of Sex Roles in British Reading Schemes," *Trends in Education* 16 (Spring 1974): 57–60. See also Judy Keiner, "Introduction to 'Mind That You Do As You Are Told,'" *Feminist Review* 3 (1979): 83–84, and Gaby Weiner, "Sex Differences in Mathematical Performance: A Review of Research and Possible Action," in *Schooling for Women's Work,* ed. Rosemary Deem (London: Routledge and Kegan Paul, 1980), pp. 82–83.

35. Alphons Silbermann and Udo Michael Krueger, *Abseits der Wirklichkeit: Das Frauenbild in Deutschen Lesebüchern, Eine soziologische Untersuchung* (Cologne: Verlag Wissenschaft und Politik, 1971), p. 93, as quoted by Zelime

Amen Ward, "Federal Republic of Germany: Disparate Government Responses to Women," in *Integrating the Neglected Majority: Government Responses to Demands for New Sex Roles*, ed. Patricia Kyle (Brunswick, Ohio: King's Court Communications, 1976), p. 49.

36. Women on Words and Images, "Look Jane Look, See Sex Stereotypes," in *And Jill Came Tumbling After: Sexism in American Education*, ed. Judith Stacey, Susan Bereaud, and Joan Daniels (New York: Dell Publishing Co., 1974), pp. 160–162, 172. Women on Words and Images was a 25-member task force of the Princeton, New Jersey chapter of NOW; their longer study, "Dick and Jane as Victims: Sex Stereotyping in Children's Literature," is reprinted in U.S., Congress, House, *Women's Educational Equity Act*, pp. 512–570.

37. Grace K. Baruch, "Sex-Role Attitudes of Fifth-Grade Girls," in *Jill*, ed. Stacey, pp. 200–201.

38. *Sondages*, nos. 3–4 (1974), p. 53.

39. INRDP, "Images," pp. 780–781.

40. "La Condition féminine," *Avenirs*, nos. 268–269 (1975), pp. 39–40.

41. Women on Words and Images, Look Jane Look," p. 177.

42. INRDP, "Images," p. 782.

43. Patrick Kay Bidelman, *Pariahs Stand Up! The Founding of the Liberal Feminist Movement in France, 1858–1889* (Westport, Conn.: Greenwood Press, 1982), p. 199.

44. Lucy Komisar, "France's Non-feminist Minister of Women," *Saturday Review* 2, no. 19 (June 14, 1975): 29–30, 57.

45. Délégation régionale à la condition féminine, *L'Image de la femme dans les manuels scolaires et les livres d'enfants* (Paris: Préfecture de la Région Ile de France, 1979).

46. INRDP, "Images," pp. 781–782.

47. Berger, *Instituteurs*, p. 42.

48. Gisèle Charzat, *Les Françaises sont-elles des citoyennes* (Paris: Denoël and Gonthier, 1972), p. 146.

49. *Nord Pédagogie*, no. 22 (1972), p. 19.

50. P. Bairoch, T. Deldycke, H. Gelders, J.-M. Limbor, *La Population active et sa structure* (Brussels: Institut de l'université libre, 1968), p. 167; "Evolution de l'emploi féminin dans la société française," *Avenirs*, nos. 268–269 (1975), pp. 11, 21; "Répertoire par académies du marché de l'emploi féminin," *Avenirs*, nos. 268–269 (1975), pp. 53–58; *Annuaire statistique de la France* (1980), p. 74.

51. Betbeder, "Maternelle," p. 21. The percentage of enrolled two-year-olds doubled between 1970 and 1981. The total number of preprimary pupils rose by 23 percent between 1958 and 1978, while the number of primary pupils actually dropped by 5 percent because of the earlier entry of pupils into secondary schools and a falling birth rate (*Annuaire statistique* [1979], p. 114).

52. "La Condition féminine," *Avenirs*, nos. 268–269 (1975), p. 43.

53. Sylviane Stein, "Femmes: les conquêtes inachevées," *L'Express* (19 March 1982), p. 56.

54. Bairoch et al., *La Population active*, p. 96; Marie-Hélène Mérino, "Les Femmes dans la hiérarchie des emplois," *Avenirs*, nos. 268–269 (1975), pp. 124, 128; Institut national de la statistique et des études économiques, *Principaux résultats du recensement de 1975* in *Collections de l'INSEE*, no. 238, série D, no. 52 (September 1977), pp. 121–122, 200.

55. Charzat, *Françaises*, pp. 282–283.

56. Pierre Giolitto, "Côté fille, côté garçon," *L'Education* (12 December 1981), p. 11; Catherine Bodard Silver, "France," in *Women, Roles and Status in Eight Countries*, ed. Janet Zollinger Giele and Audrey Chapman Smock (New York: John Wiley, 1977), pp. 282–283.

57. Silver, "France," pp. 282–283.

58. "Les Femmes chôment davantage," *MDE*, no. 44 (November 1978), p. 21.

59. Stein, "Femmes," p. 58.

60. Ibid., p. 57.

61. Roger Cans and Marc Coutty, "S'adapter à la réalité du travail," *MDE*, no. 83 (May 1982), pp. 10–11.

62. Claude Grignon, *L'Ordre des choses, les fonctions sociales de l'enseignement technique* (Paris: Editions de Minuit, 1971), p. 96.

63. Cans and Coutty, "Emploi: les filles défavorisées," *MDE*, no. 83 (May 1982), pp. 18–19.

64. Leterrier, *Programmes*, p. 465.

65. Ligue du droit des femmes, "Sexisme," p. 451; Délégation régionale, *L'Image*, pp. 9–14; Decroux-Masson, *Papa lit*, pp. 32, 69, 82, 116.

66. Association pour une école non sexiste, "Pour une école non sexiste" (Paris, 1982), pp. 1–2.

67. Letter in *MDE*, no. 64 (September 1980), p. 48.

68. "La Condition féminine," *Avenirs* (1975), p. 41; Béatrice Berge, "Les Garçons au fourneaux, les filles à l'établi," *MDE*, no. 66 (November 1980), pp. 52–54.

69. Margaret Collins Weitz, "The Status of Women in France Today: A Reassessment," *Contemporary French Civilization* 6 (1981–1982): 213–214.

70. Sylviane Stein, "Femmes: allez Roudy," *L'Express* (5 November 1982), pp. 67–68.

71. *Les Femmes en France dans une société d'inégalités* (Paris: Documentation française, 1982), pp. 134–139; Frank Deberne, "La Forêt des manuels," *MDE*, no. 46 (January 1979), pp. 15–18.

72. *Femmes en France*, p. 139; Michaele Bobasch, "Au paradis des petites filles," *L'Education* (1 April 1982), p. 4.

73. Association pour une école non sexiste, "Pour une école non sexiste," pp. 2, 4; Letter from Catherine Valabrègue, 31 January 1983.

74. *Le Monde* (9 March 1982).

75. "Circulaire no. 82–182 du 29 avril 1982, Orientation des jeunes filles," *Bulletin officiel de l'éducation nationale*, no. 18 (6 May 1982), pp. 1514–1516.

76. Huguette Debaisieux, "A quoi rêvent les jeunes filles," *L'Express* (2 August 1980), p. 59.

77. Yves-Marie Labé, "L'An II du changement," *MDE,* no. 86 (September 1982), p. 43.

78. Association pour une école non sexiste, "Nantes: ville non sexiste" (October 1982), pp. 1–2.

79. Labé, "L'An II du changement," p. 43.

Bibliography

A Note on Sources

Archival sources, government documents and reports, teachers' memoirs, pedagogical treatises, educational reference works, histories of French education, studies on the position of women in French society, and other general works are cited in the notes and are not repeated here. Readers interested in recent studies on all aspects of the history of French education and in the names of those currently working in the field should consult the annual bibliographies and lists of researchers in *Histoire de l'éducation*, which began publication in December 1978. Also useful are the articles and bibliography in *The Making of Frenchmen: Current Directions in the History of Education in France, 1679–1979*, ed. Donald N. Baker and Patrick J. Harrigan (Waterloo, Ontario: Historical Reflections Press, 1980). Standard histories of French education since 1800 are Antoine Prost, *Histoire de l'enseignement en France, 1800–1967* (Paris: Armand Colin, 1968) and Joseph N. Moody, *French Education Since Napoleon* (Syracuse, N.Y.: Syracuse University Press, 1978). The education of French girls in the nineteenth century, prior to 1880, is surveyed in Françoise Mayeur, *L'Education des filles au XIXᵉ siècle* (Paris: Hachette, 1979). Mayeur's *Enseignement secondaire des jeunes filles sous la troisième république* (Paris: Presses de la fondation nationale des sciences politiques, 1977) is the standard work on public secondary schools for girls from 1880 to 1924.

Textbooks

A complete list of textbooks approved for use in public schools by one or more departments as of 1889 was published by the Ministère de l'instruction publique (*Livres scolaires en usage dans les écoles primaires publiques*, 1889). Lists of textbooks approved for use in individual departments in 1882 and 1883 are in Archives Nationales F¹⁷ 11652–11654; lists of textbooks in use in 1909 in twenty-three departments (Ain-Creuse) are in F¹⁷ 11656.

The numbered lists below permit the citation of textbooks simply by number in footnotes where multiple references to textbooks were necessary.

I. Pre-1870 textbooks not on the 1889 list of approved textbooks

1. Caillard, Mme Paul. *Entretiens familiers d'une institutrice avec ses élèves, essai de méthode pratique sur l'éducation, spécialement destiné aux écoles primaires.* 3d ed. Paris: C. Delagrave, 1874. (1st ed., 1863).
2. ———. *Résumé d'éducation pratique par demandes et par réponses, extrait des Entretiens familiers d'une institutrice.* 7th ed. Paris: C. Delagrave, 1880. (1st ed., 1863).
3. Joigneaux, P. *Conseils à la jeune fermière.* Paris: G. Masson, 1874. (1st ed., 1859).
4. Pichard, Lilla. *Jean de Namur, ou entretiens d'un instituteur avec ses élèves sur la protection que l'homme doit aux animaux dans son intérêt personnel.* Paris: Librairie d'éducation, 1874. (1st ed., 1869).
5. Sirey, Mme. *Petit manuel d'éducation, ou lectures à l'usage des jeunes filles de 8 à 12 ans.* 2d ed. Paris: Belin, n.d. (1st ed., 1841).

II A. 1870–1914: Textbooks for Girls

(Original publication dates are indicated for textbooks predating the secularization of public schools in 1882.)

1. Barillot, V. *La Ménagère agricole à l'usage des écoles primaires.* 10th ed. Paris: Belin, 1902.
2. Bérillon, Louis-Eugène. *La bonne ménagère agricole, ou simples notions d'économie rurale et d'économie domestique.* 10th ed. Auxerre: C. Gallot, 1888 (1st ed., 1862)
3. Bertin, Marthe. *Le Bébé, notions élémentaires de puériculture.* Paris: Belin, 1906.
4. Blanc, Marie-Thérèse de Solms [Mme Thérèse Bentzon] and Chevalier, Mlle A. *Causeries de morale pratique.* Paris: Hachette, 1899.
5. Brémant, A. *Sciences et enseignement ménager.* Paris: A. Hatier, 1912.
6. Carraud, Zulma. *La petite Jeanne ou le devoir.* Paris: Hachette, 1899. (1st ed., 1852).
7. Cazes, Emilien. *Economie domestique.* Paris: C. Delagrave, 1896.
8. Chalamet, Rose-Elise. *L'Année préparatoire d'économie domestique, ménage, devoirs dans la famille, cuisine, jardinage, blanchissage, entretien du linge, couture à l'usage des écoles de filles.* Paris: A. Colin, 1893.
9. ———. *La première année d'économie domestique, Morale, soins du ménage, hygiène, jardinage, travaux manuels, suivie de notions d'instruction civique et de droit usuel.* Paris: A. Colin, 1887.
10. Chapelot, Mme, Bouchez, Mme, and Hocdé, Mme. *Morceaux choisis à l'usage des classes préparatoires.* 4th ed. Paris: Masson, 1908.
11. Cuir, A.-F. *Les petites écolières, lectures morales sur les défauts et les qualités des enfants.* Paris: Hachette, 1893.
12. Delorme, Mme Marie. *Les petits cahiers de Mme Brunet, livre de lecture à l'usage des écoles de filles, hygiène et médecine usuelles, recettes de ménage, économie domestique.* Paris: A. Colin, 1888.

13. Dereims, Alice. *Jeanne et Madeleine, livre de lecture pour les jeunes filles à l'usage des cours moyen et supérieur (enseignement primaire) et des classes élémentaires (enseignement secondaire).* Paris: A. Colin, 1902.

14. Desmaisons, Mme L. Ch. *Pour le commencement de la classe, 100 lectures morales quotidiennes (Filles).* Paris: A. Colin, 1895.

15. ———. *La première année de cuisine, préceptes, journal de Madeleine, résumés . . . à l'usage des écoles de filles.* Paris: A. Colin, 1895.

16. ———. *Tu seras ouvrière, simple histoire, livre de lecture courante, à l'usage des écoles de filles, leçons de choses, hygiène, travail manuel, économie domestique.* Paris: A. Colin, 1892.

17. Durand-Gréville, Alice Marie Céleste [Mme Henry Gréville]. *L'Instruction morale et civique des jeunes filles.* Paris: E. Weill and G. Maurice, 1882.

18. Eidenschenk-Patin, Mme A. *Les deuxièmes lectures des petites filles.* Paris: C. Delagrave, 1912.

19. ———. *Les premières lectures des petites filles.* Paris: C. Delagrave, 1911.

20. ———. *Les troisièmes lectures des petites filles.* Paris: C. Delagrave, 1913.

21. Fabre, J.-Henri. *Aurore, cent récits sur des sujets variés, lectures courantes à l'usage des écoles et des institutions de démoiselles.* 3d ed. Paris: C. Delagrave, 1879. (1st ed., 1874).

22. ———. *Le Ménage, causeries d'Aurore avec ses nièces sur l'économie domestique, lectures courantes à l'usage des écoles de filles.* 12th ed. Paris: C. Delagrave, 1887. (2d ed., 1875).

23. ———. *Les petites filles, premier livre de lecture à l'usage des écoles primaires.* 5th ed. Paris: C. Delagrave, 1884. (1st ed., 1880).

24. Fredel, Mme and Toudy, Mme. *L'Education maternelle et ménagère à l'école, lectures courantes à l'usage des jeunes filles.* Paris: F. Nathan, 1904.

25. Gérard, Jules. *Maximes morales de l'écolière française.* Paris: Gedalge, 1916.

26. Greff, Michel. *La Fermière, notions élémentaires d'économie domestique agricole.* Paris: C. Delagrave, 1896. (1st ed., 1859).

27. Hannedouche, Alfred and Demailly, Mme E. *Livret d'enseignement méager.* Paris: C. Delagrave, 1903.

28. Henrion, Victor. *Le Monde des jeunes filles.* 3d ed. Paris: Belin, 1881 (1st ed., 1876).

29. Juranville, Clarisse. *Le deuxième livre des petites filles (cours élémentaire).* 8th ed. Paris: Larousse, 1893. 47th ed., 1908.

30. ———. *Manuel d'éducation morale et d'instruction civique à l'usage des jeunes filles.* 6th ed. Paris: Larousse, 1899.

31. ———. *Le premier livre des petites filles (classe enfantine).* 9th ed. Paris: Larousse, 1893. 57th ed., 1909. (1st ed., 1873).

32. ———. *Le Savoir-faire et le savoir-vivre dans les divers circonstances de la vie, guide pratique de la vie usuelle à l'usage des jeunes filles.* 5th ed. Paris: Auguste Boyer, 1883. 28th ed. Paris: Larousse, 1919. (1st ed., 1879).

33. Juranville and Berger, Pauline. *Le Bagage littéraire de la jeune fille, livre de lecture (cours supérieur).* 4th ed. Paris: Larousse, 1910.

34. ———. *Le Bagage scientifique de la jeune fille, livre de lecture (cours supérieur)*. Paris: Larousse, 1899.

35. ———. *Le troisième livre de lecture à l'usage des jeunes filles*. 2d ed. Paris: Larousse, 1892.

36. Lalanne, Jean-Baptiste and Bidault, M. *L'Education ménagère à l'école primaire*. Paris: Bibliothèque d'éducation, 1906.

37. Lebaigue, Ch. *Pour nos filles, choix de lectures expliquées à l'usage des jeunes filles (cours moyen)*. Paris: Belin, 1892.

38. Lemoine, Alcide and Marie, Juliette. *La jeune française, 200 lectures destinées pour les jeunes filles*. Paris: Larousse, 1910.

39. Leune, Alfred and Demailly, Mme E. *Cours d'enseignement ménager, science et morale, cours moyen*. Paris: C. Delagrave, 1902.

40. Massy, Mme Henriette. *Notions d'éducation civique à l'usage des jeunes filles*. Paris: Picard-Bernheim, 1884.

41. Moniez, Mme Hélène. *Premières lectures de nos filles, morale, instruction civique, connaissances usuelles, économie domestique*. Paris: Belin, 1899.

42. Murique, Mme Louise. *Maman et petite Jeanne, premier livre de morale à l'usage des écoles primaires de filles*. Paris: Hachette, 1891.

43. Nectoux, Claire. *Journal d'une petite écolière, livre de lecture et de composition pour la préparation au certificat d'études primaires d'après les cahiers d'un élève*. 3d ed. Paris: C. Delagrave, 1893.

44. Pichard, Lilla. *La bonne petite fille*. 13th ed. Paris: Belin, 1888. (3d ed., 1872).

45. ———. *Madame Adeline, ou récits d'une institutrice à ses élèves sur l'intelligence des animaux*. 3d ed. Paris: Belin, 1874. (1st ed., 1867).

46. Pinard, Adolphe. *La Puériculture du premier age*. Paris: A. Colin, 1904.

47. Raquet, H. *La première année de ménage rural*. 13th ed. Paris: A. Colin, 1908.

48. Sage, Charlotte Chappoz. *L'Enseignement ménager*. Paris: Nony, 1901.

49. Sagnier, Louise. *La Fillette bien élevée, livre de lecture à l'usage des écoles de filles*. Paris: A. Colin, 1896.

50. Sévrette, Julie. *La jeune ménagère*. Paris: Larousse, 1904.

51. Troncet, Louis J. *Jeannette, premier livre de lecture à l'usage des petites filles de la classe enfantine et du cours élémentaire*. 3d ed. Paris: E. Cornély, 1905.

52. Valette, Aline. *La Journée de la petite ménagère*. 13th ed. Paris: E. Weill and G. Maurice, 1885.

53. Vieu, Marie Malézieux [Marie Robert Halt]. *Le droit chemin, livre de lecture courante, à l'usage des jeunes filles (degrés moyen et supérieur), éducation de la volonté, éducation du sens moral, devoirs sociaux, antialcoolisme*. Paris: P. Delaplane, 1902.

54. ———. *L'Enfance de Suzette, livre de lecture courante, à l'usage des jeunes filles (degré élémentaire)*. 17th ed. Paris: P. Delaplane, 1907.

55. ———. *Le Ménage de Mme Sylvain, livre de lecture courante à l'usage des jeunes filles*. Paris: P. Delaplane, 1895.

56. ———. *Suzette, livre de lecture courante à l'usage des jeunes filles, morale, leçons de choses, économie domestique, ménage, cuisine, couture*. Paris: P. Delaplane, 1889.

57. Wirth, Mlle C. *Le Livre de composition française des jeunes filles.* 6th ed. Paris: Hachette, 1912.

58. Wirth, Ernestine. *La future ménagère, lectures et leçons sur l'économie domestique, la science du ménage, l'hygiène, les qualités et les connaissances nécessaires à une maîtresse de maison, à l'usage des écoles et des pensionnats de demoiselles.* 10th ed. Paris: Hachette, 1904.

59. ———. *Le Livre de lecture courante des jeunes filles chrétiennes, lectures de la division élémentaire.* 21st ed. Paris: Hachette, 1910. (1st ed., 1870).

60. ———. *Le Livre de lecture courante des jeunes filles chrétiennes, lectures de la division supérieure.* 14th ed. Paris: Hachette, 1907. (1st ed., 1872).

61. Wirth, Ernestine and Bret, Mme E. *Premières leçons d'économie domestique.* Paris: Hachette, 1886.

Catholic Textbooks

62. Brocard, Mlle and Despiques, Mlle. *Lectures morales, pour les élèves des cours supérieurs et complémentaires et pour patronages.* Lyon: E. Vitte, 1911.

63. Grelet, Mme M. *Programme de l'enseignement ménager à l'école libre.* Lyon: E. Vitte, 1908.

64. Huot, Jules. *Manuel d'éducation ménagère à la ville et à la campagne.* Paris: J. de Gigord, 1912.

65. Kereven, Mlle Edmée de. *Elisabeth.* 2d ed. Lyon: E. Vitte, 1910.

66. ———. *La petite Elisabeth.* 2d ed. Lyon: E. Vitte, 1910.

67. ———. *Le premier livre d'Elisabeth.* 2d ed. Lyon: E. Vitte, 1910.

68. ———. *La Politesse des petites filles.* Lyon: E. Vitte, 1913.

69. Masson, Anne-Louise. *Manuel de morale et d'instruction civique à l'usage de l'enseignement primaire.* 3d ed. Lyon: E. Vitte, 1922. (1st ed., 1909).

70. Méchin, Abbé E. *Fleurs et épines, ou vertus et défauts, livre de lecture courante à l'usage des pensionnats et des écoles de jeunes filles.* 14th ed. Paris: Belin, 1895. (1st ed., 1866).

71. Religieuses de la Providence de Saint-Brieuc, *Notions d'économie domestique à l'école primaire et dans les pensionnats de jeunes filles.* Ploermel: Procure générale des frères de l'instruction chrétienne, 1900.

72. Société départementale d'agriculture et d'industrie d'Ille-et-Vilaine. *Leçons d'agriculture élémentaire et d'économie domestique à l'usage des jeunes filles des écoles primaires rurales.* Ploermel: Procure générale des frères de l'instruction chrétienne and Rennes: Société départementale d'agriculture et d'industrie d'Ille-et-Vilaine, 1896.

73. Stella. *Lectures pour les jeunes filles, cours moyen.* Tours: A. Mame, 1911.

74. Thiéry, Marie. *Elise.* 7th ed. Paris: A. Hatier, 1926. (1st ed., 1910).

75. ———. *Lise, deuxième livre de lecture courante.* Paris: A. Hatier, 1910.

76. ———. *Lisette, premier livre de lecture courante.* Paris: A. Hatier, 1910.

II B. 1870–1914: Textbooks for Boys or Mixed Classes

1. Aicard, Jean. *Le Livre des petits.* 7th ed. Paris: C. Delagrave, n.d.
2. Aulard, Alphonse. *Eléments d'instruction civique.* Paris: E. Cornély, 1907.
3. Bécour, Julia. *Geneviève et Michel, livre de lecture courante.* Lille: Camille Robbe, 1890.
4. Belot, Armand. *La Vie civique, lectures républicaines des écoliers et écolières de France.* Paris: C. Delagrave, 1906.
5. Bert, Paul. *L'Instruction civique à l'école.* 6th ed. Paris: Picard-Bernheim, 1882.
6. Bigot, Charles. *Le petit français.* 34th ed. Paris: G. Delarue, n.d.
7. Brémant, A. *Sciences physiques et naturelles.* 64th ed. Paris: A. Hatier, 1911.
8. Carraud, Zulma. *Maurice, ou le travail.* Paris: Hachette, 1853.
9. Carré, I. and May, L. *L'Année préparatoire de rédaction et d'élocution.* 7th ed. Paris: A. Colin, 1889.
10. Chailley-Bert, Joseph. *Tu seras commerçant.* Paris: A. Colin, 1895.
11. Compayré, Gabriel. *Eléments d'instruction morale et civique.* 119th ed. Paris: P. Delaplane, n.d. (1st ed., 1880).
12. Delapalme, Emile. *Premier livre de l'adolescence, ou exercices de lecture et leçons de morale.* Paris: Hachette, 1893. (2d ed., 1843).
13. ———. *Premier livre de l'enfance, ou exercices de lecture et leçons de morale.* Paris: Hachette, 1893. (1st ed., 1849).
14. Dès, Albert and Dès, Mme. *Education morale et civique.* 7th ed. Montluçon: A. Thorinaud, 1910.
15. Devinat, Emile. *Lectures moyennes illustrées.* Paris: C. Delagrave, n.d.
16. ———. *Livre de lecture et de morale.* 17th ed. Paris: Larousse, n.d.
17. Dufrenne, P.-A. and Soulisse, M. *Lectures héroiques et contes pour les élèves des cours moyens des écoles primaires de garçons et de filles.* Paris: Bibliothèque de l'éducation, 1911.
18. Dupuy, Charles. *L'Année du certificat d'études, livret de morale.* 2d ed. Paris: A. Colin, 1892.
19. Fouillée, Mme Alfred [G. Bruno]. *Les Enfants de Marcel.* Paris: Belin, 1887.
20. ———. *Francinet, principes de la morale, de l'industrie, du commerce et de l'agriculture.* 66th ed. Paris: Belin, 1887. (1st ed., 1869).
21. ———. *Instruction morale et leçons de choses civiques pour les petits enfants.* 21st ed. Paris: Belin, 1887.
22. ———. *Premier livre de lecture et d'instruction pour l'enfant (morale et connaissances usuelles).* 205th ed. Paris: Belin, 1894.
23. ———. *Le Tour de la France par deux enfants, devoir et patrie.* 120th ed. Paris: Belin, 1884. (1st ed., 1877).
24. Friedberg, Mme E. de. *Petit formulaire de l'enseignement civique à l'usage des écoles primaires.* Paris: C. Delagrave, 1883.
25. Emile Ganneron. *Tu seras citoyen.* Paris: A. Colin, 1892.
26. Jeannel, Charles. *Petit Jean.* Paris: C. Delagrave, 1882. (1st ed., 1846).
27. Jost, G. and Braeunig, F. *Lectures pratiques destinées aux élèves des cours moyen et supérieur.* 7th ed. Paris: Hachette, 1893.

28. Jost, G. and Humbert, V. *Lectures pratiques destinées aux élèves du cours élémentaire.* 6th ed. Paris: Hachette, 1883.
29. Lacelf, Auguste and Bergeron, E. *La Récitation aux cours préparatoire et élémentaire.* 5th ed. Paris: Delalain, n.d.
30. ———. *La Récitation aux cours moyen et supérieur.* Paris: Delalain, n.d.
31. Larive and Fleury. *Exercices français de première année.* 46th ed. Paris: A. Colin, 1899.
32. Lavisse, Emile. *Tu seras soldat, histoire d'un soldat français, récits et leçons patriotiques d'instruction et d'éducation militaires.* 10th ed. Paris: A. Colin, 1894.
33. Lavisse, Ernest. *La nouvelle première année d'histoire de France.* Paris: A. Colin, 1898.
34. ———. [Laloi]. *La première année d'instruction civique.* Paris: A. Colin, 1880.
35. Lemoine, Alcide and Aymard, Aubin. *Le jeune français, lectures éducatives, morales et littéraires.* Paris: Larousse, 1914.
36. Leroux, Louis and Montillot, J. C. *Une famille.* 4th ed. Paris: A. Colin, 1893.
37. Liard, Louis. *Morale et enseignement civique.* Paris: L. Cerf, 1886.
38. Ligny, Armand. *En route pour la vie.* 7th ed. Paris: A. Colin, 1919. (1st ed., 1907).
39. Marchand, H. *Tu seras agriculteur.* Paris: A. Colin, 1892.
40. Matrat, Paul. *Tu seras prévoyant.* Paris: A. Colin, 1892.
41. Mézières, A. *Education morale et instruction civique.* Paris: C. Delagrave, 1883.
42. Nicolas, Georges. *Tu seras chef de famille.* Paris: A. Colin, 1891.
43. Pavette, O. *L'Instruction civique.* 11th ed. Paris: Belin, 1909.
44. Payot, Jules *La Morale à l'école.* 3d ed. Paris: A. Colin, 1908.
45. Primaire, E. *Manuel d'éducation morale, civique et sociale.* Paris: Bibliothèque d'éducation, 1901.
46. Rocherolles, Ed. *Les premières lectures enfantines.* 36th ed. Paris: A. Colin, 1887. (1st ed., 1877).
47. Rogie, L.-E. and Despiques, P. *Histoire de la France et de sa civilisation.* Paris: F. Juven, 1905.
48. Steeg, Jules. *Les Dangers de l'alcoolisme, lectures scolaires, maximes.* Paris: F. Nathan, 1896.
49. ———. *Instruction morale et civique.* Paris: N. Fauvé and F. Nathan, 1882.
50. Vieu, Marie Malézieux [Marie Robert Halt]. *Ecoliers et écolières.* Paris: P. Delaplane, 1891.

Catholic Textbooks

51. Allou, Marie Ferdinand. *Cours de morale et notions d'enseignement civique.* Amiens: Delattre-Lenoel, 1882.
52. Audley, Charles Félix. *Instruction civique à l'usage des écoles primaires.* 3d ed. Paris: Poussielgue, 1883.

53. Dantu, Abbé Gustave. *Manuel de morale pratique.* 2d ed. Paris: G. Beau-chesne, 1910.
54. Ecole libre. *Le premier livre d'André.* 5th ed. Lyon: E. Vitte, 1921. (1st ed., 1910).
55. ———. *Le deuxième livre d'André.* 4th ed. Lyon: E. Vitte, 1922. (1st ed., 1910).
56. Frères des écoles chrétiennes [F.F.]. *Lectures courantes (cours moyen).* Tours: A. Mame, 1901.
57. H. D., F. A. *Le deuxième livre de lecture de l'enfance chrétienne.* 8th ed. Paris and Lille: A. Taffin-Lefort, 1913.
58. Huguenot, Abbé V. *Manuel chrétien d'enseignement civique.* Paris: Gaume, 1882.
59. Rondelet, Antonin. *Manuel chrétien d'instruction civique.* Paris: Louis Vivès, 1882.
60. Valentin, Théophile. *Les Fleurs de l'histoire, dialogues, biographies et récits à l'usage de la jeunesse.* 2d série. Toulouse: E. Privat, 1890.

III A. 1914–1940: Textbooks for Girls

1. Allard, A. and Bergevin, Mlle. *Cours méthodique de sciences physiques et naturelles et d'enseignement ménager.* Paris: Belin, 1923.
2. Brisset, L. and Scordia, Blanche. *Leçons de science, avec applications à l'hygiène et à l'enseignement ménager.* Paris: A. Hatier, 1915.
3. Coulon, Mme Georges. *Enseignement ménager.* Paris: Hachette, 1922.
4. ———. *Puériculture.* Paris: Hachette, 1925.
5. Dolidon, M., Munié, Mlle, Rosenthal, Georges, Rosenthal, Gabrielle, Rosenthal, Léon, Vérone, Maria. *Le Livre de la jeune fille, mémento de connaissances nécessaires dans la vie.* Paris: Larousse, 1925.
6. Nonus, S. A. and P. C. *Résumés des leçons de morale et d'instruction civique à l'école primaire.* Amiens: Poiré-Choquet, 1930.
7. Pastouriaux, L., Le Brun, E., and Lassalle, Mme. *Les Sciences et l'enseignement ménager au cours supérieur.* Paris: C. Delagrave, 1935.
8. Roudil, A. and Bartoli, Mme. *Les Sciences physiques et naturelles au certificat d'études primaires, avec application à l'enseignement ménager.* Paris: Larousse, 1932.
9. Souché, Aimé. *Le premier livre de morale de la jeune française.* Paris: Librairie d'éducation nationale, A. Picard, 1923
10. ———. *Le second livre de morale de la jeune française.* Paris: Librairie d'éducation nationale, A. Picard, 1926.

Catholic Textbooks

11. Chênelette, Mlle de. *La Journée ménagère à l'école.* Lyon: E. Vitte, 1930.
12. Darcey, Mlle. *Petit cours d'enseignement ménager.* 7th ed. Lyon: E. Vitte, 1924.
13. Foulon-Lefranc, Mme. *La Femme au foyer.* Paris: L'Ecole, 1938.
14. Foulon-Lefranc, Mme. and Laurent, G. *L'Ecole du bonheur.* Paris: Magnard, 1938.

15. Grill, Chanoine C. and Le Floch, P. *L'Enseignement scientifique par l'observation et l'expérience (Filles)*. Paris: L'Ecole, 1937.
16. Guennard, Mlle. *Le Trésor de la ménagère*. Lyon: E. Vitte, 1935.
17. Leday, J. *Mon petit livre, lectures courantes pour les jeunes filles*. Paris: J. de Gigord, 1921.
18. Marduel, Mme Fleury. *La Morale de la ménagère*. Paris: L'Ecole, 1938.
19. Segond, E. *Mes premières lectures, à l'usage des écoles et maisons d'éducation de jeunes filles*. Paris: A. Hatier, 1927.

III B. 1914–1940: Textbooks for Boys or Mixed Classes

1. Ab der Halden, Charles. *Hors du nid, lectures suivies, cours moyen*. Paris: Editions Bourrelier, 1934.
2. Bodin, Marguerite. *Jacques et Zette, livre de lecture courante, cours préparatoire*. Paris: A. Colin, 1928.
3. Broutet, Félix and Reynier, Marguerite. *Le Livre des métiers, livre de lecture courante pour le cours élémentaire*. 5th ed. Paris: Delalain, 1938.
4. Chadeyras, F. *Belles lectures françaises*. Paris: C. Delagrave, 1921.
5. Cressot, J. *Pour la vie morale de nos enfants*. Paris and Strasburg: Istra, 1936.
6. Dès, Laetitia. *Jean et Lucie, histoire de deux jeunes réfugiés, livre de lecture pour les cours moyen et supérieur*. Paris: F. Nathan, 1920.
7. Emery, L. *Devant la vie, entretiens moraux à l'usage des classes du cours supérieur et du cours complémentaire*. Paris: Société universitaire d'éditions et de librairie, 1936.
8. Fouillée, Mme Alfred [G. Bruno]. *Le Tour de l'Europe pendant la guerre*. Paris: Belin, 1916.
9. Forsant, Octave and Dudouit, Pierre. *La Vie des champs, livre de lecture pour les écoles rurales*. Paris: Larousse, 1930.
10. Franchet, Antonin and Franchet, Léon. *La Lecture vivante, cours supérieur*. Paris: Bibliothèque de l'éducation, 1926.
11. Gautier, M. and Cornet, M. *Monique et François découvrent le monde*. Paris: Delalain, 1932.
12. Habert, P. and Boulot, V. *Lectures choisies d'auteurs contemporains*. Paris: Hachette, 1919.
13. Hébert, Max. *Ton métier d'homme, mon enfant*. Paris: Rieder, 1931.
14. Imbert, G. *Leçons de morale*. 3d ed. Paris: Belin, 1935.
15. Jeanne, W. and Jeanne, Mme. *Frère et soeur*. 4th ed. Paris: L. Martinet, 1923.
16. Miraton, M. and Farges, M. *L'Education morale et civique par la suggestion artistique et littéraire*. 9th ed. Paris: Delalain, 1923.
17. Rogie, Louis-Eugène, Bornecque, M. and Coupin, M. *Nouvelles lectures littéraires, scientifiques et artistiques, cours supérieur*. Paris: Gedalge, 1924.
18. Roudil, A. and Bartoli, Mme. *Les Sciences physiques et naturelles au certificat d'études primaires (Garçons, écoles urbaines)*. Paris: Larousse, 1932.

19. Seguin, Kléber. *Histoire de trois enfants, cours moyen.* Paris: Hachette, 1927.
20. Souché, Aimé. *Petite maman et ses trois enfants.* Paris: F. Nathan, 1938.
21. Vasseur, Lucien. *Enfants du vingtième siècle.* Paris: Hachette, 1935.

Catholic Textbooks

22. Bazin, R. and Dufrenne, P. *Lectures françaises, Il était quatre petits enfants, cours élémentaire et moyen.* Tours: Mame, 1923.
23. ————. *Lectures françaises, Il était quatre petits enfants, cours moyen et supérieur.* Tours: Mame, 1923.
24. Bellenoue, M. *Entretiens familiers sur la morale sociale.* Paris: Spes, 1923.
25. Bourceau, Abbé E. and Fabry, Raymond. *Lectures expliquées avec enseignement morale et civique, cours élémentaire.* 15th ed. Paris: Editions de l'école, 1925.
26. ————. *Lectures littéraires expliquées avec enseignement moral et civique, cours supérieur.* Paris: Librairie de l'Ecole, 1933.
27. Grill, Chanoine and Le Floch, P. *L'Enseignement scientifique par l'observation et l'expérience (Garçons).* Paris: L'Ecole, 1937.
28. Hamayon, Mgr Marcel and Bragade, Abbé A. *André et Jacqueline, deux enfants de France.* Paris: Editions de l'Ecole, 1940.
29. Une Réunion de professeurs. *Lectures courantes, cours moyen.* Tours: A. Mame, and Paris: J. De Gigord, 1919.
30. Vesco de Kereven, E. and Martin, J. *La Famille Aubert.* Lyon: E. Vitte, 1920.

IV A. 1940–1944: Textbooks for Girls

1. Bressan, Nelly. *La Puériculture à l'école.* 5th ed. Chambéry: Maison d'édition des primaires.
2. Foulon-Lefranc, Mme and Laurent, G. *L'Ecole du bonheur.* 6th ed. Paris: Magnard, 1943.
3. Guillaume, Rose. *Sciences appliquées et travaux pratiques, enseignement ménager, puériculture, hygiène.* Paris: Bourrelier, 1943.

IV B. 1940–1944: Textbooks for Boys or Mixed Classes

1. Ballot, Marc. *Carnet de l'enfant bien élevé.* Paris: C. Lavauzelle, 1942.
2. Jauffret, Edouard. *Au pays bleu.* Paris: Belin, 1941.
3. Miller, André. *Nicole et Victor.* Paris: Larousse, 1943.
4. Poirot, M. *Cours d'éducation morale et patriotique.* Paris: Ecole universelle par correspondance, 1941.
5. Renaud, L.-P. *Notre morale "servir".* Paris: C. Lavauzelle, 1944.
6. Rouable, Maurice. *150 lectures de morale vivante.* Paris: Vuibert, 1943.

Catholic Textbooks

7. Bazin, René and Dufrenne, P. *Lectures françaises, Il était quatre petits enfants, cours moyen et supérieur.* Tours: Mame, 1942.
8. Bourceau, Abbé E. and Fabry, Raymond. *Lectures expliquées avec l'enseignement moral et civique, cours moyen.* Paris: Editions Ecole et Collège, 1941.

V A. 1945–1958: Textbooks for Girls

1. Anscombre, Jean. *Mon mémento de sciences (Filles, écoles rurales et urbaines).* Saint-Germain-en-Laye: Maison des instituteurs, 1956.
2. Bressan, Nelly. *La Puériculture à l'école.* 7th ed. Chambéry: Maison d'édition des primaires, 1946.
3. Coulon, Mme G. *Enseignement ménager.* Paris: Hachette, 1947.
4. Guillaume, Rose. *La Vie familiale et ménagère.* Paris: Editions Bourrelier, 1949.
5. Jolly, René. *Les Sciences appliquées (Filles).* Paris: F. Nathan, 1948.
6. Séguin, Jeanne and Millett, Pauline. *Pour nos filles.* Paris: Larousse, 1957.
7. Vérel, L. and Bressan, Nelly. *Sciences appliquées, ecoles de filles.* Chambéry: Editions scolaires, 1949.
8. Vernay, L., Guillaume, Rose, and Pierre, P. *Sciences, écoles rurales de garçons et de filles, supplément pour les filles.* Paris: Editions Bourrelier, 1955.

Catholic Textbooks

9. Durand, Marie-Louise. *Devant la vie.* Paris: Editions de l'Ecole, 1953.
10. Foulon-Lefranc, Mme. *La Femme au foyer.* 11th ed. Paris: L'Ecole, 1953.
11. Guennard, Mlle. *Le Trésor de la ménagère.* Lyon: E. Vitte, 1950.
12. Lecordier, Gaston. *Morale du travail, pour des jeunes filles des milieux urbains, industriels et commerciaux.* Paris: Spes, 1947.

V B. 1945–1958: Textbooks for Boys or Mixed Classes

1. Ab der Halden, Charles. *Hors du nid.* Paris: Editions Bourrelier, 1950.
2. Anscombre, Jean. *Mon mémento de sciences (Garçons, écoles rurales).* Saint-Germain-en-Laye: Maison des instituteurs, 1956.
3. ———. *Mon mémento de sciences (Garçons, écoles urbaines).* Saint-Germain-en-Laye: Maison des instituteurs, 1956.
4. Aubin, A., Prévot, G., and Rossignol, M. *Lectures modernes.* 11th ed. Paris: A. Hatier, 1955.
5. Ballot, Marc. *Carnet de l'enfant bien élevé.* Paris: C. Lavauzelle, 1952.
6. Ballot, Marc and Aveillé, R. *Education morale et civique.* Paris: C. Lavauzelle, 1952.
7. Besseige, Henri. *Présentation de la France, textes choisis et groupés en vue de la formation civique des jeunes.* Paris and Strasburg: Istra, 1946.

8. Dubus, Hermin. *Dans la ronde des métiers et des jours.* Paris: Société universitaire d'éditions, 1948.
9. Gardet, E. and Pechenard, M.-L. *Chez nous en France.* Paris: Hachette, 1956.
10. Godier, A. and Salesse, G. *Préparons-nous à la vie sociale.* Paris: Editions Bourrelier, 1954.
11. Jolly, René. *Les Sciences appliquées (Garçons, écoles urbaines).* Paris: F. Nathan, 1948.
12. Pouron, Maurice, Picard, Marguerite, and Leroy, Emile. *Choix de lectures.* Paris: C. Delagrave, 1951.
13. Ravaudet, Marie. *L'Age de raison, cours de morale à l'usage des petits.* Villefranche: Editions du c.e.p. beaujolais, 1950.
14. ———. *Courage, cours de morale à l'usage des cours moyen et cours supérieur.* Villefranche: Editions du c.e.p. beaujolais, 1950.
15. Renaud, L.-P. *La Vie morale de l'enfant.* Paris: C. Lavauzelle, 1948.
16. Souché, Aimé. *Les nouvelles leçons de morale au cours moyen.* Paris: F. Nathan, 1947.
17. Vernay, L., Guillaume, Rose, and Pierre, P. *Sciences, écoles rurales de garçons et de filles.* Paris: Editions Bourrelier, 1955.

Catholic Textbooks

18. Bourceau, Abbé E. and Fabry, Raymond. *Lectures expliquées avec enseignement moral et civique.* Paris: Editions de l'Ecole, 1949.
19. ———. *Lectures littéraires expliquées, éducation morale, civique et patriotique, cours supérieur.* Paris: Editions de l'Ecole, 1950.
20. Grill, Chanoine C. *Cent dictées à l'usage des candidats au certificat d'études par un inspecteur diocésain.* Paris: Editions de l'Ecole, 1947.
21. Hamayon, Mgr Marcel and Bragade, Abbé A. *André et Jacqueline, deux enfants de France.* 7th ed. Paris: Editions de l'Ecole, 1951.
22. Réunion de professeurs. *La Légende et l'histoire.* Paris: Ligel, 1954.
23. ———. *Le Livre de la morale.* Paris: Librairie générale de l'enseignement libre, 1951.
24. ———. *La Vie heureuse.* Paris: Librairie générale de l'enseignement libre, 1948.
25. Tallois, Jacqueline. *Grand frère et petite soeur.* Tours: Mame, 1947.

VI. Since 1958

1. Lecordier, Gaston. *Morale civique et sociale, première année.* Paris: Bloud and Gay, 1959.
2. ———. *Morale civique et sociale, deuxième année.* Paris: Bloud and Gay, 1959.
3. Marion, François. *Marchands de courage.* Paris: Ligel, 1958.
4. Souché, Aimé. *Les nouvelles leçons de morale au cours moyen.* Paris: F. Nathan, 1959.
5. Villard, G. *La Morale en action.* Paris: F. Nathan, 1960.

VII. *Textbooks for Higher Primary Schools*

1. Bruno, Mlle and Bruno, A. *Le Livre de la ménagère.* 9th ed. Paris: Belin, 1934. (1st ed., 1912).
2. Challaye, Félicien and Reynier, Marguerite. *Cours de morale à l'usage des écoles primaires supérieures et cours complémentaires.* 8th ed. rev. Paris: Félix Alcan, 1939.
3. ———. *Cours de morale et instruction civique, adaptation aux nouveaux programmes.* Paris: Presses universitaires de France, 1941.
4. Ecole primaire supérieure de jeunes filles d'Orléans. *Résumés de morale.* Orléans: Bertrand, 1912.
5. Perier, Arsène. *Leçons de droit à ma fille.* Paris: Belin, 1885.
6. Pierre, Albert and Martin, Mlle A. *Cours de morale théorique et pratique à l'usage des écoles primaires supérieures (filles et garçons) et des aspirants aux écoles normales, au certificat d'études primaires supérieures et aux brevets.* 9th ed. Paris: F. Nathan, 1911.
7. Rogie, Louis-Eugène, Bornecque, M. and Levesque, Mme. *Nouvelles lectures professionnelles.* Paris: Gedalge, 1928.
8. Salomon, Mathilde. *A nos jeunes filles, lectures et leçons de morale.* Paris: L. Cerf, 1893.

Index

Ab der Halden, Charles, 86, 91, 135, 157
Aicard, Jean, 43
Alcoholism and anti-alcoholism: depicted in textbooks, 39, 47, 56–57, 59; in curriculum, 29, 56; pupils' attitudes toward lessons on, 68, 70
Aline et René, 164
Amicales, 76, 77–78
Anarchists' views of girls' education, 79
André et Jacqueline, 92, 139
André textbooks, 48
Annuaire officiel de l'enseignement libre catholique, 28
Arithmetic lessons, 9, 16, 93
Association pour une école non sexiste, 164, 167
Avec les mots de tous les jours, 158

Baccalauréat, 16, 98, 100, 108, 121, 147, 163
Barangé law, 1951, 152
Barrès, Maurice, 69, 134, 150
Bartoli, Mme, 94
Basses-Alpes, girls' education in, 113, 115, 116, 127
Bazin, René, 91
Beauvoir, Simone de, 70, 100, 156
Bédorez, Léon, 65
Belin (publisher), 21, 28, 42
Bellenoue, M., 129
Belot, Inspector, 61
Bentzon, Mme Thérèse. *See* Blanc, Marie-Thérèse de Solms
Berger, Pauline, 51, 52, 57
Bérillon, Louis-Eugène, 100
Bertillon, Jacques, 83
Bert, Paul, 30, 43
Blanc, Marie-Thérèse de Solms [pseud. Mem Thérèse Bentzon], 37–39, 104
Blum, Léon, 97, 98
Bodin, Marguerite, 76, 81
Bornecque, M., 132
Bouchor, Maurice, 86

Bourbon Restoration, education, 8
Bourceau, Abbé E., 89
Bourdieu, Pierre, 10
Bouvier, Jeanne, 70
Braeunig, F., 103
Bragade, Abbé A., 92
Brevet de capacité, 8, 9, 11
Brevet supérieur, 17, 18
Brittany, educational trends in, 9, 110–112, 126
Broussin, Marthe, 142
Broutet, Félix, 104
Bruno. *See* Fouillée, Augustine Tuillerie
Brunschwig, Cécile, 78
Buisson, Ferdinand, 30, 87

Caillard, Mme Paul, 23–24
Carcopino, Jérôme, 134
Carraud, Zulma, 22–23, 27, 28
Catholic schools. *See* Schools, Catholic
Catholic views of republican textbooks, 30, 40, 48
Certificate of primary studies (*certificat d'études primaires; c.e.p.*), 15, 62, 66, 69, 98, 108–18, 145, 147; examinations for, 66–68, 92, 96, 108, 135; trends in girls' earning of, 109–18
Chabot, C., 68
Chalamet, Rose-Elise, 35, 36–37, 54, 57, 79
Challaye, Félicien, 131–32
Charity, depicted in textbooks, 39, 48, 49
Charrier, Charles, 86, 93
Chatreix, Henri, 85
Chevalier, A., 37–39, 104
Chevalier, Jacques, 134
Childhood, changes in textbooks' depiction of, 42, 90
Children's duties: depicted in textbooks, 24, 124; in curriculum, 29

Civics instruction: emphasis for women, 141; in curriculum, 28; textbooks for, 29, 35, 37, 133, 136
Civil code, article 213, 33, 85, 97, 131
Classe de fin d'études. See Schools, primary: grade levels
Coeducation, 2, 3, 6, 7, 9, 15–16, 71–72, 74, 76, 77–78, 140, 154–55
Colette, Sidonie Gabrielle, 70, 140
Colin, Armand (publisher), 36, 37, 46
Collèges. See Schools, secondary
Compayré, Gabriel, 30, 40–41
Compulsory schooling, 5, 13; age for, 2, 3, 13, 99, 151
Concordat of 1801, 8
Condorcet, Marie Jean Nicolas, Marquis de, 7, 8
Confédération générale du travail, 137
Congress on primary education, 1889, 71–74
Conseil national des femmes françaises, 156, 161
Constitution (1946), women's rights, 136
Contraception, 83, 88, 165, 166
Cornec, Josette, 88
Cours complémentaires. See Schools, primary: complementary courses
Cours élémentaire. See Schools, primary: grade levels
Cours moyen. See Schools, primary: grade levels
Cours normaux, 9, 12
Cours préparatoire. See Schools, primary, grade levels
Cours secondaires. See Schools, secondary
Cours supérieur. See Schools, primary: grade levels
Croiset, Alfred, 76–77
Cuir, A.-F., 42
Curriculum. See Schools, primary: curriculum; Schools, higher primary
Curie, Marie, 139, 140

Daniel et Valérie, 156–57, 164
Debré law, 1959, 152
Decroux-Masson, Annie: Papa lit, maman coud, 1, 158
Defodon, Charles, 19
De Gaulle, Charles, 136, 138
Dejean de la Bâtie, Jeanne Adèle, 19, 78
Delagrave (publisher), 24, 36
Demailly, E., 54
Depopulation, concern about, 83, 106–7, 135; in curriculum, 83; in textbooks, 87–88, 89, 124, 131, 138–39

Deraismes, Maria, 33
Dereims, Alice, 49–51
Dès, Laetitia, 91
Desmaisons, L. C., 44, 46
Dictionnaire pédagogique, 5
Divorce, depiction in textbooks, 89, 97
Dolidon, Charles, 93
Domestic economy. See Home economics
Donnet, Cardinal, 24
Donzelot, Jacques, 10
Drawing, in curriculum, 9, 16, 17, 82, 100
Dreyfus, Alfred, 15, 28
Drouard, Charles, 43
Dudouit, Pierre, 91
Dufrenne, P., 91
Dupanloup, 13, 24
Durand-Gréville, Alice [pseud. Mme Henry Gréville], 30–34, 37, 79, 87
Duruy, Victor, 11012, 13, 20

Ecole française, L', 67
Ecoles libres. See Schools, private
Ecoles maternelles, 15, 18, 72, 153–54, 162
Ecoles mixtes. See Coeducation
Ecoles normales. See Normal schools
Ecole normale supérieure pour l'enseignement primaire, Fontenay-aux-Roses, 17, 31, 78
Ecoles pratiques du commerce et d'industrie (apprenticeship schools), 119
Ecoles primaires. See Schools, primary
Ecoles primaires supérieures. See Schools, higher primary
Ecole unique, 98, 152
Economie domestique. See Home economics
Eidenschenk-Patin, Albertine, 26, 42, 52, 78
Elisabeth readers, 48–49, 57, 90
Elise readers, 48–49, 135
Emery, Léon, 88
England: recent concern about sex discrimination, 157, 159; textbooks, 58; teachers' attitudes, 77

Fabry, Raymond, 89
Falloux law, 11, 171 n. 28
Family, depiction in textbooks, 31, 43, 91, 131, 134, 135, 138; husband's role in, 33, 39, 40, 88–89, 124; wife's role in, 23, 25, 32–34, 37, 40, 52, 56–57, 59, 87, 124
Family finances, control of: depiction in textbooks, 33, 58, 88; surveys on, 88

Family, post-World War II policies affecting, 138
Farges, M., 85, 86
Féderation de l'éducation nationale (FEN), 152
Féderation unitaire de l'enseignement, 106
Feminism: among teachers, 76, 77, 78, 80, 106; opposition to, 46, 64, 78, 142; pre-1914, 19, 33, 59, 77, 79; since 1960s, 156, 160–61, 164–67. *See also* Votes for women
Femmes en France dans une société d'inégalités, Les, 166
Fénelon, Abbé, 10, 18–19, 23, 31, 32, 36, 42, 47
Ferry, Jules, 2, 13, 18, 21, 168
Ferry Laws, 2, 10, 13, 24
Fifth Republic, education, 3, 151–68
Foncin, Pierre, 36
Fontenay-aux-Roses. *See* Ecole normale supérieure pour l'enseignement primaire, Fontenay-aux-Roses
Fourth Republic, education, 2, 3, 136–50
Fouillée, Augustine, Tuillerie (Mme Alfred Fouillée) [pseud. Bruno], 27, 42, 52
Foulon-Lefranc, Mme, 96, 97, 135–36
Franchet, Antonin, 85
Franchet, Léon, 85
Francinet, 42, 52
Fredel, Mme, 93
French Revolution, education, 7–8
Frères de l'instruction chrétienne, 27
Friedan, Betty: *Feminine Mystique,* 166

Gambetta, Léon, 30
Gasquet, Amédée, 83
Gasquet, Marie, 70
Gayraud, Amélie, 123
Germany, recent concern about sex discrimination, 159; textbooks, 58; women teachers' attitudes, 77
Ginier, Marguerite, 61, 79
Giroud, Françoise, 1, 157, 160
Giscard d'Estaing, Valéry, 157, 164
Gréard, Octave, 71, 72, 74
Grégoire, Ménie, 123
Gréville, Mme Henry. *See* Durand-Gréville, Alice
Grill, C., 94
Groult, Benoîte, 166–67
Guizot, François, 9, 121
Guizot law, 1833, 9
Gymnastique. See Physical education

Hachette (publisher), 19, 21, 22, 24, 25, 27, 36, 37, 167
Halt, Marie Robert. *See* Vieu, Marie Malézieux
Hamayon, Marcel, 92
Hannedouche, Alfred, 54
Hatier, A. (publisher), 28
Hautes-Alpes, girls' education in, 113, 115, 127, 128
Hébert-Duperron, Abbé, 5
Herr, Lucien, 131
Historical role models in girls' textbooks, 24–25, 49, 52, 140
History: in curriculum, 16; in textbooks, 36; teaching of, 25
Home economics, 24; in curriculum, 17, 54, 92, 94, 122; instruction in, 61, 62, 92–94, 99, 100, 135, 165; students' attitudes toward, 69, 70, 122; teachers' attitude toward, 92–93, 141–42; textbooks for, 36–37, 54–57, 94, 96–97, 137
Hygiene: in curriculum, 16; instruction, 70, 83, 93

Inspection of primary schools, 60–61; reports on, 18, 65, 90
Inspectrices primaires, 31, 71–75, 79
Institut national pour la recherche pédagogique (INRDP), 1, 157, 160

Jaurés, Jean, 85, 86, 131
Jeanne et Madeleine, 49–51
Jeannel, Charles, 27
Joan of Arc, 25, 49, 52, 140, 147
Jospin, Lionel, 167
Jost, G., 103
July Monarchy, education, 9–10, 21
Juranville, Clarisse, 28, 35–36, 37, 39, 42, 51–54, 57, 60, 139–40

Kant, Immanuel, 35
Kereven, Edmée de, 48
Kergomard, Pauline, 74, 77

Lakanal, J., 7
Lapie, Paul, 81
Larive and Fleury, grammar books, 36
Larousse (publisher), 28, 36, 139–40
Lavaut, Marguerite, 86
Lavisse, Ernest, 36, 37, 40, 41, 43, 58, 87
League of Nations, mentioned in textbooks, 88, 90
Lecordier, Gaston, 139
Le Floch, P., 94

Legal position of women, 33, 35, 37, 136, 157, 166. *See also* Civil code, article 213
Lemoine, Alcide, 42
Leroux, L., 43
Leune, A., 54
Levesque, Mme, 132
Liard, Louis, 83
Ligue de l'enseignement, 87, 93; comité des dames, 47
Lisons, 158
Literacy rates, 5–7, 13, 26, 110, 113
Lycées. See Schools, secondary

Macé, Jean, 47
Magnard (publisher), 164
Maintenon, Mme de, 10, 19, 25, 32
Mame, Alfred (publisher), 28, 91
Manual works: in curriculum, 16, 17, 81–82, 100; students' attitudes toward, 69–70; teachers' attitudes toward, 69, 81, 92
Manuel général de l'instruction primaire, 19, 67, 78
Marangé, James, 108
Marianne, as a republican symbol, 3
Marriage, depiction in textbooks, 32–33
Martin, A., 124
Masson, Anne-Louise, 39–40
Massy, Henriette, 35, 37
Maulny, Germaine de, 70
Maurice ou le travail, 23, 27
Mézières, A., 41, 43
Military education in primary curriculum, 17
Millett, Pauline, 139–41
Ministry for the Rights of Women, 166, 167
Ministry of National Education (formerly Ministry of Public Instruction), 2, 21
Miraton, M., 85, 86
Mireaux, Emile, 134
Mitterrand, François, 166
Mixité. See Coeducation
Mollo, Suzanne, 156
Monde de l'éducation, Le, 165, 167, 168
Montillot, J. C., 43
Morale lessons: in curriculum, 9, 14, 16, 28–29, 105; in students' notebooks, 64; in textbooks, 16, 28–41, 85–90, 96, 138–39; students' attitudes toward, 68–69; teaching of, 79, 85
Morceaux choisis, 90–91
Mother's role: educators' view of, 5, 19, 22; in textbooks, 21–22, 36, 88. *See also* Family, depiction in textbooks of wife's role

Myot, Renée, 158

Napoleon I and education, 8
Napoleon III and education, 11
Nathan, F. (publisher), 164, 165
Nicolas, Georges, 43
Nord, education in, 17, 19, 69
Normal schools, 12, 13, 14, 17, 18, 19, 83
Obedience of women, depicted in textbooks, 33, 40, 97
Old Regime, education, 5–7, 10

Pankhurst, Emmeline, 59
Paris, education in, 9–10, 14, 18, 28, 60, 61, 64, 109–10
Passeron, Jean-Claude, 10
Patriotism: depicted in textbooks, 34, 88, 90; examination questions, 68; in curriculum, 30
Payot, Jules, 20, 86
Peasants, schools' message for, 20, 22–23, 29, 47, 54–56
Pécaut, Félix, 17, 19, 30, 31
Pedagogical manuals. *See* Teachers' manuals
Pelletier, Monique, 161
Person, Jeanne, 101
Personality traits of boys and men: depicted in textbooks, 40–41, 42, 88–89, 91, 124, 131, 135, 158, 165; presented to teachers, 86
Personality traits of girls and women: depicted in textbooks, 22–25, 31–59, 86–97, 124, 131, 135, 139, 158, 165; educators' views of, 72–73, 76–77, 100, 101; in students' notebooks, 63; listed in curriculum, 29; surveys on attitudes toward, 144–45, 160; taught to teachers, 18–20, 64, 86
Pétain, Philippe, 133, 139
Petite Jeanne ou le devoir, La, 22–23, 24, 25, 27, 28
Physical education, 17, 82
Pichard, Lilla, 23
Pierre, Albert, 124
Pinard, Adolphe, 83, 84, 96
Pius XI, 154
Pius XII, 137, 154
Politics and women, 136–37, 141; depicted in textbooks, 33, 35, 59, 89
Pompidou, Georges, 157
Popular Front, educational policies, 97–101
Poussièlgue, Charles (publisher), 28
Primary schools. *See* Schools, primary
Prost, Antoine, 16

Protestant educators and textbook authors, 30, 37
Puériculture, 17, 83, 94–97, 122, 138

Raquet, Hector, 54–56
Reading, in curriculum, 9, 16, 90; instruction in, 6, 41; textbooks for, 16, 41–54, 90–92, 139–40, 156–57, 167
Redoublement, 153
Religion: in curriculum, 5–6, 7, 9, 10, 12, 14, 29, 85, 134; in textbooks, 22–25, 27, 36, 39–40, 48, 52, 58, 97, 136; women's interest in, 14, 39, 48, 73. *See also* Schools, Catholic
Religious congregations and schools, 7, 8, 9, 11–12, 14, 25, 134
Renaud, L. P., 135, 136
Revue pédagogique, La, 78
Reynier, Marguerite, 104, 131–32
Ripert, Georges, 134
Roger-Lévy, Jeanne, 78
Rogie, Louis-Eugène, 132
Roudil, A., 94
Roudy, Yvette, 166
Rouland, Gustave, 11
Rousseau, Jean Jacques: *Emile*, 32, 78
Rural life: depicted in textbooks, 47, 54–56, 85, 90–91, 137; in student notebooks, 63, 67

Salomon, Mathilde, 123–24
Sandre, Marie, 75–76, 80
Sauvan, Lucille, 9–10, 18, 22, 24
Savary, Alain, 168
Schools, Catholic, 2, 11, 14, 15–16, 48, 63, 67, 69, 83, 101, 110–12, 123; ratio of girls to boys in, 14–15
Schools, higher primary, 29, 43, 98, 99, 119–22, 134, 149; curriculum for boys, 122–23; curriculum for girls, 29–30, 122; graduates' activities, 125–26. *See also* Textbooks for higher primary schools
Schools, primary: complementary courses, 66, 98, 105, 119–21, 149, 151; graduates' activities, 125–29
Schools, primary: curriculum, pre-1880s, 5–6, 7, 9; 1882, 1887, 16–17, 81; 1923, 81; 1938, 81; Vichy Regime, 134; Fourth Republic, 152; Fifth Republic, 152. *See also* the listings for subjects: Arithmetic, Civic instruction, Drawing, Home economics, History, Manual works, Military education, Physical education, *Puériculture*, Reading, Science, Sewing, Singing

Schools, primary: grade levels, 16; *classe de fin d'études*, 99, 100, 134, 151; *cours élémentaire*, 16, 29; *cours moyen*, 16, 29, 82, 152; *cours préparatoire*, 16; *cours supérieur*, 16, 29, 82, 90, 100, 151
Schools, primary: mission of, 2–3, 16–17, 81, 134, 151–52
Schools, private, 2, 8, 14, 35, 48, 101, 109, 132, 152, 154; textbooks for, 21. *See also* Schools, Catholic
Schools, secondary *(lycées* and *collèges)*, 2, 3, 8, 11, 12–13, 16, 98, 99, 100, 104, 119–21, 123; elementary classes of, 2, 37–38, 81, 98, 151; post-1940, 134, 149, 150, 151–52
Science: curriculum, 16, 82, 100, 137; examination questions on, 67; teaching of, 61, 79, 82–83, 94; textbooks, 16, 54, 82, 94, 137, 138
Second Empire, education, 11–13
Second Republic, plans for education, 11
Secretary of State for the Feminine Condition, 157, 160, 161
Secularization of public schools, 2, 10, 13–14, 22, 23, 28, 29, 35, 47, 63, 78
Séguin, Jeanne, 139–41
Seguin, Kléber, 85, 92
Seine, education in the department, 17, 60, 68, 71, 93–94, 109–11
Separate spheres for men and women: depicted in textbooks, 22, 32, 39, 42, 50, 56, 57–58, 102, 142; in student notebooks, 64
Sévrette, Julie, 54
Sewing, school lessons on, 7, 8, 9, 25, 36, 54, 62, 67, 70, 92–93
Sexism, French and international concern about, 156–61, 164–68
Simon, Jules, 11, 46, 87
Singing, in curriculum, 9, 16
Sirey, Josephine, 21–22
Socialism: and teachers, 85, 106; and textbooks, 85, 86, 89, 131
Socialist views of women, 79, 168
Social mobility and immobility: depicted in textbooks, 41, 42–43, 46, 57, 63–64, 67–68, 104, 137; schools' role in promoting, 59, 70, 99, 105, 108, 126–27, 148, 153, 163
Solidarity, social: depicted in textbooks and by schools, 49–50, 105, 142
Souché, Aimé, 87–88, 138
Sourgen, Hélène, 141
Sourgen, Henriette, 141
Spuller, Eugène, 19
Stanton, Theodore, 30

Steeg, Jules, 30
Strikes and labor unions, depicted in textbooks, 34, 49, 86
Student attitudes toward: adult roles, 156, 161; coeducation, 154; educational and occupational choices, 69–70, 107–8, 122–23, 125–29, 132, 144–45, 147–48, 150, 159–60, 163–64, 168; politics, 141; school subjects, 68–70
Students' notebooks, themes in, 12, 62–64, 93, 96
Sullerot, Evelyne, 135
Suzette textbooks, 45, 46–47, 48, 54, 60, 90
Syndicats for teachers; Syndicat national des instituteurs (SNI), 78, 106, 108

Talleyrand-Périgord, Charles Maurice de, 7
Teachers' attitudes toward: advancement of women teachers, 71–74; nature of womanhood, 71–80, 106–7; own status, 105, 106; problems of women teachers, 57, 71, 75; women's work, 142, 143, 161
Teachers' manuals, 9–10, 18–20, 86
Teachers, women, 13–14, 15, 17–18, 20, 61, 65, 71–75, 115, 130, 153
Technical education, 8, 163–64
Temps modernes, Les, 156
Textbook authors, 30–31, 167, 176 n. 23
Textbooks, Catholic, 27, 28, 47, 86, 90, 94, 95; history, 28; home economics, 54, 56, 97, 135; *morale*, 39–40, 89–90, 139; readers, 48–49, 92
Textbooks, depiction of women: before 1880, 8, 21–25; recent studies of, 156–60, 164–67
Textbooks, elementary classes of secondary schools, 37, 49
Textbooks, higher primary schools, 123–24, 131–32
Textbooks, primary schools: availability of special girls' books, 21–25, 27, 90, 140; policy on adoption, 20–21; sales of, 36, 46, 48, 49, 51, 54, 56, 91, 94, 103, 140; types required, 26–27. *See also* Arithmetic, History, Home economics, *Morale*, Reading, Science
Textbooks, primary schools: themes. *See* Alcoholism and anti-alcoholism; Charity; Children's duties; Depopulation; Divorce; Family; Family finances; Historical role models in girls' textbooks; Marriage; Mother's role; Obedience of wives; Patriotism;

Personality traits of boys and men; Personality traits of girls and women; Politics and women; *Puériculture*; Rural life; Separate spheres for men and women; Social mobility and immobility; Solidarity; Strikes and labor unions; Urban life; Work, for men, for women
Thiery, Marie, 48, 135
Third Republic, education, 2, 5, 13–132
Tour de la France par deux enfants, Le, 27, 28, 35, 36, 42, 51, 90, 135
Travaux manuels. See Manual works

United States: recent concern about sex discrimination and textbooks, 157, 159; textbooks, 58
Universities, women students in, 163
Urban life, depicted in textbooks, 49, 56, 91, 137; examination questions on, 67

Valabrègue, Catherine, 165, 167
Valentin, Théophile, 28
Vichy Regime, education, 133–36
Vieu, Marie Malézieux [pseud. Marie Robert Halt], 43, 45, 46–47, 54
Vieu, Robert, 47
Vitte, Emmanuel (publisher), 28, 36, 48
Votes for women, 136; opponents and supporters, 59, 76, 85, 101; textbook references to, 36, 40, 58, 88, 89, 181 n. 104

Weiss, Louise, 123
Wirth, Ernestine, 24–25, 27, 28, 52
Work, attitudes toward: in curriculum, 29; for men, textbooks, 32, 43, 46, 57, 87; for women, in textbooks, 32, 33, 35, 36–37, 38, 43, 46, 47, 51–52, 54, 57–58, 87, 88, 89, 102–6, 123, 131–32, 135, 138–40, 157–58, 165; held by women educators, 74, 76; in student notebooks, 63; on examination questions, 68; surveys on women's work, 143–45, 150, 161–62
Work, statistics on, 3, 49, 102, 103, 113–14, 116–18, 124–25, 129–31, 143, 162–63
Working classes, schools' messages for, 10, 22, 29, 32, 34, 41, 49, 58, 85, 105, 140
Writing: in curriculum, 9, 16; teaching of during Old Regime, 6

Xenophon, 22

Zay, Jean, 97, 98–99, 100, 134

DATE DUE